...C & Sons Ltd

Scotland.

Every drop
12 years old

WALKER'S
KILMARNOCK
WHISKIES.

WHITE LABEL	over	**5**	years old.
RED LABEL	over	**9**	years old.
BLACK LABEL	over	**12**	years old.

A LONG STRIDE

A LONG STRIDE

The Story of the World's No. 1 Scotch Whisky

NICHOLAS MORGAN

CANONGATE

First published in Great Britain, the USA and Canada in 2020
by Canongate Books Ltd, 14 High Street, Edinburgh EH1 1TE

Distributed in the USA by Publishers Group West
and in Canada by Publishers Group Canada

canongate.co.uk

1

Text by Nicholas Morgan

British Library Cataloguing-in-Publication Data
A catalogue record for this book is available on
request from the British Library

ISBN 978 1 83885 207 8

Typeset in Johnnie Walker by 3btype.com

Printed and bound in Great Britain by Clays Ltd, Elcograf S.p.A.

CONTENTS

PROLOGUE

'In no other district in Scotland
has the blending and bottling
of whisky been brought to such
perfection.'[1]

*Tom Browne's cricketing cartoon, which first appeared as a full-colour
poster in 1909*

THIS BOOK TELLS THE STORY, seen through the lens of a single business, of how Scotch became Scotland's gift to the world, a gift that keeps on giving to a remarkable degree today. It's a story of two hundred years of relentless endeavour; of prosperity in the face of adversity: how a business not just survived the great flood of Kilmarnock in 1852, the early death of two generations of its business leaders, two world wars, penal tax regimes and Prohibition, and global and national depressions and recessions, but came back stronger each time. And it's the story of how a brand of Scotch whisky became a national, no, an international institution, its fame based largely on a promise of the same quality the whole world over, an instantly recognisable square bottle with a slanting label, and an instantly recognisable man who walked all over the world.

The Scotch industry as we know it today is the result of the endeavours of a hugely talented group of men, mostly (but not entirely) Scots, in the late Victorian and Edwardian period. There has been a tendency to view the entrepreneurs who made Scotch such a global success as a collective, the 'whisky barons', with shared characteristics and values. As we shall see, the 'thrawn' Walkers of Kilmarnock were very different from many of their counterparts, and these differences defined some of the core values of their business. It would be a considerable mistake to think of them in the same way as one might some of the whisky celebrities who sought out social advancement and political place to help build their personal reputations and those of their businesses. The Walkers eschewed publicity and self-promotion; when members of the Walker business were honoured by titles it was for exceptional service to the country in its deepest time of need.

With unbroken family management from its foundation to 1940, this is the story of three generations of quite remarkable

Kilmarnock men who rose from obscurity to lead the world of whisky. And important though the family was, it's also the story of the remarkable men who helped them, very often in the earlier years also men of Kilmarnock or its environs; after all, who else could you trust? Whisky is a remarkable drink and tends (in the author's experience) to attract, like moths to a flame, remarkable people into its seductive orbit. The story of the Walker business shows it was ever thus. Families, of course, come with their own particular advantages and problems, and even the odd rivalry. For the Walkers, family and its responsibilities certainly drove the need to acquire wealth far and above any desire for conspicuous consumption; and in the case of the Walker business the family, not just those active in its management, held some sway over its destiny as a result of shareholdings very deliberately split equally between siblings regardless of gender. Four men from the third generation of the family, Jack, George, Alex and Thomas, worked in the family firm. Business historians like to talk about second, or third, generational entrepreneurial decline as if it was some obligation or duty of the children of the successful to be as talented as their forebears, but who can blame their youngest brother, James Borland Walker, after a war in Africa and a war in Europe, for taking the money and living a comfortable life as a horse-breeder? Families also love their lore and legend, and there is no doubt that he who lives longest lives to tell the tale. Such was certainly the case with Sir Alexander Walker, whose often repeated (and occasionally wonderfully inconsistent) recollections of the past came to be one of the main sources for future copywriters and publicists interested in the 'history' of the brand.

At its simplest (and no one said Scotch whisky should be complicated), Scotland principally makes three kinds of whisky. The production of the first kind, *single malt Scotch whisky*, is a conversion process as starches from malted barley are converted into sugar in the mashing process, the sugars converted to alcohol by the addition of yeast during the fermentation stage, and the weak beer that results distilled (normally twice) in copper pot stills to produce a spirit of around 70% alcohol by volume (abv). This basic conversion process is the same for the production of the second kind, *single grain Scotch whisky*, except it is made from a mixture of malted barley and other cereals (normally wheat or maize), on a much larger scale than most malt whiskies, and in a continuous (rather than a batch) process using 'Coffey' or 'patent' stills rather than pot stills. The production of a single malt or a single grain Scotch whisky must take place at a single distillery. Once distilled, the spirit must, by law, be matured in Scotland in oak casks for at least three years before it can be called *whisky*. The third kind of whisky is *blended Scotch whisky*, the product of mixing together single malt and single grain Scotch whisky. Around the world today about 90 per cent of all the whisky that's sold is blended; the remainder mostly single malt. Almost all of the single grain Scotch whisky that is made is used in the production of blends. Originally crude mixtures of two or three different single malt and single grain Scotch whiskies, blended Scotch whiskies today are often made from over thirty different individual whiskies, each brand closely guarding the secrets of its particular recipe. If a whisky carries an age statement on its label, then that must apply to the youngest whisky in the blend. The world's largest-selling blended Scotch whisky variant is Johnnie Walker Red Label.

The origins of distilling in Scotland are obscure. Or, as Aeneas MacDonald wrote in 1930, 'The origin of whisky is, as it ought to be, hidden in the clouds of mystery that veil the youth of human race.'[2]

And as befits a book concerned with the history of whisky in the nineteenth, twentieth and twenty-first centuries, when Scotch had been dragged kicking and screaming from illicit bothies in sequestered glens and licensed Lowland distilleries in the commercial heart of Scotland onto a world stage, that's as far as we need to concern ourselves with the 'olden days'. Suffice to say that when John Walker's business commenced, production of single malt Scotch whisky was fragmented, pre-industrial, often illegal, and the quality of the product at best variable, often undrinkable without the addition of amelioratives. Single grain Scotch whisky, produced in highly capitalised but still technologically crude distilleries (the Coffey or patent still did not come into use until the 1830s), was sold raw and hot from the still for local consumption, and much was exported to London to be rectified as gin or as whisky, when it was known as 'Scotch blue beer'. Scotch whisky was little known or appreciated outside of its locales. No one had really thought of 'blended Scotch whisky'.

This book follows a broadly chronological narrative, beginning with the death of Alexander Walker in 1819, and the establishment of a grocery business in Kilmarnock the following year for his son John. Details of John's career are sparse, for like his sons and grandsons he avoided the limelight. But whilst their careers are illuminated by voluminous series of business records, John's remains in the shadows. And while it is a common belief, popularised in film and song, that the beginning is a very good place to start a story, this is one that in many respects starts not at the beginning, but rather like some Homeric epic, *in medias res*. And as the past collides with the present, it is hard to offer more than a summary of the defining events of the final decades of the tale. So as with a good sandwich, or a well-made pie, the diligent carnivorous reader will find that the meat is in the middle.

Over the past thirty years Diageo, and United Distillers before it, has invested heavily in building up the world's largest archive of historical material relating to the alcohol beverage industry, the idea of Ian Ross, formerly of White Horse Distillers and John Walker & Sons and a scion of the family of William H. Ross, and Colonel Michael Burkham, formerly of the Royal Welch Fusiliers. The John Walker & Sons collection is the largest component of this archive and spans a period from 1819 to the present day. For many years this material lay in the basement of a building at Hill Street in Kilmarnock, watched over like Smaug the dragon by the last of the Johnnie Walker blenders there, before being transferred to what is now the Diageo Archive. The bulk of the material in the collection dates from the 1880s onwards and tells us little about the critical decisions made by Alexander Walker, son of John, in the early years of the business. We are lucky to have a fragment of Alexander's voluminous correspondence ('I must confess that I am just about the worst correspondent you could possibly meet,' he wrote to Daniel Wilson, a partner in Walker's Sydney distributors, in November 1882) but sadly have been left with nothing so intimate from his sons.[3] The carefully written minute books of John Walker & Sons Ltd, have survived, but financial and sales records are harder to interpret. The author, with some assistance, has created series of data relating to the value of sales, profitability and the like; due to his numerical failings and the opaqueness of some of the ledgers, these may not be perfectly accurate to the last digit, but there is no doubt that indicatively they absolutely reflect the development of the Walker business. Data for sales and business performance from 1985 are taken from *International Wine and Spirits Record*. The archives of the Distillers Company Ltd, which include details of the merger discussions between the 'big three' in the early twentieth century, and those of

W. & A. Gilbey (the self-styled aristocracy of the wine and spirits trade in the late nineteenth and early twentieth century), also held in the Diageo Archive, were invaluable to this study. Sir James Stevenson, Baron Stevenson of Holmbury, one of the most important characters in this story, was by his own admission an assiduous diary-keeper, but sadly neither diaries nor business correspondence have survived in the small collection of his papers deposited in the East Sussex Record Office by his family, which relate mostly to his period as director of the 1924 Empire Exhibition.

Despite its much greater profitability and marketing proficiency, the Victorian and Edwardian Scotch whisky business was something of a poor relation to the wine trade. Even the principals of a firm like Walker's, who as we shall see had little time for the wine business, preferred the respectable designation of 'wine merchant' to that of 'distiller'. The wine trade was replete with trade journals, many of which gave extensive (and not always favourable) coverage to the rise of blended Scotch whisky in the last quarter of the century, and the consequent demise and virtual disappearance of single malt from the shelves and counters of late Victorian and Edwardian bars and wine merchants. They also provide a telling commentary on the irresponsible financial speculation in whisky stocks (and later distilleries) that accompanied the rise of blends, and which so nearly brought the industry to its knees. By the late nineteenth century, the advertising industry in the United Kingdom was far more sophisticated than is generally imagined. Journals established in the early twentieth century gave extensive and normally thoughtful coverage to the development of whisky advertising and the crucial role of agencies and illustrators, and have provided critical insights into the Johnnie Walker story. For the record, these pioneers of the science and art of advertising spoke a language little different from that used by the marketing men and women of today. Those who decry the influence of marketing on Scotch whisky as if it was some late twentieth century arriviste should understand that without it Scotch whisky would be nothing today. Historical newspapers (both national and local) and illustrated weekly magazines often fill in the gaps in the absence of detailed business records, and certainly act as a barometer for the place of Scotch in the popular culture of the nation.

Of course, Scotch has its own secret language, a sort of Polari to keep insiders in, and outsiders out. When it comes to making whisky, the industry has words like 'mashing' and 'fermenting', but in addition there's 'sparge', 'lyne arms' and 'worm tubs' to contend with, to name but a few. There are books that will help find a way through this often-contradictory maze of tortuous terminology.[4] One important phrase is 'get-up'; it refers to the package: the bottle, the label, the closure, the capsule. Today a 'case' is a standard measure by which most companies quantify sales; it refers to an 'accountant's case' of 9 litres of whisky. As the bottled whisky trade began to take over in the 1880s from 'bulk' (the sale of whisky in casks), so the case became the predominant measure. However, when Walker's refer to a case in the late nineteenth or early twentieth century it's not always clear whether they mean six or twelve bottles. From 1924 to the 1970s we have fairly detailed sales for Johnnie Walker in British proof gallons – these have all been converted to 9-litre cases. Today the Scotch whisky industry as a whole sells nearly 100 million 9-litre cases a year around the world. Another key term is 'proof', a measure of alcoholic strength; '100 proof' is equivalent to today's 57% abv. In the nineteenth century Walker whiskies tended to be bottled at 'proof' or '10 up' (10 under proof), the equivalent of 51.4% abv. In 1917 the wartime government introduced a standard strength of '20 up', or 40% abv, which is now the minimum strength at which Scotch whisky can be bottled.

For all its simplicity, Scotch whisky plays a hugely important role in today's Scottish economy. In 2018 the industry sold 95 million cases; American whisky (bourbons, Tennessee whisky and blends) sold 51 million, Canadian 28 million, Japanese (blends and single whiskies) 15 million and Irish whisky 10 million. Scotch whisky accounts for 10,000 jobs in Scotland and over 40,000 jobs across the United Kingdom. Some 7,000 of these jobs are in rural areas of Scotland, providing vital employment and investment to communities across the Highlands and Islands. Scotch whisky exports are worth £4.7 billion, representing 70 per cent of Scottish food and drink exports and 21 per cent of the United Kingdom's. With almost 20 per cent of global Scotch sales, 3,000 jobs in Scotland support Johnnie Walker at over 50 operating sites, including 28 single malt distilleries the length and breadth of Scotland, and 1½ single grain distilleries (Diageo has a half share in the North British Distillery in Edinburgh). Over 2 million visitors to Scotland in 2018 included whisky distilleries in their itineraries; nearly 500,000 visited distilleries connected with Johnnie Walker.

Alexander Walker cared so much about his father that he named his firm after him; he cared so much about his own family that he was driven to increase the size and scale of his business to a degree that caused him sleepless nights and fits of anxiety. And he cared about his blends; he was passionate about *his* whisky. The quality of his whisky was the standard by which he measured himself. He had an obsession for quality (which he had no doubt inherited from his father) that was passed on to his sons, and which was written into the life blood of the business, and of the brand. It's still at its heart today. It's hard to be neutral about whisky once it gets into your blood, once it gets into your heart. This is a book written from a passion for facts, a passion for Scotch whisky, and a passion for the people who made it, and who make it today. It's a book written from the heart. It's a book about one of the simplest things, Scotch whisky, and in particular it's a book about a small group of remarkable people, from a rather unremarkable town in the west of Scotland. In John Walker's grocery shop one of them laid the foundations for a brand of blended Scotch whisky which set out on a long journey from Kilmarnock till it strode the world like a Colossus. A simple thing, a wonder of the world.

CHAPTER 1
TEA & WHISKY: A GROCERY SHOP IN KILMARNOCK

'There is every probability that Kilmarnock will
still further increase in wealth and population,
and become a formidable rival to the famed
"Metropolis of the West"'[1]

Founded in 1820, John Walker's shop in King Street, Kilmarnock, image c. 1830s

1

GIVEN THAT HE IS without doubt Kilmarnock's most famous
son, whose name is spoken every day by people around the world,
surprisingly little is known about the life of John (later 'Johnnie')
Walker. We do know that John was born at Todriggs Farm on the
Caprington Estate, a few miles south-west of Kilmarnock, on 25 July
1805. Tradition has it that the Walker family had farmed at Todriggs
for generations. A substantial stone-built farmhouse, currently derelict,
stands on the site, but this may have post-dated John's time there.
John's father, Alexander, had been born in 1780, and in 1804 married
Elizabeth Gemmel. John was born the following year. Alexander died
in 1819, aged only thirty-nine (relatively early deaths, as it was to turn
out, were something of an affliction for Walker men), at which point
the contents of the farm, now the property of John, were sold and in
1820 some of the proceeds invested in a grocery business in Kilmarnock
as a source of income for John and his mother Elizabeth. Valued by
Elizabeth, John's maternal uncle Thomas Todd, his paternal uncle John
(also resident at Todriggs), and neighbouring farmers Thomas Borland
and Hugh Paton, the estate, including debts worth £120, totalled £537
15s. By far the largest component was cattle and calves valued at £236,
and horses, sheep and swine (£50), although there was also seed corn,
beans, barley and seed potatoes listed amongst everyday farming tools
and implements.[2] Despite being a minor, John was technically able to
run his business himself, but seems to have agreed to the wishes of his
curators (his mother and uncles) that it initially be managed on his
behalf by one Robert Caldwell, named in the first surviving inventory
of the shop's stock-in-trade in 1825, while John learned the skills of the
grocery trade from him for the first few years.

By the time John Walker's business was established in
Kilmarnock the town was being described as 'the largest and most

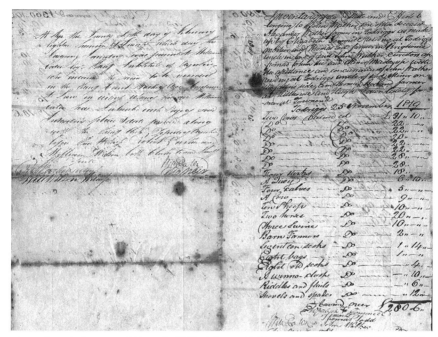

A page from the inventory of Alexander Walker's farm at Todriggs, near Kilmarnock, which John Walker inherited in 1819

elegant in Ayrshire ... with a series of modern streets, little inferior to those of the New Town of Edinburgh ... and [which] possesses to all appearances, many of the attributes of a great capital'.[3] This was a result of a transformation over the previous fifty years or more, 'from a mean village into a minor city'.[4] The population, only 4,400 in 1755, was nearly 13,000 by 1821, making it the ninth-largest settlement in Scotland. With a haphazard arrangement of narrow streets, the old town had been dark and difficult to navigate: 'It is easily enough got into,' wrote one visitor in the 1790s, 'but the devil himself had surely a hand in its formation, for I can't for the life of me discover a way out of it ...'[5] Having obtained an Act of Parliament to improve the town, the burgh council literally opened up the old town from its medieval focus, the Cross, in 1804. To the south ran King Street (where the new Town Buildings were built in 1805) and to the north Portland Street and Wellington Street. The result was that 'the town as a whole presented an air of comfort and elegance to the eye of a stranger and impressed him with a favourable impression of the taste and industry of the inhabitants'.[6] And no doubt any stranger visiting Kilmarnock would also have been impressed not only by the dramatic improvements effected to the principal road to Glasgow, but also by the (horse-drawn) railway which ran from the town to Troon, built in 1812 in order to connect coal mines around the town to Troon Harbour, which had been substantially developed by the Duke of Portland, Kilmarnock's principal landowner, the railway's principal promoter, and the proprietor of the coal mines that fed the railway.[7]

Kilmarnock was surrounded by Ayrshire's rich and much improved farmland, famous for its dairy produce, particularly Ayrshire

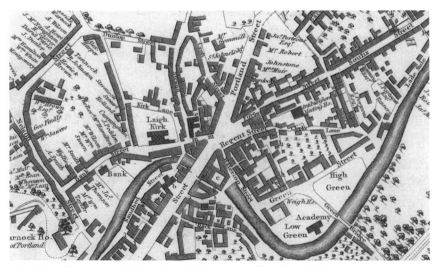

King Street Kilmarnock in 1819, running south from Portland Street. John Walker's shop was next to the Sun Inn, marked by the letter 'b'

(or Dunlop) cheese, it's most valuable product, and cattle which were admired, and sent, all over the world.[8] In addition the land around Kilmarnock was rich in mineral deposits, most notably iron and coal. Wool and leather had principally driven the growth of the town up to the 1820s, with weaving introduced in the early eighteenth century, and, in 1743, a large weaving manufactory set up in the town specialising in carpet production. Leather-working and boot and shoe manufacture began around the same time.[9] Fluctuating trade conditions brought considerable economic insecurity, particularly to the weaving community, who were already threatened by the effect of increasing mechanisation.[10] In 1821, of almost 2,700 households in the town, the overwhelming majority were dependant on the trades and industries that had been increasingly depressed since the end of the Napoleonic Wars, and would continue to be till the middle of the century. With this came demands for assistance for the impoverished, a growing radicalism and demand for reform of the franchise, and the threat of 'riotous proceedings' and 'outrages', which the town council met with an equal mixture of relief programmes and repression.[11]

If poverty and politics were potentially divisive forces in Kilmarnock's life, then alcohol could be a cohesive factor, both uniting the town in celebration at high days and holidays, and helping to reinforce and legitimise the social order of the day. On the King's birthday shops were decorated with greenery, and shopkeepers stood at their doors 'watching what was going on in the street'. The 'chief event of the day' was when the city fathers took to the balcony of the Town Buildings and 'pledged the King's health': 'Other toasts followed, and I remember', wrote an onlooker, 'how the common folks, assembled below on the street, used to look up to, and envy, these big-wigs – who occupied such an exalted station.' After this they would adjourn to 'the Sun Inn, kept by Mr John Murray, where the loyal health were drunk under all the usual demonstrations of joy'.[12] Both the *Old* and *New Statistical Account of Scotland* lamented the number of inns and alehouses (around 150 by 1840), and regretted the 'evidences of intemperance'.[13] If Kilmarnock liked to drink, then so did Scotland. It has been calculated that in the 1830s the per capita consumption of spirits among the Scottish population aged fifteen years and more averaged a little under a pint a week, and drink permeated almost all aspects of daily business and leisure, even, as we shall see, shopping for groceries.[14] Elizabeth Grant of Rothiemurchus complained that whisky-drinking was the bane of Morayshire, from the poorest cottage to the most genteel breakfast table. In the urbanised Lowlands of Scotland, commentators criticised the consumption of cheap, 'coarse and deleterious spirit', rapidly distilled and principally from grain, rather than 'pure' malted barley.[15]

For those with a greater disposable income, there was already some nascent sense of connoisseurship or discernment when it came to choosing what whiskies to drink: 'There are some places more famed for the goodness of their whisky than others, such as Glenlivet, Ferintosh, Campbeltown, Crieff, etc. of which intimation is given in the houses where it is sold upon tickets almost in every spirit dealer's window in Glasgow, Edinburgh and other places.'[16] Not that whisky was the only spirit of choice in early nineteenth-century Scotland. Apart from Speyside breakfast tables, it was rarely to be seen amongst the fine wines and cognacs of the gentry or aristocrats. In 1820s Glasgow, a city whose economic engine room was largely driven by sugar, slavery and smoking, long before smelting and shipbuilding came on the scene, 'Rum punch, with the lemons and limes from Trinidad and Jamaica, was the ruling element at all dinner parties in Glasgow.'[17] In Edinburgh in the 1820s rum too held sway: 'It was computed that above 2000 private stills were constantly employed in producing molasses spirit. The common people got so universally into the habit of drinking this spirit, that when a porter or labourer was seen reeling along the street, the common saying was that *he has got molassed.*'[18] Whether drunk by the dram, or in punch or toddies served by the half-mutchkin, the consumption of spirits was all-pervasive. 'In no other country does spiritous liquor seem to have assumed so much the attitude of the authorised instrument of compliment and kindness as in North Britain.'[19] Clearly for distillers, innkeepers and grocers, this was a considerable opportunity.

Before entering the grocery business it was normal for a boy to be apprenticed to the trade for between five and seven years, so it appears likely that around 1820, John Walker was indentured to Robert Caldwell to learn the complexities of the trade.[20] According to the *Shopkeeper's Guide*, the virtues required of an early nineteenth-century grocer were relatively straightforward: early rising, self-denial, industry, arrangement, calculation, punctuality, perseverance, health, cheerfulness, courage and civility, good address, integrity and, last but not least, economy.[21] In addition, grocers in the 1820s, despite the modern perception of the generality of their trade, required to learn specific skills and mysteries – bookkeeping, the law (particularly with regard to licences and excisable goods), salesmanship, window dressing, and the nature and qualities of the multiplicity of goods they dealt in. These could include tea, coffee, cocoa and chocolate, sugar, dried fruits and nuts, spices (including rice and grains), confectionery (preserved and crystallised fruits and peels, jams and juices), oils, pickles, sauces, hard cheeses, vinegars, and a variety of 'miscellaneous' household goods such as soaps, black lead, pipe clay and bath bricks.[22] To this should be added, for the 'grocer and spirit dealer' (as was most common in Scotland), wines, fortified wines and liqueurs, spirits (British and foreign), and beers and porters. Critically the grocer had to learn how to select, store and care for this multiplicity of mostly imported goods, and in instances where quality was poor or had deteriorated, how to restore, or 'improve' their quality.[23] The grocer's trade was not passive; through selection and receipt of goods to preparing, weighing or measuring for sale, it required a series of sometimes highly skilled interventions, all dependant on an understanding (within any category of goods) of flavour, relative qualities, and cost. One of the most important skills, which for some defined the grocer's trade, was blending, or 'the skills to enable them to change and alter' goods 'by mixture, confections, and possession of simple ingredients'.[24]

The goods that grocers like John Walker offered to their customers ranged from the mundane to the exotic, from soap and starch to sweet almonds and orange peel. The latter sort were the 'small luxuries that were increasingly important in the lives of consumers, both the middling sorts and the lower orders', and reflected the significant changes that had taken place both in the consumption and availability of such luxuries during the second half of the eighteenth and early nineteenth century, and the nature of retailing itself.[25] Of all the goods that grocers handled, few had been such an engine of change as tea, still at this point sourced exclusively from China, and until 1834 sold in the United Kingdom through the monopoly of the East India Company. In 1820 the annual per capita consumption of tea was 1.22 pounds per person, which would almost double by the time of John Walker's death in 1857. Imports averaged £29 million per year, a figure that had increased enormously since the Commutation Act of 1784 had drastically reduced duties on tea and ended a vast illicit trade in smuggled tea that (like the trade in smuggled whisky) was particularly strong in Scotland. Tea had also changed from being the drink that transformed manners, and shaped polite society, public spaces and domestic ritual (and even household furniture and tableware), to the drink that could be found at even the poorest table. Tea blending, although originally a luxurious, bespoke experience for the most exclusive customers to produce unique flavours to suit individual tastes, was at the heart of this democratisation of the drink.[26] Chinese tea varied in style and quality, from the black-leafed Bohea and congous, oolongs and scented pekoes, to the very finest green teas such as gunpowder (rarely sold as single varieties due to their costs).[27] From harvest to harvest, from year to year, and from variety to variety there could be an enormous variation in taste and quality, and price. Traders used a classification system that ranged from 'Very Fine' through 'Ordinary' to 'Musty & Mouldy' and 'Dusty'.[28]

One way for the dealer or grocer to deal with this continual variation was to mix, or blend, types of tea. Blending could also help improve the character of some of the less flavoursome varieties, in ways which were long understood by the trade: 'One ounce of Pekoe in a pound of fine Souchong, gives an excellent flavour; as do two ounces of Pekoe to two pounds of Congou or Souchong, mixed equally together.'[29] Blenders were dependant at the outset on receiving pure tea in the very best condition from China. Yet a veil of secrecy shrouded tea growing and manufacturing in China in an attempt to prevent any possible loss of their global monopoly on its production. Despite the larger tea-houses sending representatives out to the Chinese mainland to gain both expertise and advanced knowledge of the quantities and qualities of tea that would be heading for London, some still felt that 'no article of consumption is more subject to adulteration than the pleasant one which forms the principal ingredient of the tea table. It is not only adulterated by the Chinese vendor, but it undergoes sophistication by the Chinese artist.'[30] Tea might have been mixed with the leaves of other shrubs such as japonica, or cheap Boheas – the lowest quality of black tea – dyed to take on the appearance of more expensive green teas. Shipments damaged by saltwater in transit might be fumigated and dried before being mixed with Bohea. As more cheap teas were demanded by a less discerning clientele, so it became easier for the adulterers to flourish. It was estimated by a House of Commons committee that the value of adulterated tea put on the market in 1783 was £4 million (about £600 million today), when the value of teas sold by the East India Company totalled £6 million.[31]

The issue of adulteration became a cause célèbre in the period after the Napoleonic Wars when high demand for cheaper teas was frustrated by high duties, leaving the field open for unscrupulous purveyors of 'poisonous and imitative teas'. At the same time a new breed of retailers, selling direct to consumers from London and through networks of local agents, exploited consumer fears of adulteration, and in nationwide newspaper advertising deliberately sowed the seeds of doubt as to the quality of blended teas. These disruptive businesses, promising teas 'pure as imported', 'tried to arouse suspicion of a hallowed practice in the trade and asperse the honour and integrity of other dealers' by undermining the legitimacy of the tea-blending process. Their legacy, an enduring suspicion (particularly among public health officials) that 'blending' was synonymous with 'adulteration' was to haunt Scotch whisky in both the nineteenth and twentieth century like Marley's ghost.[32]

Tea totalling £52 13s. 6d. was the second largest item by value in John Walker's business by 1825: two chests of 'fine tea' (166 pounds), no doubt black tea and blended, and at around 6s. a pound the cheapest one might expect to buy, and two smaller canisters of green tea, Hyson at 10s. 6d. per pound and one of Twankay at 7s. 4d. (plus reams of 'tea paper' for packaging small parcels for customers). This was hardly enough stock to suggest that Caldwell and John had been blending tea commercially themselves by 1825 – more likely it was purchased from one of the large tea-houses in Glasgow or Edinburgh.[33] That's not to say that they would have been unaware of the flavours and qualities of the various teas on offer, and the intricacies of blending them. In all likelihood they would also have been acutely aware of the importance of the art of blending teas, and of local preferences for tea styles, tastes which varied distinctly across Scotland.[34] Scotch whisky was the most valuable item in the shop at £64 13s. 3d. Amongst the small casks of rum, brandy, gin and 'shrub' there were two large casks, probably puncheons, of 'aqua' at two qualities – 'No 1' at 5s. 9d. per gallon, and 'No 2', at 6s. In addition there were 5 'small casks', most probably octaves, of Islay whisky at 11s. 4d., and one from the newly built distillery at Largs, at 9s. 6d.[35] In total, by 1825, he held just over 175 gallons (including around 125 of 'aqua' and 45 of Islay), likely not enough in either quantity or variety to be commercially blending from, or at least not as it would be understood today.

And what exactly was the 'aqua', a term used through the nineteenth century (and occasionally into the twentieth) in the whisky industry in a bewildering variety of ways? By way of example, in March 1805 John Munro in Edinburgh offered his customers 'Fine Old Aqua Shrub'. In December 1808 Robert Taylor, also in Edinburgh, was offering for sale 20 puncheons of 'Old Grain Aqua'. In September 1821 over 800

gallons of 'old Highland Malt and sugar aqua' were being sold.[36] In
November 1824, Thomas Miller of the newly built Abbey Hill distillery
in Edinburgh announced that he had commenced making 'Grain Aqua,
and that early next month he intends to make Malt Whisky'.[37] Most
likely, however, the 'aqua' in the Kilmarnock shop in the early 1820s
was Lowland single grain whisky, 'the long use' of which, lamented
a *Scotsman* editorial in June 1823, had 'in some measure vitiated the
taste of the people in Scotland'.[38] The prices charged elsewhere for
grain whisky seem to match the Kilmarnock price for 'aqua'. In 1823
the Genuine Tea Wine and Spirit Warehouse in Edinburgh's High Street
offered the following for sale by the gallon to its discerning clientele:

> Plain Grain Whisky 6s;
> Good Old Grain Whisky 6s 6d;
> Fine Old Grain Whisky 7s;
> Very Fine Grain Whisky 7s 6d;
> Strong Grain Whisky 8s;
> Double Strong Grain Whisky 8s 6d.

Further up the road, James Hardie's Genuine Tea, Wine, Foreign and
British Spirit Warehouse advertised 'Fine Grain Whisky' at 6s. to 7s. per
gallon, and 'Fine Strong Grain Whisky' at 7s. 6d. to 8s. per gallon.[39] There
was certainly no shortage of pot-still grain whisky on the market, albeit
much of it was still being shipped to England for rectification into gin.
Both the techniques and economics of production of whisky from 'raw
grain' were fully understood, as were in particular the economies of
scale that resulted from producing raw grain spirit in larger distilleries
as opposed to the typical Highland small stills, highly prized for the
production of full-flavoured single malt whisky.[40]

The blending of grain and malt whisky was also a common and well-understood, if unspoken, practice which it is impossible to think was not influenced by the skills of the tea blender, given shared practitioners and a common approach of blending light and heavy, the expensive with the less expensive, the good with the less good. Giving evidence to the Royal Commission on Whisky in 1908, James Mackinlay of Leith recalled a handbook in the firm's office that showed that 'blending or mixing was a very old affair'.[41] Alexander Peddie's *The Hotel Inn Keeper Vintner and Spirit Dealer's Assistant*, published in Glasgow in 1825, was intended for the young publican and innkeeper so that:

> *He will rise by easy steps to be a proficient in the art of making, mixing, managing, flavouring, colouring, and bottling of wines, foreign and British spirits, porter and ales; and will be capable of producing liquor of every description, pleasing to the eye, and grateful to the palate; which at all times will command a run, and the respect, attention, and support of the public.*

Unlike the many similar London-published handbooks which offered guidance on how to manage, preserve and 'improve' stocks, and manufacture a bewildering variety of compounds and cordials which barely (if at all) mentioned whisky, Peddie dedicated a whole chapter to the subject. He explained how whisky 'may be mixed up in such a way to be of considerable advantage to the seller, and be as equally good, agreeable and palatable, to the buyer'. Peddie's exemplar recipes were simple, merely offering different proportions of either grain or malt, and not going to the level of particular makes or styles. The overriding importance of quality and age, both in the grain and malt whiskies used, was essential, 'as two bads will never make a good', and the 'whiskies should be bought from the distiller as old as possible'. If both were of a high quality, 'two thirds of grain whisky may be added to one third of malt whisky ... without the mixture being known by those who reckon themselves judges'. The longer the blend could be kept in the cask, the better it would become, and 'by the mellowness it acquires by age ... it is impossible to know it from that extracted from malt'. Small beer and even strong ale could be added to give additional richness and a tinge of colour ('There are a great many people fonder of a dram that has received a tinge than that which is clear and transparent'), but porter would have the effect of making the spirit too dark, like a brandy. A good quality blend could easily be sold as a malt whisky, 'and no judge whatever will know that it is so', the blenders intent being to produce something that was 'wholesome and good for the consumer'. Blends, Peddie concluded, were 'not only palatable, but highly beneficial and conducive to health as they change the effect which a perpetual round of sameness would have on the system'.[42]

In addition to pleasing both his customer and his pocket there was another reason why a grocer or spirit dealer might choose to think of producing their own blends of whisky, or for that matter, tea. A grocer might well possess all those virtuous prerequisites demanded by the *Shopkeeper's Guide*, and the particular skills of his trade, but in a crowded market, over and above service (including, importantly, the offer of sales on credit), distinctiveness was the key to both survival and success. In larger towns and cities with more and wealthier shoppers and more heavily capitalised businesses, this might be achieved through an extensive range of goods with some exclusive lines; in smaller communities a unique and well-priced popular blend of tea or whisky might just be enough to guarantee customer loyalty.

Authorities on the subject were clear what commercial benefits a distinctive blend could bring:

> *The chief objects to keep in view in making up a blend are that ... it shall possess a flavour which shall please the taste of your customers and at the same time be sufficiently distinctive to make the blend your own spécialité, and he who secures these objects at the least cost will be the most successful blender.*[43]

> *Our grocer will aim to give his blends a distinctive character if he finds he can do so. The aim of the smart houses is to produce a blend which customers cannot find elsewhere ... this is the secret of success with most of the best known blends and blenders ... to give your blend a character of its own, and differentiate it from that of your neighbour, you have to introduce some striking ingredient – striking enough to please your customers, not to excite their dislike!*[44]

With the redevelopment of the old town centre, and the continuing growth of Kilmarnock's population, retailing had flourished since the Shop Tax of 1786, which had assessed only twenty-six businesses, perhaps a handful of which were grocers.[45] As we shall see, by the time John Walker began in business some thirty years later the retailing trades had mushroomed. With a low cost of entry the grocery trade was highly aspirational for those who sought a path to both social and economic improvement, but the chances of failure were high. For John Walker, blending – of both tea and whisky – was soon to become the thing that defined his business and guaranteed him a lifetime of success, something that eluded so many others in the grocery business.

Despite having been in business since 1820, it is only in 1833 that the first of a handful of references to John Walker and his shop in Kilmarnock appears in the surviving public records. Rarely can the founder of what was to become a worldwide business have been so anonymous. It has been suggested that his first premises may have been in Sandbeds, running along the Kilmarnock Water parallel to King Street, but there is no evidence to support this.[46] But in the 1833 directory of the town, the earliest that survives, John was listed as a 'grocer and spirit dealer' at 25 King Street; in the Register of Electors (newly compiled under the terms of the 1832 Reform Act) for the same year he is described simply as a 'grocer'. With a single square-paned bow window fronting onto King Street, the shop and its cellar was one of the more valuable properties in the street.[47] Close to Kilmarnock Cross, almost opposite the new council buildings (with the Flesh Market at its rear), and next door to the Sun Inn so beloved of the councillors 'for demonstrations of joy', this was an enviable position to capture the town's more prosperous shoppers. 'There are', wrote one commentator, 'two weekly markets, during which a degree of bustle and animation prevail, seldom seen in a provincial town. The inhabitants are accommodated with a convenient flesh-market, together with others for butter and cheese; that for meal has fallen into disuse, in consequence of the number of victualling shops in the town.' The Cross, the traditional market place, was still the heart of the town; milk sellers would gather there in the morning, while in the afternoons (particularly on a Friday) a more varied selection of traders, with butter, eggs, poultry, fish, seasonal fruit and vegetables ('I do not remember a single fruit shop being in the town at that time; potatoes were rarely sold by provision merchants') and even treacle toffee, would take their place.[48] Around the Cross and leading down the main thoroughfares were a variety of different shops: grocers, seedsmen, bakers, booksellers and printers, ironmongers, chemists and wine merchants, all of the same or relatively similar appearance, with 'comparatively small bow windows, with small panes of glass', all no doubt with 'proprietors keenly alive to business ... morning noon and night behind his counter with his apron on', and most spotlessly clean, despite the dust which led the shopkeepers of Portland Street and King Street to petition the Police Committee, 'pointing out the great necessity of watering the streets in droughty weather to prevent the goods in their shops being injured by dust which in other respects was a positive nuisance'.[49] Inside, the shop would have been configured as much for social interaction as for commercial transaction. In addition to the show-cups to display teas and sugars, and the scales, weights, measures and paper required to dispense goods, Walker's shop had 'tumblers, dram glasses, and beer glasses' to serve customers with drinks while they shopped (common practice in Scotland until the passing of the Forbes Mackenzie Act in 1853).[50]

In addition to tea, whisky, brandy and rum, the most valuable items in John's shop were sugar and soap. He also sold a range of confections, preserved fruits and nuts, and a small selection of spices, coffee and rice. He was also brewing his own ginger beer. Commentators may have fancied that this improved Kilmarnock was as grand as the avenues and boulevards of Edinburgh's New Town, but it has to be said that the stock in John Walker's shop in 1825 was mean in both range and quality of goods compared to the inventories trumpeted in hand bills and newspaper advertisements by contemporaries in the capital's new shopping paradise of Princes Street and the High Street.[51] And there was no shortage of competition closer to hand. The 1833 *Kilmarnock Directory* calculated there were 230 'grocers and hucksters' in the town, along with 105 inns, public houses and spirit-dealers;

Pigot's 1837 directory listed 38 established 'grocer's and spirit dealers', nine of whom (not including Walker) were also wine merchants. As well as the Sun Inn, John's immediate neighbours included the draper and haberdasher Hugh Craig, and tailors and clothiers John and Andrew Stewart. Across the road were the confectioner Hugh Beckett, Joseph Thomson the baker, and Isabella Young and her sister, straw hat makers. Including Walker's, there were eight grocers in King Street, six in Portland Street, and a couple around the Cross.

We almost know more about some of these competitors than we do about John, who in a taciturn spirit that came to typify his family, refused the opportunity to promote his business in directories or newspaper advertisements. William Calderwood, a wine and spirit merchant in Regent Street (heading north-east from the Cross), advertised in 1833 'the following qualities: viz Arran, Islay, Campbeltown, and Common Malt Whisky', and offered his 'sincere thanks to his Friends and the Public in general, for the very liberal encouragement he has received in the Spirit, Porter, and Ale trade'; James Tyrie on Cheapside announced he had just 'commenced business in the Spirit Line; and from his having formed a correspondence with the first distillers in Scotland, is enabled to sell at the following low prices: Good Malt Aqua at 6s 6d per gallon, Fine Malt Aqua at 7s, Superior Malt Aqua at 8s, Campbeltown at 9s, and Islay & Arran at 10s'.[52]

Walker's most formidable competitors, however, were William Wallace & Co., who were based in Portland Street (the eponymous principal partner living in the large Hacket House in Hill Street), and William Rankin & Co., who in 1833 were close by at 30 King Street. Both were grocers and wine merchants, as well as 'spirit dealers'. Rankin's would later be described as 'one of the oldest and most aristocratic businesses of the kind in the town', being 'patronised by nearly all the gentry of the town and surrounding district'.[53] In a double-page advertisement in the 1846 *Kilmarnock Post Office Directory* (which listed 87 'Grocers, tea and spirit dealers'), William Rankin advertised an extensive range of ports and sherries, porters and beers. Whiskies, sold by the gallon, included Campbeltown, Islay, Glenlivet, Jura and Royal Brackla, as well as blends – 'a mixture of finest whiskies, very old, much recommended' – priced as high as his most expensive malts (10s. a gallon). He was also selling a variety of black and green teas, and a 'very fine' mixture of 'the finest teas'. In the 1851 *Ayr Directory*, following the growing fashion for fortified wines, Rankin

An advert for William Rankin & Son of Kilmarnock in 1846, 'one of the oldest and most aristocratic businesses of the kind in the town'

emphasised the quality, variety and relative cheapness of his bottled ports and sherries, urging 'Gentlemen whose purchases have heretofore been chiefly confined to the larger cities of England and Scotland' to try samples; his whiskies included old Glenlivets, Islays and Campbeltowns. William Wallace's advert of the same year focused on Chinese teas, spices, dried fruits, nuts and provisions, and their extensive range of spirits, wines and beers.[54] Both families were extensively involved in Kilmarnock society, two generations of the Rankins holding the office of postmaster, and the Wallaces being prominent in charitable affairs.[55] As we shall see, these businesses continued to grow in the nineteenth century, although both would ultimately become part of John Walker & Sons.

In 1833 John married Elizabeth Purvis, daughter of the gardener on the Caprington Estate where his father had farmed. We know that by this time John's business must have been relatively successful, as he had qualified as a £10 householder to vote under the terms of the 1832 Reform Act, which in Scotland had admitted 'small shopkeepers, weavers, shoemakers and other tradesmen' to the electorate, now about 1 in 8 of the male adult population.[56] For the record, John chose not to vote in the election of 1837, but in 1844 and 1852 he cast his ballot in favour of the successful candidate, the Liberal Edward Pleydell-Bouverie.[57] In this he may have been influenced by the experience of William Forrest, a grocer and spirit dealer in King Street, and then Portland Street, who had cast his vote in 1837 for the successful Tory candidate, John Campbell Colquhoun. Forrest subsequently fell foul of radical sentiment, a lesson to Kilmarnock shopkeepers that knowing your customers' politics was as important as knowing their taste:

His shop for a number of days was almost deserted; nay, more, it was, to use a modern phrase, boycotted and guarded by a rabble of louts, who while they loudly clamoured for liberty to themselves, yet threatened to maltreat those who exercised their liberty of spending their money where they thought they were likely to be best served ... a poor old man who had ventured to enter the shop and purchase a small quantity of tea and sugar, after he came out was followed ... and sadly abused by a miserable miscreant[58]

The Walkers' first daughter, Margaret, was born in 1835, followed two years later by Alexander, and then Robert (1839), Elizabeth (1841) and John (1844). By this time the business must have been prospering; since 1835 the family had been living in a house in the northern fringes of the town off the Kilmaurs Road, with a domestic servant and a shop-worker (seventeen-year-old David Rud) employed by John. Sometimes described as 'Walker's Land' and later called 'Glenbank', this was a newly built property in India Street, owned by John, where the family remained until his widow died in 1890.[59] This was a fashionable and developing part of town, away from the congested centre, with modern houses and substantial gardens (John, it was said, was a keen horticulturalist). Three of the houses in the street, including the Walkers', had an annual value of £19, one of £16, and the remaining three of £10. Their neighbours were a teacher, an auctioneer, an ironmonger, two seedsmen and a hatter. In 1851 Robert, Elizabeth and John were all still attending school, though it's possible that by now Alexander, aged fourteen, was already working in his father's shop. Both Robert and John followed him into the family firm.[60]

An undated silhouette of John Walker

John Walker was now in his prime, but unlike so many other successful small business owners he eschewed the temptations of local politics, trade associations and civil society, choosing instead to focus on his shop, his family, and his garden. Compared to the many colourful local worthies whose stories fill the pages of James Walker's *Reminiscences of Old Kilmarnock*, John remains a mere cipher. This studied reticence was a trait inherited by his eldest son in both personal and business matters, and by his grandsons. The only image of John is a silhouette of uncertain provenance, which bears a striking similarity to a portrait that can be seen hanging on a wall in a painting of John's grandson George Paterson Walker. It shows a smartly turned out, strong-featured man with fashionable long sideboards in late-Regency dress, with a high velvet collared jacket and an even higher-collared shirt and cravat. Not extravagant, and by no means a dandy, but very fastidious. Appearance was everything in the grocery trade, from shop window to the shop counter, and as the master of ceremonies presiding over the shopping experience, the shopkeeper was no exception. From what few family paintings and portraits survive it's clear that John's male descendants, in addition to inheriting his reserve, also shared his very particular dress sense.[61]

Between the 1820s and 1850s Kilmarnock was transformed by the arrival of steam power, railways and heavy industry. The population had increased from some 13,000 in 1821 to 18,000 in 1831, and 21,000 in 1851. Whilst shoe, carpet and woollen manufacture remained important, mechanisation (much of it home-grown) had slowly supplanted many of the old craft skills. There was an undoubted spirit of innovation about the town, whether from landowners such as the Duke of Portland with his pioneering of tile-drainage (and tile manufacture) or the artisan Thomas Morton, whose inventions revolutionised carpet-production, and who later started the manufacture of telescopes in the town.[62] The arrival of the railway from Glasgow in 1843 was critical; it cut a swath through the north of the town and was followed by foundries and locomotive works, established by Andrew Barclay and the Glasgow and South-Western Railway amongst others. Outside of Kilmarnock the Portland Ironworks was established at Hurlford in 1846. The tramway from Kilmarnock to Troon was rebuilt the following year to allow steam locomotives to haul coal from the mines surrounding the town to the expanded harbour there. In 1852 manufacture began of the Kennedy Patent Water Meter, invented by Thomas Kennedy and John Cameron, a local clockmaker. Two years earlier the Kilmarnock Water Company had been established to provide piped water to businesses and private homes in the town, a gas company (in which John Walker was a modest investor) having been set up in 1822 to provide, amongst other things, lighting for the town's shops and offices.

Growth was not unabated, hardship continued in times of depression, and in the 1840s the town council found itself again setting up soup kitchens and make-work schemes for the unemployed, mostly from the textile industries. Following food riots in Glasgow in March 1848, during which businesses were attacked and looted, and five protestors shot by troops, a crowd gathered at Kilmarnock Cross, 'hallooing, and yelling, and smashing lamps' and breaking shop windows before being dispersed by baton-wielding special constables, with a 'few of the turbulent or ringleaders being lodged in gaol'.[63] However, despite the privations of the poor the growth of the 'comfortable classes' was remorseless; as one historian wrote, 'Many neat and beautiful residences have been built within the last few years … which give ample evidence of a prevailing taste for the elegancies and refinements of life.'[64] Such 'tastes for elegancies' were catered for by firms such as Daniel MacDougall's Kilmarnock Confectionary Warehouse in King Street, which advertised in the most extravagant terms 'confectionaries of every description', for 'dinners, routs, balls, suppers, banquets and soirées'.[65] John Walker tried to tempt genteel customers not with advertising but with a window display of brazil nuts, figs and plums, boxes of fancy soaps, bottles of sultana sauce, jars of marmalade and Brighton biscuits, but perhaps surprisingly no alcohol.[66]

This polite Kilmarnock society could not have anticipated the storm that would descend on the town in July 1852, when the Great Flood of Kilmarnock laid waste to 'fields, bridges, mills, dams, houses, gardens and orchards'. The dramatic storm resulted in torrents of water running off the moors and fields into the tributaries that fed the Kilmarnock Water, leaving a trail of destruction as the spate headed for the town itself at about four o'clock in the morning of 14 July. At the Kilmarnock Foundry in the north-east of the town, buildings were destroyed and workers' housing flooded to the depth of ten feet, as occupants fled from their beds. Similarly machinery and goods were destroyed at Laughland, Roxburgh and Gilchrist's woollen factory, whilst a 'huge boiler' from another factory was carried away by the water: 'buoyant as some canoe, it sailed along, adding to the intense sublimity of the scene, yet filling the spectators with horror'. As the waters raced to the town centre and Flesh Market Bridge, on which stood the council chambers and prison, their destructive velocity was increased by the narrowness of the water course and the tight bends as it passed under the town buildings and down Sandilands Street. 'To those who could look upon it without thoughts of danger, King Street presented a novel spectacle. It was converted into a broad river, which rolled along in sullen grandeur, carrying upon its waves trees, planks of timber, tubs, casks, chairs and other articles.' No doubt some of these tubs and casks belonged to John Walker, 'as a vast quantity of goods belonging to all, from the Cross downward, was greatly damaged or destroyed'. In all, about £15,000 of damage (equivalent to over £2 million today) was sustained in the town in about two hours, the provost and magistrates establishing a subscription fund for the ninety-nine families 'of the poorest classes . . . totally unable to withstand the loss of clothing, furniture and damage to their dwellings'.[67] One popular story has it that John Walker's entire stock was destroyed as the flood submerged the rear shop and cellars that backed on to Sandbeds, forcing him to make 'a fresh beginning', dismissing his shopman and working only alongside his wife.[68] The evidence, however, tends to suggest otherwise. John may have lost stock in the 1852 flood but the fact that his business, only five years later, held stock worth £1,434, and had £1,140 cash in the bank indicates either a truly miraculous recovery, or a far less traumatic outcome.[69]

John Walker died at his house in India Street, Kilmarnock, on 19 October 1857, aged fifty-two years old. He left personal estate of £4,256, to be divided equally between his widow and his five children, instructing his trustees that one or more of his heirs were to take over his business in full, providing they met their obligations to their mother and siblings.[70] Despite his relative anonymity during his lifetime, his apparent refusal to advertise or promote his business, and the possible damage inflicted on it by the Great Flood of 1852, the grocery was a prosperous, growing concern. The business he left, worth around £2,425 (his stock-in-trade being valued at some £1,400), was far bigger, and far more complex, than in 1825 (then worth a little over £200). On the traditional grocery side John held a much wider and more sophisticated range of goods and had added, for example, hams, preserves, sauces and pickles to his stock. He carried a wide range of teas, both in bond (worth £130) and ready for sale in the shop, including Imperial, gunpowder, Young Hyson, congou and pekoe. With these quantities and varieties, it seems certain that he was blending his own teas. He held bottled stocks of champagne, fortified wines and spirits as well as bulk of brandy, rum, sherry, bass ale and porter.

Whisky, however, overshadowed everything else, accounting for over half the value of the entire stock, some £750 (of which around £370 was under bond).[71] The holdings were dominated by Campbeltown whiskies, now mostly forgotten names like Kinloch, Lochhead, Lochruan, Riechlachan, Springside and (the still very well known) Springbank. There were also Islay and 'patent' grain whiskies (unidentified). Geography, or rather proximity, apparently dictated what John used in his blends, possibly along with a local preference for the stronger flavours of the West Coast and island distilleries, relatively easily available through the ports of Troon and Ayr. In the shop there were six casks on the front of the counter selling different styles of whisky ranging in price from 10s. 10d. to 14s. per gallon, and also 'aqua' for sale in gallon jars and bottles. There can be little doubt that these would have been rudimentary blends of both malt and grain whiskies, strong in both alcohol and flavour and drunk most likely with warm water and sugar (and possibly lemon) as toddies. Elsewhere in the cellars and back rooms there were over 2,000 bottles, corks by the gross, and 'jar labels'.[72] Moreover, the extensive debts owed to John at his death by numerous creditors, over £800 in all, make it clear that he was conducting a wholesale as well as a retail whisky business, with substantial sums being owed by grocers, spirit-dealers and innkeepers in Kilmarnock and the surrounding area.[73] The ability to offer and manage credit was a critical way of obtaining and retaining customers in the grocery trade; it was also fundamental to building the business further. If John's inheritance had been a grocery shop, then his legacy was a whisky business with a grocery shop attached. Perhaps this is why John was described, for the first time, as a 'Grocer and Spirit Merchant' on his death certificate.

While it's surprising that so little is known about Kilmarnock's most famous son, the exact details of his business career obscured by time and a paucity of surviving documents, the picture we get at John Walker's death is of a very well-established retail and wholesale whisky-blending business with both private and trade customers in and around the thriving industrial town of Kilmarnock. With this growing trade would have come an accrued knowledge and expertise in the field of whisky and whisky blending, the latter no doubt partly transferred from working with teas. And with the knowledge and expertise would also have come an expanding network of trusted business contacts. However, John's principal asset was his hard won reputation, encapsulated in the name John Walker under which he had always traded, the name that guaranteed the quality of every bottle of blended whisky sold from the shop. As we shall see, circumstances which had contrived to limit the possibilities for growth in the blended Scotch whisky trade were about to change dramatically, and John's business was perfectly placed to exploit these altered conditions. All it needed now was a leader of vision, drive and relentless determination to succeed.

CHAPTER 2
A 'GREAT GULF STREAM OF TODDY'

Opened in 1879 the complex of buildings erected by Walker's in the Strand came to dominate the centre of Kilmarnock – John Walker & Sons illustrated brochure by A. Barnard, 1894

'Like that great gulf stream of toddy which flows through my native land – softening our natural severity, tempering our old fanaticism, and modifying our rugged climate.'[1]

ALEXANDER WALKER was in sole control of the family business for almost thirty years. During this time it was transformed from a grocery shop in Kilmarnock to a massive concern whose premises dominated the centre of the town and had offices in London and agents all over the world. By the 1880s it was, it was claimed, the largest single exporter of Scotch whisky, and also the most profitable. Blended Scotch whisky had grown to become the preeminent spirit in the world, the fashionable drink of choice in clubs, hotels, theatre bars, railway refreshment rooms and restaurants. Alexander Walker was a man of considerable business vision and organisational skills, keen to take advantage of these developing consumer trends, and anxious that his firm should provide for his growing family. When it came to growing the business, it was almost as if nothing was new enough, whether in terms of production, marketing or route to market. But his business principles were rooted in something far more old-fashioned: an overwhelming belief that quality (and value) was the principal and necessary condition for growth, something learned, no doubt, from his father.

As a remarkable collection of correspondence from the last ten years of his life reveals, although obsessed by his business Alexander was a rounded personality with a wide variety of interests. He maintained a close circle of friends and acquaintances in and around Kilmarnock and Glasgow to whom he was both generous and loyal, and often revealed to them concerns and anxieties about business affairs which he never shared with the small group with which he trusted the management of the firm, mostly men of Kilmarnock, including two of his sons. To them (and to others in matters of commerce, local affairs or religion) he could be stern, fierce, impatient, ill-tempered and forthright, with often a stinging turn of phrase. To write, as one obituarist did, 'that he didn't suffer fools gladly', was to exhibit a masterful control of the understatement. 'I am greatly perplexed', Walker wrote to the manager of his London office in July 1886, about Thomas Inglis (manager of the Royal Caledonian Asylum in London), 'as to how I am to get on with that "Bletherin bitch" Inglis as I am afraid I am very likely to lose my temper with such a loquacious gentleman.'[2] He described himself as being of a 'mercurial temperament'.[3] However beneath this gruff exterior he was modest and unassuming ('I don't like making an exhibition of myself'), caring, generous to a fault, sometimes deeply compassionate, occasionally romantic, and very often exceptionally humorous.[4] Most of all he was driven by a passion to make the best blended whisky in the world.

When John Walker wrote his will in November 1846 he stipulated that Elizabeth and his three executors (all fellow business owners in King Street) would act as curators and tutors for the children, and were to oversee the estate until the youngest child, John, attained majority in May 1865.[5] Alexander, by this time aged twenty and most likely already working for his father, took over the running of the business following John's death in 1857 in a partnership with his mother and brother Robert, then aged seventeen. Young John may also have started working for the company sometime after 1861, when he was lodging in Glasgow as an 'agent's clerk, spirits etc.'.[6] During this time the size of the business more than doubled (as did the value of the spirits and wines kept in bond) while the wholesale trade increased to around two-thirds of sales by value. But in November 1864 Robert Walker 'retired' from the partnership, setting up his own grocery shop briefly in King Street, before travelling out to Sydney.[7] On 18 May 1865, the young John Walker's twenty-first birthday, the partnership with his mother was dissolved, and Alexander, 'having in terms of my late father's will allotted all shares & funds belonging to the trust estate of

my late father', took sole ownership and control of the firm of John
Walker & Sons with a capital of £840.[8] Alexander had married Georgina
Paterson, the daughter of an Edinburgh builder, in 1861 and was already
the widowed father of a daughter, Mary, and two sons, John and George
Paterson Walker, their mother having died from heart disease weeks
after George's birth in October 1864. The family were living in a new
residential development of houses with large gardens, Wallacebank,
on Wellington Street, not far from Elizabeth Walker's house.

     In the United Kingdom consumption of spirits, both domestic
and foreign, had increased from 0.63 gallons per head in 1820, to 0.93
in 1860, although the consumption of whisky in Scotland had declined,
partly due to its increased cost, and also the growing influence of the
temperance movement that had its first stirrings in Scotland in 1829.
Wine consumption had remained almost static. In Scotland in 1820,
around 3.2 million gallons of spirits were distilled; in 1860 the figure
stood at 13.3 million. Seven million gallons were grain whisky, 6 million
malt whisky. In the same year over 1.5 million gallons of spirits were
exported from Scotland to England. There were 125 distilleries in
operation in Scotland (compared to 117 in 1820) but the size and scale of
these would have made them unrecognisable compared to four decades
earlier. Although not entirely absent, illicit distillation and smuggling
had been almost wiped out since the changes in the law of 1823. Home
consumption of imported spirits in 1860 stood at 5.5 million gallons, of
which rum (3.7) and brandy (1.4) comprised the overwhelming quantity.
And although per capita consumption had not grown, imports of wines
increased from 5 million gallons in 1820 to 12 million in 1860, with Spain
being the largest source (5.3) followed by Portugal (2.5) and France (2.4).
As with spirits (particularly rum), many of these wines were re-exported
from the United Kingdom. Beer production stood at over 20 million

barrels in the country as a whole; Scotland produced only 816,000.
The consumption of tea, still sourced almost exclusively from China,
had more than doubled since 1820 to 2.67 pounds per person.[9]

Against this background a number of changes in the law
were to be of particular significance to changing patterns of drink
consumption, and particularly to the growth in the sale of Scotch
whisky both at home and abroad, and to Alexander Walker's business.
In 1860 Gladstone slashed the duties on imported wines, subsequently
eased licensing restrictions on restaurants and eating houses, and
introduced a 'Grocers' Licence' for the sale of wines. Excise duties on
spirits in England and Scotland had been equalised in 1855; a few years
before, in 1853, 'vatting', or the mixing of whiskies, had been permitted
under bond; blending under bond was permitted by the Spirit Act of
1860, then the bottling of spirits under bond for export in 1864, and
finally for home consumption in 1867.[10] The effect of this was to open up
the English and export markets to Scotch whisky, and to allow blenders
to operate at scale without the need for the capital that was required
whilst restricted to blending duty-paid whiskies.

Many have suggested that these changes alone were
responsible for the development of blending (primacy in which is often
attributed to Andrew Usher & Co of Edinburgh) and the growth of
blended Scotch in the second half of the nineteenth century. However,
as we have already seen, blending and mixing whiskies was a well-
established practice as early as the 1820s, and by 1860 blended whisky
was already the drink of choice for many. Charles Tovey, veteran of the
wine trade and early drinks hack, wrote in 1864: 'The prevalent notion
among whisky drinkers, especially in Scotland, is that several varieties
of whisky blended is superior to that of any one kind.'[11] Tovey also
commented on the pervasive popularity of drinking 'toddy':

*You may find it at the after-dinner table of the aristocracy,
mingling its fumes with the odours of Lafitte or Romanee Conti
[sic], and many a nobleman will leave the choicest wine to
indulge in his glass of toddy. The middle classes and tradesmen
most prefer it to any other spirit or wine.*[12]

Mixed to taste by each drinker at the table – in a ritual that, like tea, was surrounded with a degree of domestic paraphernalia such as toddy kettles, jugs, ladles and spoons – this combination of whisky, hot water and sugar (and sometimes a slice of lemon) 'aids digestion [and] promotes cheerfulness, sociability and happiness'. It was also perhaps the most common 'respectable' form of whisky consumption (as opposed to 'dram drinking'), and had become increasingly popular in Scotland in the 1840s and 1850s, partly due to the sometimes high duties on rum which had 'induced the Glasgow citizen to give up his cold rum punch and betake him to hot toddy'.[13] Such was its popularity that wine and spirit merchants produced 'toddy mixtures', some sweetened, which were possibly some of the earliest blended whiskies. In 1848 an Inverness newspaper advertised 'old highland whisky for toddy, being a judicious mixture of the manufacture of the most favourite distillers', while in Glasgow David Chrystal advertised 'a fine old Toddy mixture free of flavour', and John and Thomas Prentice in Greenock 'a superior toddy mixture' at 9s. 6d. a gallon.[14] Few, however, promoted themselves as heavily as David M'Lachlan, from Laurieston in Glasgow, who explained that:

*It has been proved beyond doubt that Highland Whiskies
are only in perfection when the produce of several distilleries
situated in different localities are blended or mixed together*

in certain proportions and as each distiller can only sell whisky of his own distillation great difficulty is experienced by gentlemen in selecting whiskies of the proper character to embody or infuse with each other so as to produce a glass of genuine toddy.

M'Lachlan's toddy mixture was 'designed to satisfy the greatest connoisseur as to its age and purity'. Available in gallon jugs or heavily branded bottles (partly to guard against imitation and counterfeit) by the dozen, and protected by registered trademarks, it was sold not only in Scotland but throughout England and Wales by the early 1860s. Notably, however, as the market for blended Scotch quickly developed, M'Lachlan dropped the reference to 'toddy mixture' in 1866 and was instead promoting 'McLachlan's Scotch Whisky' in the *Morning Advertiser*, 'blended in such proportions as to produce a mixture that no single whisky can ever equal'.[15] However, as late as 1891 the *Victualling Trades Review* reported that '"Whisky Toddyology" is how a Glasgow publican intimates his ability to brew the national drink.'[16]

Two other factors were critical in shaping the competitive environment that Alexander Walker operated in, both at home and in export markets. The first was the decline in sales of brandy following the impact of the grapevine pest *phylloxera*, which first appeared in France in 1863. This infestation destroyed almost three-quarters of France's vineyards by the late 1880s, and the subsequent decline in brandy consumption is often cited as the major reason for Scotch whisky's success. However, although consumption of brandy peaked at 4.5 million gallons in 1876, falling to just less than 2.5 million in 1887 and ending up at 2.7 million gallons in 1900, the decline in volume was hardly catastrophic. A far greater issue for both the trade press and consumers was the decline in quality and reputation of much of what was sold as 'brandy', and the almost institutionalised adulteration of French spirit with German.[17] Discussing this matter, the board of W. & J. Gilbey, the darlings of the wine trade establishment, agreed that should they use this spirit they would lay themselves open to have all the prejudices surrounding German Spirit levelled at them.[18]

Those who could find the real thing had to dig deep into their pockets to afford almost double what they would pay for a bottle of whisky. Far more dramatic was the decline in the consumption of sherry, a drink which was almost at the peak of its popularity. In 1871 a record 6 million gallons were consumed in the United Kingdom, after which consumption plummeted to a mere 1.5 million in 1900.[19] 'The ordinary sherry of commerce', wrote the *Saturday Review* in 1873, which had complained about the way that sherry drinking had infiltrated both the counting house and the drawing room, 'is about the most unwholesome thing under the sun, and everything should be done to discredit it.'[20] A perceived decline in quality, rumours of adulteration and falsification, the loss of favour amongst the medical fraternity, all contributed to this astonishing demise.

> *There can be no doubt that the seeds of the popular disfavour were laid at the time when the Sherry Trade seemed as stable as a rock, and extra profits induced the shipment of a class of article which brought a bad name to Jerez products, the goods being tarred with the same brush as the bad. Since the downward career was once started there has been no check, and popular taste has apparently taken up the cudgels against this once highly-esteemed beverage.[21]*

The decline in the consumption of these two favoured drinks of the genteel and bourgeois certainly opened a market for a competitively priced and palatable spirit whose quality and authenticity could be guaranteed. Of course the catastrophic decline in the sherry trade would also have another, less favourable impact on Scotch as the number of genuine sherry casks available for maturing both malt and grain spirit declined rapidly, just as Scotch production was increasing.[22]

Sherry certainly featured heavily in the Walker business in 1866. Stocks in bond and in the shop were valued at just under £1,000 – not much less than the entire whisky stock, which were worth £1,113 – reflecting both the popularity of the drink, and Alexander Walker's understanding of consumer tastes.[23] Although Alexander clearly had some personal understanding of the technical side of the wine trade, it was to be of diminishing importance to the business, as interest in sherry in particular fell away. In 1883 he complained that 'I am so much over head & cats just now, and with several of my folks away their holidays I cannot get the wine trade looked to.' Two years later, refusing an offer to purchase sherries, he confessed, 'The fact of the matter is the wine trade gets no attention in this establishment.'[24]

The whisky stocks held by Alexander Walker in 1866 certainly suggest that his Scotch whisky blending business was well established, although he was, like his father, reluctant to publicise his goods directly to consumers, making it difficult in the absence of complete records to know exactly what was being produced and sold, and in what quantities. The value of whisky stocks had increased by around a third since John died, and although there was still a very distinct West Coast flavour to the holdings, with Campbeltowns such as Springbank and Riechlachan, and Ardbeg and Laphroaig from Islay (with only a small quantity of 'Glenlivet, duty-paid'), the largest single quantity was grain whisky from MacFarlane's Port Dundas distillery in Glasgow. In the shop's cellars there was one, if not two, large blending tuns of 'whisky' (this was, of course, still a year before bottling in bond for home consumption was allowed), whilst in the front shop there were casks of 'whisky' (graded No. 1 to No. 6) and dozens of bottles of 'aqua' ready for sale. At the back of the shop there was a profusion of dry goods, including small flasks, glass jars, bottles of all types, corks and bungs, labels and capsules, the latter required to seal bottles and guarantee the integrity of the contents.[25] The whiskies would have been sold at between 57% abv (proof) and 51% (10 under proof), weighty in both strength and flavour, despite the moderating character of the grain whiskies. The Campbeltowns, 'though they would change in style dramatically later in the century', were 'distilled in stills of small size,

John Walker & Son's grocery shop in Portland Street, Kilmarnock, c.1906

and made from peat dried malt . . . [with] a flavour about it peculiar to itself, and which was much relished by consumers of that kind of spirits', and were known to find a good market in Ayrshire.[26] The Islays, more so than today, would have been smoky, heavy and pungent. In all, then, blends not designed for the fainthearted, but rather for the toddy-drinking aficionados of Kilmarnock and the surrounding countryside. Others in the town's grocery trade followed the same path, advertising the 'finest Campbeltown whiskies' and 'excellent mixtures' of Islays and Campbeltowns for toddy, and 'superior toddy mixtures'.[27]

Over the next fifteen years the scale of the business was transformed. By 1880 the total Annual Balance increased more than fourfold to £42,000; the value of stock-in-bond, now dominated by whiskies, sevenfold. The wholesale trade was six times bigger than 'retail', and now specified export sales.[28] The business had long outgrown John's shop in King Street. The shop had moved to Portland Street in the early 1870s, and in 1873 Alexander had purchased property for use as a bonded warehouse in Croft Street, which ran north-east from the Cross; he had also purchased, but let, the adjoining Commercial Hotel. Within five years this space too had become inadequate. In 1873 Walker had begun to purchase residential properties in 'the unsavoury locality known as the Strand' (which ran north-east from Cheapside and converged with Croft Street), where 'a few wretched thatched cottages lingered in the shade of the Laigh Kirk'.[29] In 1878 the old buildings were cleared and he began the construction of what was to become a massive bonding, blending and bottling complex, with a cooperage, case-making department, stores and stables, that would dominate the centre of the town. It should be said it's not entirely clear how these building projects were financed although the cost of building was certainly written off partly against profits. Walker's very well-connected lawyer, James McCosh of Dalry, was also critical in sourcing heritable loans to support these projects, a particularly challenging task in the wake of the failure of the City of Glasgow Bank in 1878.[30]

These first striking buildings were designed 'in a French renaissance style' by a young Kilmarnock architect, Gabriel Andrew, who became house-architect for Alexander Walker, with a drawing office in the Croft Street property.[31] The first phase, 'fitted up with the most approved modern appliances', was opened in February 1879, comprising a bonded warehouse on four floors, which also contained two 2,000-gallon blending vats 'for mixing the well-known Highland Blend which has taken the name of Kilmarnock to almost every portion of the world'. The hydraulic lift that connected the four floors, 'where every arrangement has been made for the safety of the workers at the hoists', was the wonder of local journalists, and an example of 'liberality with which every requisite detail has been attended to'. Next door, existing buildings had been repurposed as the bottling warehouse, and 'introduced into Kilmarnock an entirely new industry,

Alexander Walker's original Old Highland Whisky label, produced in the Court of Session in Edinburgh as evidence in a trademark dispute in 1882

that of box making and packing' (which was carried out in the old Croft Street Bond), required to produce several hundreds of cases each week. Offices were also built for the Inland Revenue, 'a want that has long been felt – a public office near our market place where officers can be readily seen', meaning that the general revenue business would no longer need to be conducted at the George Hotel.[32] In 1881 the offices in the Strand and Croft Street were connected by telephone, the first in the town.[33]

As the newspapers correctly observed, the engine behind the company's growth was their 'well-known Highland Blend', known to the business as John Walker & Sons' Old Highland Whisky, and to the trade and consumers variously as John Walker's Old Highland Whisky, Walker's Kilmarnock Whisky, or simply John Walker's Whisky, a brand name he had been using since the mid-1860s. 'Old Highland' was a Scotch whisky generic that had been used since at least the late eighteenth century and into the mid-nineteenth, in a trade which avoided the word 'blended' wherever possible for fear of accusations of adulteration. It became for many wine and spirit merchants a useful shorthand (like 'toddy mixture' had been) to indicate a blend of malt and grain whiskies.[34] For some, with a nod and a wink, it also conjured up the notion of 'the good old days' of smuggled whisky, and played on the belief, common at the time, that the illicit was often going to be better than the legal article. It was perhaps the first of a number of increasingly romantic descriptions that blenders deployed to describe their whiskies ('The real Mountain Dew: the best old Highland Whisky' was being advertised for shipment from Aberdeen to Newcastle in 1855) which earned increasingly scornful comment from those in the trade press fighting a losing battle to uphold the primacy of single whiskies over blends.[35]

For Alexander Walker the brand was in the name, 'John Walker & Sons', of which he was fiercely proud, and the personal guarantee of quality that went with it. And it was also in the place. In 1874 Walker registered the copyright of his label for Old Highland Whisky (and at the same time a label for 'Old Irish Whisky') at Stationers' Hall in London. He also registered the Kilmarnock coat of arms as a trademark. The labels were designed by Smith Brothers of Kilmarnock.[36] The label was subsequently registered under the new Trademark Act in 1877, claiming first use since before 1867.[37]

Even in a market in its earliest stages of development, Alexander Walker had chosen a 'get-up' (as the whisky trade calls the packaging of a product) that would stand out from competitors'. As was explained in the Court of Session in Edinburgh in 1881, John Walker & Sons had 'for a number of years past used a peculiar trade mark label for their whisky, and the bottles have been made up in a particular manner, with the intention of rendering the complainer's whisky easily recognisable in the market'. 'The bottle', it continued,

> is made of clear greenish glass, has the label affixed to it in an oblique or slanting way near the middle of the bottle, and has a capsule in white metal, with a black stamp on the top, bearing the arms of Kilmarnock, with the letters 'W & S' on the shield, and the words 'J Walker & Sons, Kilmarnock', round the margin of the impression. There is also on the side of the metallic capsule in black raised letters the words in cursive writing, 'John Walker & Sons', and these words run in a slanting or oblique direction.[38]

And of course in addition to the label being in an 'oblique or slanting way', designed to capture the eye's attention, it was very often on an equally distinctive square bottle. The iconic square bottles were most likely being used in some markets from the time of introduction of the label in the 1860s and they first appear in the London stock records in 1874.[39] Square bottles were not entirely new; they were widely used for patent medicines and cures, for table sauces, and traditionally for gin. However, square bottles were unusual for Scotch and highly distinctive in a sea of round bottles. By the 1870s Walker's were also not the only company using them for whisky. They were relatively expensive to produce but in turn provided packaging optimisation during shipping and may have offered some savings in freight costs. Unfortunately the use of the iconic square bottle was not without issue, as we shall see later. But combined with the oblique or slanting label, the impact on shelf, or for that matter on showcards or mirrors, was outstanding and instantly recognisable, then as it is now. Between Alexander Walker and his designers at Smith Brothers, they had produced one of the most enduringly distinctive alcohol 'get-ups' ever designed.

John Walker & Sons of course had long ceased to be a one-man business. As early as 1862, when Robert was still a partner, the firm was looking for 'a young man, who has been two or three years at the Grocery, or Grocery, Wine and Spirit Trade'.[40] John Walker, Alexander's younger brother, had started working for the firm as a traveller in the 1860s, dying in 1875 aged thirty in Rothesay, where he may have been sent to attend to his health.[41] Around 1867 John Blaikie, formerly a grocer and wine merchant in Glasgow, had joined Alexander in Kilmarnock as a commercial traveller. Shortly afterwards James Boyd joined as a bookkeeper or cashier. Archibald Stevenson became manager of the shop in Portland Street at some point in the 1870s. These three, like so many others in the business, would never leave. The move to the bond in Croft Street would have required numerous hands, even more so the new premises in the Strand. Moreover, around 1873 Alexander Walker opened a London office at 3 Crosby Square, off Bishopsgate, adding more employees and more complexity to his role as general manager, but critically opening up huge opportunities to expand the business in both the English and export markets. This, above all, was probably his biggest gamble. For what was in effect a new product, blended Scotch needed visibility, and London was the city that led fashions and consumption trends for the rest of the world.

London was not wanting in long-established wine and spirit merchants jealously eyeing the potential profits that blended Scotch could bring, or other pioneers from Scotland like Greenlees Brothers, who were trying to make London their own. John Blaikie moved to London to manage the Walker office there, at least initially on a fifty–fifty profit share with Alexander, but it proved to be a difficult business to establish. Looking back in 1886, Alexander wrote to his son George that 'I am glad that you say that the prospect of our London business is so bright. I never expected anything else since I first started there but no one but myself knows the hard work I had to make it.'[42] Blaikie's first few years witnessed a succession of bad results which nearly exhausted his principal's fragile-enough mood and caused Blaikie to offer effusive and repeated apology: 'I now enclose balance as at Saturday and am really sorry it shows so badly. I am very sorry it shows so badly . . . I know you will be very much disappointed' (1874); 'I had fully expected a more satisfactory one for the trade we have been doing . . . I can only hope that by this time next year if all's well to show a better sheet' (1875); 'I now enclose balance sheet as at 1st Feb and am sorry to say it does not show well these beastly bad debts have completely swamped any little profit that would have been' (1876); 'herewith note of balance which I am sorry to say is very far behind. I have been pushing about for cash and have not got it' (1877); 'Yours read! . . . I have no doubt this next year will show a different result and will guarantee that there is not £20 of bad debt as unless I find they are Al I won't sell' (1878). The problem it seemed was not finding business – 'our Old Highland seems to have got a hold and there is no question about it keeping the same' – but in managing it.[43] And Blaikie, in Alexander's eyes, was wanting in the sense of urgency that drove him: 'You will see that I am writing this in a temper but you will bear in mind what I have said in the past and realise that I worry every day for money.'[44]

Scotch whisky may have been distilled in the Highlands and blended in the Lowlands of Scotland, but as Alexander Walker realised, its reputation would be made in London. The difficulty he faced was finding the right people: trusted salesmen who could open accounts and collect their bills, and customers who could be relied upon to pay their bills. He also had to manage John Blaikie, whose judgement he sometimes doubted. There were two sides to the business: wholesale selling in London to the increasingly important railway companies, catering and restaurant houses such as Spiers & Pond, and individual hotels and public houses; and then private clients. The intent here was not just to sell casks, cases and bottles, but also to achieve visibility for the brand in the right places and with the right people. Blaikie's first salesman, Mr Cocks, rarely made a profit so great were his expenses; he was then seduced by the apparent entrée into the world of London's social influencers that a certain John Piper seemed to promise, engaging him first on commission, and then on the payroll, despite the fact that John Kilgour, Walker's accountant in Kilmarnock, warned in April 1882 that 'Mr Piper's connection may ultimately be of little profit, as just now it is absorbing a large amount of Capital, with very slow return, and consequently tending largely to our present tight financial position here'. Like all salesmen, Piper talked a good game. He did count some society names among his customers, such as Lord Beresford and Baron Ernest de Caters, but with annual accounts totalling £1,411 of which £1,119 was unpaid, Walker soon became 'sick and tired of promises of large results in the end', determining to send Kilgour to London as Blaikie had signally failed 'to let Piper understand that you really are the man in charge'. Piper continued to open up new accounts unabated whilst miserably failing to bring in outstanding debts, and much to Alexander's annoyance allegedly blurred the lines between his Walker business and private customers. At the same time as seeking legal advice from his lawyer and fixer, McCosh, on how proceedings with Piper might work in Chancery, he wrote to Kilgour with some resignation that though the affair was 'looking blacker and blacker . . . there is no use in losing temper, paper and ink in my trying to help you. Make the best or worst of his "splendid connection" as he called it, and we must just submit as there is no use in crying over spilled milk.' At the end of 1883 he wrote to the lawyer Edward Upton in London: 'The connection has not been at all a satisfactory one, and while it has paid Mr Piper it has been a serious loss to John Walker & Sons', the London accounts for that year showing 'heavy losses sustained through Mr Piper's connections'.[45] Under the circumstances it was hardly surprising that Walker turned to a trusted son of Kilmarnock, James Hodge, to turn the London trade around.

For Walker's, London was also a hub from which to develop their export trade in the 1880s, surrounded as they were at Crosby Square by merchants and commission agents whose commercial webs of interest, and entrepreneurial appetites, spread all over the world. The beginnings of Walker's export business are unclear, but treasured tales of bottles of whisky secreted in Kilmarnock carpets and shipped all over the world, like Cleopatra being rolled in a rug and taken to Caesar, bear little scrutiny. In 1881 Alexander Walker claimed to have exported about 57,000 12-bottle cases which, along with bulk shipments in casks, amounted to 126,000 gallons of whisky. Old Highland Whisky was being sent from Glasgow, Liverpool and London to agents and wholesale merchants in Sydney, Melbourne, Brisbane, Adelaide, Townsville, Launceston, all the principal ports of New Zealand, South Africa, and the West Indies, to Alexandria, Honolulu, Bombay, Calcutta, Karachi, Penang, Singapore, and 'many other ports'. Of all these markets, Australia was the most important.[46]

According to correspondence of John Blaikie the company had been doing business in Australia with the Bank of New South Wales since at least 1867. It is also possible that having left the business in Kilmarnock, Robert Walker travelled to Australia in the 1860s with the intention of developing the trade there.[47] Sadly it's hard to disaggregate details of the export side of the Walker business from the surviving records of the 1860s to 1880s, so we have only a fragmentary picture for the most part. However, given the prodigious sales already achieved by 1880, and the sustained export growth that was to follow, it's clear that the world beyond the United Kingdom was a key part of Alexander's vision for his business from the start.

It is quite likely that the earliest shipments of whisky from Kilmarnock to Australia and elsewhere were casks sent on consignment with ships' captains taking the risk and responsibility for their sale on arrival in port, along with a share of the receipts. Scotch whisky was certainly well established in the colony, and advertised for sale as early as 1832 (and no doubt well before), when 'superior Scotch whisky' from Thomson Elmsie & Co, proprietors of the Gilcomston distillery in Aberdeen, was consigned for auction in Sydney. At this point distilling was illegal in New South Wales, yet despite high duties, 'spirits were abundant'.[48] However, it was only following the well-publicised gold strikes of the 1850s in New South Wales and Victoria that Scotch imports visibly increased, just as the laws around exports were to be liberalised in the United Kingdom. Starting in Australia, and then moving through the colonies, Scotch exports grew in line with the mineral wealth and unrestrained appetite for luxury consumables that gold created. In 1847 'the only batch of genuine Islay and Campbeltown whisky' was on sale in Sydney, where demand 'was great'. In July 1857 hogsheads and quarter casks of 'Mitchell's whisky', 'Paisley whisky', 'Dundas Hill whisky', Islay and Scotch whisky, plus cases of bottled Islay, Campbeltown and 'Scotch malt whisky', were being auctioned in Melbourne, alongside Old Tom and Geneva gins, Hennessy, Martell and a host of other upmarket alcoholic beverages.[49] In 1856 Mason Brothers, importers of china, crockery and glassware into Sydney, were advertising 'fine Scotch malt whisky'; they went on to sell 'Jamison's' Irish whisky, Campbeltown and Fettercairn malt whiskies, 'Mason's Old Scotch Malt, specially distilled for the Australian market', Cameron's Inverness Whisky, Old Davanah Highland Whisky and 'the favourite brand', Macfarlane's whisky ('in bottle'), before advertising Walker's Old Highland Whisky in 1874.[50] By 1879 (if not before) they were sole agents for Walker's in New South Wales, from which point their fates would be closely and occasionally painfully intertwined for well over a decade.[51]

Mason Brothers had been established in Sydney in 1854 by Robert Mason, who also had mercantile businesses in London (where he resided) and Glasgow, and his brother Gavin.[52] They were importers of a wide range of durable domestic goods and ironmongery, and from the 1850s began to develop a business as wine and spirits distributors in New South Wales. Of the three partners resident there, James Cullen,

James Gould and David Wilson, Cullen, who had been there since 1870, was a cousin of Alexander Walker, and it may have been this kinship that brought Old Highland Whisky into their portfolio of brands, which also included Sorin cognac, Cork Distilleries Irish Whisky and Gayen's Schiedam schnapps.[53] Robert Walker, described as a 'merchant', was still in the city in 1874, and despite illness was involved in some work with Mason's.[54] Unlike the home market, Walker's whiskies were advertised with increasing frequency in the local press – by Mason Brothers themselves, by hoteliers and retailers, and even in editorials purchased in new magazines like the *Bulletin*, where witty bon mots were to be found scattered through their pages ('Favourite study of Solicitor's Clerks? Walker on whisky bottles').[55] 'I am still of opinion that you charge us pretty sweetly for this,' wrote Walker to Cullen; 'It takes a big slice off the profits.'[56] But the market was exceptionally competitive and as in other colonies agents demanded allowances (which they rarely got) for the sort of promotional activity that Walker's would never have allowed in the home market. Advertising increased, and became more sophisticated (for example, with illustrations of the Old Highland bottle), during and following the Sydney Exhibition of 1880, which saw Walker's Old Highland Whisky win its first major international award, very quickly heralded not just in the press ('Walker's Whisky – Special 1st Prize!') but also on a foot label added to the bottle.[57] These sought-after third-party endorsements, discussed in more detail later, were of huge importance in establishing the reputation of brands in overseas markets, and distinguishing them from the competition.

Mason's also developed an early sponsorship vehicle for the brand, the Walker Whisky Trophy, donating £300 as prize money for a professional sculling race on the Parramatta River; sculling was

Medal from the Sydney International Exhibition of 1879–80: 'Walker's Whisky – Special 1st Prize!'

a popular sport in Australia with a large following. Won by Elias Laycock, who had professional victories behind him both in Australia and England, the sponsorship was in place, explained Cullen, because 'something was due to the colony, and they should do what they could to encourage manly sports'. Speaking of his 'relative', Mr Walker (who no doubt abhorred such extravagant expenditure) had 'expressed a regret that he could not be personally present on the occasion but wished it every success'.[58] Gibbs, Bright & Co., who were agents for the brand in Victoria, were equally active in growing its sales.[59]

Despite occasional losses on shipments, and concerns about the management of Mason Brothers following the death in London of Robert Mason in 1881, the Australian business remained of critical importance.[60] In 1879 Walker had launched a new brand there, 'Glencairn', in bulk and in bottle, to work alongside Old Highland Whisky against the competition: he 'meant it to be totally different from OH, so that it would not interfere with it and yet be a whisky in value which no other house could compare with ... it is distinct, has a character of its own'. The response from the market was not encouraging (nor apparently in London, where it was sold but without gaining much traction).[61] He sought to protect the reputation of Old Highland by preventing agents undercutting each other on price in disputed territories – 'I think this is the law we must lay down and stick to' – and was determined to defend his trademarks.[62] In November 1882, on the advice of his Glasgow lawyer ('the best authority in Scotland on such matters'), he raised an action in the Court of Session in Edinburgh against an Edinburgh merchant, claiming that he had sent whisky to Australia under the name 'James Walker's Edinburgh Old Highland Whisky', with labels designed and positioned on their bottles in order to deceive consumers – much to the damage of Walker's business. They also sought an injunction against the merchant and his distributor in New South Wales to the same effect. Despite the best advice, success was not assured, 'but', said Walker, 'in my opinion the exposure would do us as much good as if we did [win the case]'. The defendants attempted to defuse the issue first by withdrawing the labels, and then arguing that neither the wording nor appearance of Walker's whisky ('generally known in the Colonies as Walker's Kilmarnock Whisky') was particularly unique, but Walker was determined to carry the matter through 'to strengthen the hands of Masons & others', ultimately winning both actions.[63]

Alexander Walker certainly had good personal reason to protect the business that he had created so quickly. He had remarried in 1867, and since then his new wife, Isabella McKimmie, had delivered seven children: three sons (Alexander, Thomas and James) and four daughters (Helen, Isabella, Elizabeth and Margaret), to add to the three borne by his first wife: Mary, John (or Jack) and George. In 1873 Alexander had begun building a large new house with an equally large garden in London Road which the family moved into two years later – it was named Piersland House after a farm that had belonged to his wife's family (and which Alexander later acquired). After Margaret's birth he wrote to his cousin in Sydney: 'That makes four sons [he had apparently forgotten one!] and five daughters[;] I sincerely hope the number is completed now as the responsibility is no small one and will necessitate the sale of a good lot of Old Highland to keep matters straight.'[64]

He also had an ongoing responsibility to financially support his brother Robert and his family in Sydney.[65] Alexander had acquired Marine Cottage in Troon in the late 1870s, and in 1883 feued a substantial piece of ground in the same town from the Duke of Portland's estate and began the construction of Crosbie Tower, a large mansion with substantial grounds to the designs of Gabriel Andrew. He also sought to develop the adjacent site: 'I was just a little afraid that some speculator would put down some garrison next to Crosbie Tower which I did not at all care for.'[66] Gardening was a passion for Walker (he was Honorary President of the Kilmarnock Horticultural Society) and he exhibited at local shows – in 1881 his 'collection of stove and greenhouse plants and model flower garden (with rockery)' were the focus of attention.[67] At Troon he took great personal interest in the construction of an 'Orchard House' at Crosbie Tower ('Which I can show my friends'); he wrote to Henry Norrie, an old Kilmarnock acquaintance who had been agent at the Union Bank there, 'with regard to the vandas [a type of orchid] I must tell you that I have no accommodation for them. You are altogether mistaken about the Orchid Glass. It is an Orchard House I am erecting and will have plenty to fill it.'[68] Both houses were also built with sufficient stable space to allow Alexander to indulge his interest in keeping and breeding cobs, both for show and for driving. His success at the former was not always fully acknowledged, as he complained after one particularly successful year: 'The proprietor of the Kilmarnock Standard here is a very strong radical and because I take an interest in the other paper he did not even mention them; he has heard plenty about it since.' It was also his pleasure not just to take his small coach down to his offices in the town from Piersland House, but also, like a free spirit, to take to the open road with his wife: 'In a day or two we are off for a ten-day drive with the two cobs, just our two selves with the coachman and a lad.'[69]

The house at Troon also allowed Alexander Walker to
indulge in his passion for golf ('the golf and the shooting I have
takes up all of my spare time').[70] It was literally built next door to
the newly established Troon Golf Club (now Royal Troon), of which
he was a founder member, jealously guarding the interests of Troon
and Kilmarnock members against the much-resented incursions of
Glaswegians, who he criticised for trying to take over its management.[71]
Crosbie Tower, and Piersland House in Kilmarnock, were the focus for
both domestic and business entertainment. For despite his occasional
misanthropic outbursts it's clear from his correspondence that,
alongside his family, Alexander Walker relished nothing more than
good company and companionship, and shared food and drink.[72] Few
visitors were discouraged, but sometimes for all its critical importance
in oiling the wheels of the business the duty of hospitality took a heavy
toll. 'I am beginning to think that my health is of more importance
to me than other people's enjoyment,' he complained. 'We have had
to do so much entertaining to Colonials & Cockneys etc.,' he wrote in
October 1885,

> *that we hardly knew what it was to have a quiet day to*
> *ourselves, the consequence being that I am not all the man*
> *I should like to be and I am determined that I shall never*
> *attempt to do anything of the kind again. It seems so different*
> *entertaining strangers whom you may never see again*
> *compared with your real friends.*

Blaikie, aware of the 'constant stream of visitors' to Scotland,
apologised that the irrepressible Robert McKilligin, of R. Marquis
McKilligin & Co., a frequent visitor to the London office in search of

sherry and a biscuit, and an important customer, 'told me he intended to look you up as he is a chap not calculated to forward one's work'. On the other hand a visit from Bernard Lewis, who held the company's New Zealand agency, promised little distraction: 'I daresay he will be a bit of a bore but we must get through it as best we can.'[73] Family and friends were much preferred: 'We had a great party last night, about 50 I suppose. They seemed to enjoy themselves well, which was all that was wanted. Kept me a little from sleeping but that was no matter'. 'With the youngsters here,' he wrote to William Calder early in January 1886, 'all around it has been parties, parties, every night. I expect we shall have the result of it bye and bye.' And generosity did not only extend to hosting. At Christmas in particular gifts of wine and whisky were carefully dispatched to friends and customers; game from the shoot he rented was sent to London 'to distribute as judiciously as possible'; Kilmarnock cheese was a very special gift. But for all his love of whisky and good wines, of local cheese, freshly shot game, pork pies and even snails and frog's legs, it was something far more simple that stole his heart, as he wrote to a friend at Christmas 1888: 'It occurred to me that you might still have a Scotch tooth in your head and I have sent you a small box of Kilmarnock shortbread. I always tell my wife it is one of the shortest roads to heaven that I know of.'[74]

CHAPTER 3
'OUR BLEND CANNOT BE BEAT'

Alexander Walker, photographed shortly before his death in July 1889

'I remember the time when three hogsheads of Irish to one of Scotch were sold in London, but a short time afterwards these fine blends of Scotch came in, and the tastes changed altogether, and it became the other way round.'[1]

FOR ALL THE SUCCESS Alexander Walker had enjoyed during the
first two decades of his tenure of the business, the third and final
decade would be quite remarkable in terms of growth and profitability.
Between 1880 and 1886, when Alexander converted the firm into a
limited liability company, the annual balance of the business had more
than doubled from £41,000 to nearly £88,000. Profits averaged just
over £15,000 each year, dented somewhat by the impact of increased
duties in New South Wales in 1885, as a result of which 'our Export trade
has fallen off very largely'.[2] The value of stock-in-bond had also more
than doubled. Over three-quarters of the business was now going to
wholesale rather than private customers. In October 1883 Walker wrote:
'I find that we have bottled nearly 12000 dozens more for the first six
months of this year, than we did last, which is pretty fair.' In 1885 he
confided in an old friend that 'if you would not think it too egotistic on
my part I may tell you that our business is increasing at a greater ratio
than I can well undertake,' later complaining that 'while other people
are dull it seems that my business doubles itself every year and I feel
sometimes as if I could almost wish it would double itself back because
it is really more than one head can carry'.[3]

The burden of the sole management of such a rapidly growing
business, along with increasingly frequent bouts of ill-health, no
doubt prompted the thought to change the structure of the business,
and to broaden both managerial and fiscal responsibilities among
his family and the small team he had brought together in the 1870s.
Walker's principal assistant had been George Lipscombe, who seems
to have joined the firm around 1874 when he was only sixteen, and
whose contribution to the growth of the business in the early 1880s
was exceptional.[4] Walker and his small group of senior managers were
all devastated when Lipscombe succumbed to illness in 1885, and did

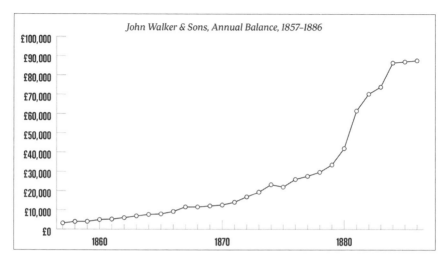

John Walker & Sons, Annual Balance, 1857–1886

everything they could to assist his recovery whilst trying to maintain his involvement with the firm, even as he travelled overseas to improve his health. Eventually he was retained in an ambassadorial role on an annual retainer – 'Put this to what use you choose, as the spirit moves you, and as you feel inclined crack up the "Old Highland", but don't go out of your way to take orders ... this £150 we will place to advertising. Do not look upon this in the light of charity. It is not so. Your talking up the "blend" is worth this to us.'[5]

Jack Walker had been sent down to work in the London office in 1881, aged eighteen. However, his physical health and well-being was fragile.[6] In 1882 he was ill and unable to work, and in 1883 Alexander sent him and his older sister Mary to Australia. 'My oldest boy was growing rather fast and did not feel at all well, so I sent him off along with his sister.' The trip included visits to Melbourne, Sydney, Queensland and New Zealand, and a return journey via San Francisco. 'I think', he wrote to his cousin Cullen, that 'Jack's trip should do him good in many ways, and perhaps be for our mutual benefit in the end.'[7]

There was a business intention here too, although Alexander was clear how much his son could be expected to achieve:

> *I have been talking to him as well as I could as to how he is to*
> *talk over the Old Highland to his customers. I wish him simply*
> *not to understand much either about the quality, blending,*
> *or prices; he has simply been a clerk in the London office, and*
> *knows little about the details of what is done at home.*[8]

The trip was not without incident. On the return journey in April 1884 the brother and sister only narrowly avoided serious injury in a dramatic railway crash in Oklahoma, when the sleeper carriage they were travelling in left the rails at high speed on a steep curve near the banks of the Arkansas River. Rescued from the wreckage, Mary Walker was one of the most seriously injured.[9] It took her some time to recover from the incident once back from New York; Jack returned to the London office but continued to flirt with ill-health, spending time in a sanatorium in early 1885. In September 1886 he returned to Australia for a short business trip, on which he also married Colina Campbell in 'a very pretty wedding' in a suburb of Melbourne, returning to London in early 1887.

The newly married couple found a house in Putney, where their daughter was born in August, but Jack soon incurred the wrath of his father by, not for the first time, overdrawing his account with the business. Alexander wrote in anger to Kilgour, 'If you can possibly give me an explanation of what is being done with the money I should like [it] very much. I cannot see how a furnished house needs any extra expenditure,' although he subsequently apologised: 'I naturally felt very much annoyed that Jack should have, or been allowed to overdraw his a/c.'[10] Alexander also began to doubt Jack's judgement in some business matters, and was cautious not to be drawn into financial speculations with his son.[11] When at the end of 1887 Jack was sent out to work at Mason Brothers, Sydney, to try and resolve the serious business issues there, his father was deeply concerned that his lack of experience and impulsive temperament (it seemed he had inherited some of his father's brusqueness but little of his tact) would lead to only more difficulties, noting however that 'at the same time he is much older than I was when I had to take the whole concern in hand'.[12]

In the absence of Lipscombe, and with Jack in London and then travelling to Australia, Alexander began to rely more and more on his second son, George Paterson Walker. Still a sixteen-year-old 'scholar' in 1881, he was sent to London during his brother's first illness the following year to cover for him in the office; when he returned to Kilmarnock his abilities gave his father the confidence to make Kilgour's posting to London permanent, George becoming his 'principal assistant'. However, even he was soon 'a little overtaxed with work' and Alexander began searching for another assistant, eventually landing on James Blair, 'a good buyer and a very steady fellow', and a partner with Kilmarnock competitors William Rankin & Co.[13] George was increasingly taken into his father's confidence on business issues and by late 1887 was responsible for the 'greater part of the work' in Kilmarnock. That notwithstanding, when Jack went back out to Mason Brothers, George took his place in London.[14] Also in London was James Hodge, who had formerly run a wine and spirit merchant's business in Kilmarnock and then Glasgow, before joining Walker's. He quickly became the 'head traveller' and clearly helped make amends for the losses that had been suffered when John Piper was causing mayhem with his 'good-as-gold customers'.[15]

Opening new accounts, retaining business, and ensuring prompt payments were the keys to Walker's success in London and beyond, and much preferred to heavy expenditure on advertising or promotion. James Hodge's impact can be assessed by his rewards; originally paid less than Blaikie, they were at parity a few years later (£600 per annum), with Hodge receiving what would become regular, generous bonuses 'for his extra service'.[16] While he clearly had, as the Scots would say, a fine conceit of himself – Blaikie complaining that 'he comes in and goes out without vouchsafing a word on business and has a good time as no one interferes with him in his travels or expenses' – he was becoming increasingly indispensable. Indeed Alexander Walker worried, when Hodge was ill and orders and payments stuttered, that 'it will never do to let the business depend on the services of one man'. Hodge was also remarkably sensitive to criticism ('I am afraid Mr Hodge is too thin-skinned,' wrote Walker) and not only took offence very easily, but also took his many grievances direct to the company's principal, who disliked 'these unpleasant matters'. However, when in March 1886 Hodge responded to an off-hand remark made by Kilgour questioning his contribution to the London business by calling his colleagues 'illiterate, ignorant, twaddlers', Walker had to put his

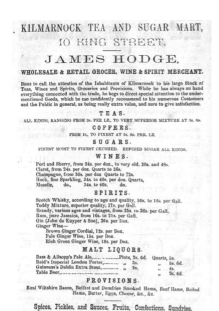

James Hodge, who went to London to become Walker's principal salesman, had run his own grocery business in Kilmarnock in the late 1860s

foot down, promising Blaikie that should Hodge visit Kilmarnock to complain, 'I mean to be very independent with one who has such a high opinion of his own abilities.'[17] Despite pleading with all parties for a reconciliation in the London office, peace seemed a distant prize. Walker wrote to Blaikie: 'I am exceedingly sorry that he rides such a high horse . . . if this continues, but we must part,' adding, 'You know, and we know, we can perfectly well do without him.' Nevertheless, when setting up the new limited company he added: 'I think it would be judicious that Mr Hodge should have a small share as well. It would encourage him and keep him together and with such a large family he really needs it.' Even then, Hodge disputed the financial arrangements around his shareholding, leaving an exasperated Walker to write that 'If Mr Hodge wishes so thoroughly to quarrel with his bread and butter by attempting to put me in a corner he is very much mistaken.'[18] Only with this matter resolved, and Hodge's regular bonus put in place, was an uneasy truce maintained between the warring parties in the capital.

As a man of increasing wealth, importance and influence in Kilmarnock and far beyond, Alexander Walker was the recipient of appeals for help from all and sundry. Distant relatives seeking handouts, neighbours in search of positions for their sons in London or Australia, churchmen or charities begging for funding, indigent widows wanting assistance for themselves and their children, entrepreneurs in need of capital, candidates for public posts seeking the benefit of his discreet influence, men with cupboards hiding one or more skeletons seeking to start new lives overseas; they all found their way to his door. And like some fictional godfather he turned no one away. Not all supplicants were successful (as we shall see) but all were heard, many were helped, the majority in receipt of at least sympathy, if not some small token. For a man of such short temper Walker took these responsibilities very seriously, often with an undue degree of patience. For although the engine of Victorian Kilmarnock may have been fuelled by a ruthless breed of capitalism, it was oiled by a hidden web of obligation and influence that extended well into the colonies, based on friends and favours. Favours given, and favours returned. Or at least that was the expectation.

In 1883 the son of a good customer, John Dunlop, asked Alexander Walker for help setting up a business in Paris, where he hoped to sell whisky. Alexander was doubtful of the connection, writing 'I don't think John Dunlop is one we would work very harmoniously with, from his inexperience and inability to cope with older hands,' and whilst he wished the Paris venture success he was concerned that 'much greater care is required on his part than if he had been bred to the business'.[19] Walker was understandably reluctant to accept any financial burden, but John's father had owned the Refreshment Rooms at both Kilmarnock and Ayr railway stations, and Walker was his executor and trustee, managing a fund on behalf of his wife and children, a responsibility he took very seriously.[20] Reluctantly he agreed to guarantee a £500 loan, despite his scepticism about the whisky trade ever succeeding in France. 'As far as the whisky trade, we must first wait till the Parisians are a little better educated as I am perfectly satisfied it will be a trade some day as it is now in almost every market in the world.' Sadly his opinion of Dunlop was to prove only too true a few years later: 'I am much afraid that John Dunlop's opinion of his business capacity is very much as I predicted. I never expected him to do much good, and now I feel I am duty bound to look after my own interests.' Although he had apparently assisted Walker's in winning a gold medal at the Paris Exhibition, his business had been far less successful. As Walker had predicted, 'It would be a most difficult thing to get the French induced to drink Scotch Whisky.' Having taken an unsecured loan from the Walker London office to assist with a shop in the Place de l'Opéra, Dunlop absconded, leaving a trail of debts behind him. And Alexander Walker was not only dented by this 'sad and disheartening business' in pocket ('I have made a very heavy bad debt through a friend whom I assisted in Paris, and he has bolted, leaving me with the big end of the stick to carry') but also in reputation, something for which he cared for dearly.[21]

Nor could he have anticipated how much his standing would be threatened by the business affairs of Mason Brothers in New South Wales.[22] After Robert Mason's death the remaining partners struggled to capitalise the firm and sought assistance in London and Scotland to finance a limited liability company. Both James Cullen and Daniel Wilson spent time in London and Kilmarnock with Walker's (who had a considerable interest in keeping Mason's going), and the result of the discussions was the flotation of a new business, Mason Brothers Ltd of London, in 1884, with a promise to investors of high dividends.[23] Along with Alexander Walker, the directors of the new business were but one of three constantly warring factions in the management of Mason Brothers, the others being the Sydney management committee (the former partners Cullen, Wilson and Gould), and the senior staff of Mason's London office in Billiter Street, none of whom appear to have had a high opinion of the others. At issue was the competence and ability of Cullen et al. 'Although an outside relative[,] I don't think he has the brains to carry out anything to a success,' Alexander wrote in a letter to Blaikie; 'My opinion', wrote Blaikie, is that 'he has yet to learn the most rudimentary principles of business'. As for Wilson, '[He] feels that too many of the employees have been there longer than himself and he has not the heart to tackle them as to the discharge of their duties.' And Gould, wrote Alexander, 'is simply a drag on the whole business'. Then there were the jealousies that existed between them and their London office.[24] A constant source of tension with the former partners in Sydney were the demands of Robert Mason's trustees for disputed payments for which the new limited company refused responsibility. For Alexander Walker, for whom financial probity – represented by the annual balance of the business – was crucial, the inability of the Sydney business to report regular performance data, or meet deadlines for the balance, was exasperating, as were the increasingly poor results that came back from New South Wales. In addition to his own shareholding in the new business, he had encouraged friends and neighbours in Kilmarnock to invest and he felt his responsibility to them as much as he did to the business.

What appeared to be at the heart of the problems of Mason Brothers was weak leadership and an institutionalised workforce unable to adapt or flex to new conditions. 'There cannot be a doubt in the mind of any businessman but that matters are managed in a very hap-hazard way at Sydney,' wrote Walker in 1888.[25] The company had bought badly (particularly in crockery) and retained large quantities of unsold stock which were a burden on the books. In addition, they made some poor judgements on shipments of wool and tallow to London which led to serious losses. ('I am extremely sorry that that heavy loss should have been made on the tallow, and my opinion is that they should get a good whipping about it.') They had opened a loss-making branch in Brisbane, committed to expensive leases on new buildings, and made costly investments in the Camdenville Foundry. ('Have you not got a spare barrel of gunpowder handy, to blow up the Camdenville, you are losing at the rate of £2000 a year!')[26] In addition, both Walker

and Blaikie (who was made a director to relieve Walker of some of
the pressure) suspected the Sydney office were less than transparent
about the sales of Old Highland whisky in the colony, and were also
withholding funds from other consignees.[27]

The burdens of the management of Mason Brothers, which
involved additional trips to London to attend board meetings, and the
bewildering frequency of often contradictory correspondence from
the various embattled parties ('One detail leads to another and if I
go into one I must go into two and the second will probably lead to a
third and I think three or four sensible men with their heads properly
screwed on could get over the difficulty very easily') clearly placed an
undue strain on Walker at a time when other matters were pressing
and his health was at best indifferent; 'I have had such a terrible
worry and hard work this last three months that I have scarcely
had time for anything; the greater part of the worry & work being
caused by having our firm here and in London formed into a Limited
Liability Company.'[28]

One way to try and resolve the problem was to take more
active control of the management in Sydney by sending Jack Walker
there with a cashier from the London office.[29] 'I was against the
proposal altogether', wrote his father, 'but he having married a
Melbourne girl was most anxious to get settled in Australia.' Jack's lack
of colonial experience and impulsiveness were a concern in London,
despite the need for change: 'If he found anything not strictly aright
he would be down on it. And there is a lot of old manners and customs
in the Sydney management that require shaking up.' The Sydney
management resented his presence, were generally obstructive, and
refused to let him get close to the wine and spirits department. Wilson
wrote to London in 'rather an impertinent letter' that 'It is to be hoped

that Mr John Walker, like whisky, will improve with age.'[30] Alexander Walker was determined that those he had encouraged to invest in Mason Brothers shouldn't suffer from the poor dividend payments, and that his reputation shouldn't suffer from having made a poor recommendation. 'I certainly feel very keenly for those friends whom I introduced to the concern,' he wrote to Wilson, 'some of them unable to lose the interest they had, and I would have them feel that it will be my duty to take up the stock and await the results.' Shareholders had been assured, Blaikie wrote to Jack Walker, 'that as long as Walker's had to do with it he was safe. This was a high compliment to JW&S but it carries immense responsibility which we must face.' The final cost to Alexander Walker of buying back shares ran to thousands of pounds; hardly surprising that he wrote in 1889: 'I have lost so much money in assisting friends lately that I have really got sick and tired of it. Besides I DO not think that a business built on borrowed capital is very often a success.'[31]

It was not just Mason Brothers in Sydney that caused the firm problems. New Zealand was not without difficulties where the distributor, Bernard Lewis, was not held in high regard. 'I don't like the idea of being represented by a broken kneed horse,' wrote Walker to Jack. 'You must put it in your own words without being offensive, but Lewis needs plain speaking and firmness.' When the new company was formed in 1886, Walker surprisingly assured Lewis 'that while he lived he looked forward with every confidence that the position of Mr Lewis would not be altered, and he was perfectly sure his memory would be so respected by his successors that the same policy would be continued.' It wasn't.[32]

In South Africa, diamonds had been discovered in the 1860s and gold in the early 1880s. Walker's were certainly doing business there by then, their first agent being Mackie, Dunn & Co.[33] However with three competing agencies there in 1887 undercutting each other to the detriment of profit and brand reputation, the London office decided to give sole agency to Rolfes Nobel & Co., somewhat against the better judgement of Alexander Walker, who explained his misgivings thus: 'I have a strong opinion that after Mackie Dunn & Co have made a business for us it would be very much out of place to act unkindly towards them,' albeit he was clear that the ultimate objective was that 'Our goods should stand first in the market in South Africa.' Rolfes Nobel had promised to take 8,000 cases a year, but 'Captain' David Sneddon, a famous son of Kilmarnock who was often a source of advice for Walker in colonial matters (and close enough to the business to be a shareholder in the new limited company), asserted that 'Kimberley alone would take that quantity.'[34] The following year Walker wrote 'how pleased he was at the great advances you [Rolfes Nobel] are making with our "brand" in South Africa, and with your energy, and the quality of the article, has no doubt a vastly increased trade will get to be done'. Twelve months later Blaikie wrote to Walker: 'The latest phase of Rolfes' expectations for 1890 is 100,000 cases and upon honour we are not at all sure but that the number will approximate to this. South Africa is developing so rapidly that they must open in various places to retain their position. Johannesburg is only one of many.'[35]

Given the highly competitive nature of these new markets, distributors like Mason Brothers and Rolfes Nobel could be very demanding in terms of advertising expenditure, an expense that Alexander Walker and the London office were always trying to reduce, or at least get the agents to pay a greater part. If a competitor like Robertson's of Dundee moved on price or incentives, Walker's agents wanted to move with them, but in 1888 Mason's were urged not to follow 'Robertson's lead, but [to make] some bold and if possible unique bid for popular favour' and at less expense. Sydney dominated advertising costs; Blaikie complained to Jack Walker in 1888 that 'the advertising is a frightful item & will cause more than Mr Kilgour to tear at scanty locks. We should decidedly object to the special advertising.' While other agents operated on a £300 advertising allowance, Sydney claimed around £900. 'Sydney is getting far too much, comparing with other ports where greater business is being done, certainly three times as much as South Africa.'[36] When push came to shove, and the brand was trying to recover its position in the Melbourne market after the recent success of Usher's – 'about the only market in the world where we are occupying a third-rate position' – advertising was cut by half and the funds spent on an additional traveller to 'push the brand'. The suspicion was that 'the bar-men are tipped to push Usher to the exclusion of others equally good or better'.[37] Walker's didn't eschew all forms of promotion: they produced and distributed framed showcards and 'literature' to stockists, along with posters, mirrors and bar furniture such as glass dispensers for whisky sold in bulk; they also sent out framed photographs of their new premises in Kilmarnock to the trade. Walker had also set up Andrew Douglas, another local boy, in a grocer's shop at 43 Bishopsgate in London in 1883 as a means of promoting his brand. 'No one can deny', wrote Blaikie, 'that perhaps the happiest advertising hit was made by entering Douglas at 43.'[38] But Alexander Walker refused to support magazine and catalogue advertising:

> *You know perfectly well what my opinion is about these stupid advertisements. We paid £40 for a sheet in the Orient. I have seen it dozens of times in Pullman cars, hotels etc., and I have*

*always found it at the bottom of all other books and periodicals,
generally dirty, and no one seemed to know it was there.*

People, he said, 'simply get the smell of it as an advertising medium
and don't care to look at it'.[39] But he understood the importance of
newspapers, having taken a stake in the *Kilmarnock Herald* ('Some of us
will have to put our hands in our pockets pretty deeply') in order to get
its conservative opinions heard in a predominantly liberal town, and
clearly had a preference for the power of well-placed editorial coverage
over advertisement.[40] He certainly put a lot of effort into negotiating
a visit to Kilmarnock by a group of colonial commissioners who had
travelled to Scotland whilst attending the Indian and Empire Exhibition
in London, when he wrote personally to the editor of the *Glasgow
Herald* ('The only one [newspaper] I care to communicate with') asking
him to attend. Writing to Mason's after the visit, Blaikie explained: 'To
say the least of the visit to Kilmarnock "it was a cheap advertisement"
and as all the papers had notices of the event more or less complete, we
are all quite satisfied[;] perhaps you will get a paragraph in some of the
New South Wales or Queensland papers?'[41]

International exhibitions provided a powerful way to advertise
brands to new markets, to introduce them to new consumers (sampling
at one exhibition in London in the 1870s was described as a 'gigantic
tippling shop'), and to win awards, which were powerful third-party
endorsements of quality, of particular importance in the geographies
where they were won. There were thirty-four major Australian, English
and Indian exhibitions between 1851 and 1914 alone, and numerous
others elsewhere in the colonies, Europe and the United States.[42] And
despite a growing cynicism in the press about such events and the
merits of their awards ('For what is an exhibition medal nowadays?
We can no longer compare it to the Victoria Cross; it rather resembles

the decoration or what is literally the Legion of Honour. Everyone
has it who lays himself out to possess it'), wine and spirits producers,
including Scotch whisky blending houses, flocked to them like
prospectors in search of gold.[43] In 1880, Old Highland Whisky won at
Melbourne, being quickly advertised as 'the first prize whisky' by Gibbs,
Bright & Co.[44] The Paris award, obtained in 1885 through the work of
John Dunlop, was followed by press coverage in France and at home
which was shared with customers, although Walker wrote, 'I hope it
may be the means of doing some good but really we are kept so terribly
busy here that we are not so keen unless for your own sake, to open
up new business.'[45] When the company subsequently won the 'first'
award at Adelaide in 1887 for both bottled and bulk whisky, Blaikie
wrote that it was 'exceedingly satisfactory and ought to help us a bit all
round'. Walker (concerned about the expense involved in promoting
such victories) wrote to the London office: 'We were very much pleased
indeed to note that we had got the highest award at Adelaide. I HOPE
THERE WILL BE NO MORE EXHIBITIONS as I think we have gained
quite enough of that sort of distinction.' Nonetheless, he couldn't
help but gloat to William Sanderson, as a postscript to a letter about
the North British Distillery, 'Cablegram to hand got highest award at
Adelaide'.[46] And all these awards, plus more besides, found themselves
on the front label of Walker's Special Old Highland, becoming a fixture
in the brand's get-up, as they are in Johnnie Walker Red Label today.

What exhibition awards did was speak to the quality of Old
Highland Whisky, and it was the maintenance of this that Alexander
held most dear, his core principle of doing business. And at a time when
the art of blending on a commercial scale was still being perfected and
was challenged by the huge scale of growth in the business, Walker
was driven by a philosophy of continuous improvement. He wrote to

Cullen in 1881 describing with relish the arrangement of blending vats and equipment in the new buildings at the Strand: 'We will keep pace with the times and try to send you something finer than we have ever managed yet,' adding, 'Quality will stand on its merit.'[47] 'I hope', he wrote to Sydney in 1883, 'the whisky is still holding its own, if quality will do it, we are determined to keep that up.'[48] Consistency, the Holy Grail of the blender seeking to establish a distinctive product on the market, was not easy to achieve. When dealing with issues raised about a shipment to Melbourne, Walker wrote to Blaikie: 'You should have made them aware that it is almost impossible to make two blends alike,' adding, however, that 'The whisky ... is just about the best we ever sent.'[49]

Colonial agents were quick to panic when other brands seemed to be taking hold in their markets, often demanding that Walker's should imitate their blends or their sales practices (or both). In such circumstances the firm and experienced voice of Alexander Walker held sway. 'With regard to the different brands of whisky which you mention,' he wrote to Cullen in response to one such request:

> they may for a while detract from the sale of JW&S but we are determined to make our whisky so far as quality is concerned of such a standard that nothing in the market shall come before it ... If we had adopted all the plans which have been suggested to us I am confident our whisky would not have maintained its present position in the market, and if it is sold and judged on its own merits I have no doubt as to the results.[50]

Alexander Walker worked hard to provide blends that would meet market needs without compromising the firm's reputation, such as with Glencairn, 'a whisky in value which no other house could compare with', and he responded quickly to any suggestion of a decline in quality and was determined to act on it: 'You said the quality of the last whisky you got was not so nearly as good as formerly. This I cannot understand but if you find the last lot sent you not exactly what you would like, kindly return a small bottle of it to me.'[51] Moreover it's absolutely clear that despite the wide range of responsibilities he had to attend to, he still took these matters deeply personally, making time to study samples of his own and competitor whiskies in order to resolve the frequent pleas from markets for help with the competition.

He was equally resolved not to follow novelty at the expense of quality when Robertson's of Dundee appeared to be threatening business: 'We would simply be imitating our opponents and doing ourselves no good[,] besides you must be aware that I have been very much against any departure from the old lines . . . and as I have been saying to George this morning, supposing we should not make a penny of profit, we shall try to make Walker better than ever.'[52] 'There is not the least doubt', wrote Blaikie to Mason Brothers as the issue with Robertson's rumbled on, 'that the quality of our Old Highland is away and beyond anything supplied previously; the break-up of the whisky ring in Scotland has enabled us to buy older whiskies to better advantage and customers are having the benefit.'[53] When Rolfes in South Africa complained of the success of Usher's Grand Old Highland Whisky, samples were discreetly acquired and forensically analysed, with the 'conclusion that . . . our "special" is head and shoulders ahead.' A special bottling of 'Very Old Highland' was promised, with the label 'printed across "Special High Class" in red ink!' that would 'show the South African friends that we can produce something very old as well as our neighbours'.[54] Walker had an absolute, almost obstinate, confidence in his ability to turn out the best that blended Scotch could offer. 'I think we are quite able to cope with Usher's in any market so far as quality goes,' he wrote in 1889, and asserted he was willing to back 'our "blend"' against any in the market. As he wrote to Blaikie in London, 'Our blend cannot be beat.'[55]

For all the difficulties encountered and overcome by the Walker business, in producing the very best of whiskies a more intractable challenge was presented by the issues of adulteration and counterfeit, already a widespread problem in the world of luxury spirits that Walker's inhabited. Although substitution, the practice of refilling bottles with an inferior product, was thought to be the mainstay of impoverished publicans and managers of tied houses, it could happen anywhere. In October 1886 James Hodge was not the first of the Walker fraternity in London to suspect that he and his friends, waiting for a train north, had been served at one of the numerous bars and refreshment rooms in the Midland Grand Hotel (now the St Pancras Hotel) with whisky from a Walker bottle 'that had never seen Kilmarnock'. It had also been observed that Greenlees Brothers' Lorne Whisky was being 'pushed' by the bar staff at a lower price to Walker's.[56]

The Midland Grand was not only Alexander Walker's favourite place to stay in London ('nothing gave me greater pleasure than going into the smoking room, years ago, after coming home from the theatre or somewhere else, to find that almost everyone was having a glass of Scotch hot and praising it'), but also a significant account offering high visibility to his brand. In addition, the Midland Railway was one of his principal carriers. The manager of the hotel was even pressing Walker's to sell him bulk whisky which he wished to use to improve his own house offering – an opportunity that was naturally refused, with Walker adding, 'His experience as a "blender" we can afford to laugh at.'[57] Blaikie suggested a plan of entrapment at the hotel to catch the manager and his staff 'in the act', but Walker chose first to speak privately with the goods manager and later general manager of the Midland Railway, and also to write to the hotel manager in characteristically unrestrained language, accusing him of being responsible for the adulteration of Walker's whisky in numerous bars throughout the hotel, adding that 'If it suits you to get a commission of a few hundred pounds a year from Greenlees Brothers', it might well suit Walker's to withdraw their business from the railway, seeing that 'they, through you, refuse to do business with one of their best, and largest customers'. Writing to Blaikie he added: 'The pressure has been put on so severely . . . that he will be glad enough to get out of it some way . . . I think we need not fear the result.'[58] Whilst the problem of the Midland Grand may have been dealt with, the broader issue of adulteration was one that the business would return to with a vengeance in the early part of the twentieth century.

In response to the continued growth of the business and the increasing complexities of its management, and perhaps prompted by concerns about his health, Alexander determined to change the structure of the business. John Walker & Sons Ltd was floated in 1887 with a capital of £70,000. Alexander Walker, who received some £50,000 for the old firm, held the majority of the £20 shares (2,000), the remainder (3,250) being issued between family members, employees and intimates. At this point there was nothing to suggest that the business wanted for capital – the continued acquisition of property and extensive building that had continued in the Strand to try and keep up with the ever-increasing demand for bonded storage, bottling, case-making and cooperage had been largely funded by heritable loans. The result: a foreboding whisky garrison standing guard in the centre of the town.

Certificate of Honour from the Jamaica International Exhibition 1891

The Union Bank had provided funds for the ongoing acquisition of whisky stocks, the foundation of the firm's commitment to quality (now divided between Kilmarnock bonds and distilleries), and loans had also been taken on their security. The flotation also allowed Walker and Blair to hatch a long-standing plan to take over the business of William Rankin in Kilmarnock, that firm 'once patronised by nearly all the gentry of the town and surrounding district'.[59]

The directors of the new company, in addition to Alexander Walker who was chairman, were James Blair and John Blaikie,

Jack Walker and George Paterson Walker. The valuation of the business, its stocks and good will had been accomplished speedily by William Robertson (of Robertson & Baxter), from whom Walker's purchased a significant proportion of their whisky stocks, and William Sanderson, of the eponymous blending company and the North British Distillery (in which Walker was a shareholder). The legal side of the formation was dealt with by James McCosh ('Mr McCosh is what I would call an extreme lawyer'), whose knowledge, influence and connections had been a critical factor in the success of the Walker's business.[60]

There is no doubt that Walker saw the formation of the limited company as an opportunity to step back from his involvement in the day-to-day management: 'I have a great lot of work before me for the next month,' he wrote to William Calder in October 1886. 'In fact I intend changing the character of the whole business from which I expect to have more leisure by and by.'[61] Of course there was no guarantee of rest: 'I intended after our firm was launched as a Limited Company', he wrote to his old friend William Kirkland in Nottingham in May 1887, 'that I would have many opportunities of spending time elsewhere, but however much work is taken off my shoulders somehow or other there is always something crops up to chain me to the spot.' He had been persistently unwell for some time, and setting up the new company was simply an additional and unwanted strain. 'I have had so much to do in getting our Company pushed through and although I feel better than I did last year I am not yet so well as I would like to be.'[62]

Walker had tried to reduce his travel to London, and was increasingly precious of his time, writing to Blaikie in 1887: 'I should like to know from you when I am really required, and I should like as much of the <u>real</u> business of the firm thrown into the time I am there as possible . . . it is such a long journey that I do not care to undertake it unless there is really something to do.'[63] He was a regular visitor to hydropathic hotels and spa resorts in Scotland and England ('Glad you have sent us such a good remittance this morning,' he wrote to Blaikie in November 1885, 'and if you can only keep it up a little, you will do me more good than all the Hydropathic establishments in the Kingdom'), and he did find time for holidays.[64] As he was still dealing with the formation of the new company, and arranging the presence of the Royal Caledonian Asylum's Pipe Band at the Burns celebrations in Kilmarnock in 1886, he saw some signs of salvation:

> *Thank goodness I have got rid of the demonstration at last and am off on a yachting cruise tomorrow which I expect will last about a week. I did what I could to make the pipers happy and comfortable and I believe the boys go home with a good feeling as regards Scotland. It is a pity that the man who 'pays the piper' should have to suffer so much. I need not add more on this subject but I am very pleased it is all over and I shall think twice before I enter onto anything of the kind again.*[65]

He mused on the possibility of longer and more exotic journeys, but explained to one friend, 'I would most willingly take your advice and the advice of all my friends and go in for a long trip, but I have such a tremendous train behind me here that I cannot possibly see my way. Perhaps the principal one being my own mother who cannot let me out of her sight more than a week at a time . . .'[66] However, despite periods of being confined to home with problems with his eyesight, his legs and his chest, in 1888 he determined to make a six-week voyage to the

Mediterranean in February of the following year, travelling with his son George on the Orient Line steamer the *Garonne*. The much-longed-for trip was a disaster. Walker became unwell, first with sea-sickness and then serious internal bleeding. On 27 February he was taken off the boat by George at Gibraltar, where doctors feared for his life; having partially recovered, their train journey back to Calais suffered a derailment. He wrote to his friend Andrew Stewart, the Glasgow industrialist who had originally planned to join him on the trip, 'We had to wait for 5 hours in a miserable state the result being that I have caught a fearful dose of bronchitis.'[67]

He and George eventually found their way back to Kilmarnock at the end of March, where Alexander was confined to the house, but pretty soon confessed: 'My nose has been kept as much on the grindstone since coming home,' dealing with general business and the ongoing problems of Mason Brothers. He later thanked George 'for all your kindness to me. I don't know what I could have done without you, and if I did not comply with all your whims I hope you will let that flea stick to the wall.'[68]

His health apparently recovering (although he told Jack he had been frightened by a recurrence of the symptoms in June), he travelled to London, and then to Troon for 'the season' whilst also busying himself in a new project to develop an automatic riveting machine for which he had obtained patents.[69] On 9 July he wrote to George in London: 'We had rather an exciting match at golf last night at Troon when Craig the wine merchant from Glasgow and his step son challenged Fernie and me for a bag of potatoes and although Fernie played very badly we came in 3 up and got quite an ovation.' It was the last letter he wrote.[70] He died on 16 July at Crosbie Tower.

Crosbie Tower in Troon, the home of Alexander Walker, completed in 1885, postcard image c.1910 by William Richie & Sons

'If he leaves us,' wrote Blaikie when news of his illness in Gibraltar had arrived in London, 'it will be a sad, sad blow to all of us, a great big-hearted man, ready with his purse whenever this was wanted.'[71] 'His generosity', wrote the *Kilmarnock Standard* in their obituary, 'has long been proverbial in Kilmarnock and it is all the more praiseworthy that most of it was done in the quietest and most unostentatious manner.'[72] In fact he had shied away from almost any public connection with charities and good causes, and preferred both in matters of philanthropy and for that matter politics (where his staunch conservative principles allied with most of those in the drinks trade) to work quietly in the background through the strong networks of influence he maintained in the town and beyond. 'His brusque manner, downrightness of speech and characteristic impatience of everything that savoured of sham, rendered him liable to misinterpretation,' continued the obituary, but his letter books reveal a man who despite his sometimes harsh words could barely refuse any appeal for either personal or business assistance, and indeed someone who often gave thoughtlessly in total contradiction to the way he ran his business, where money was everything. In his letters to family and friends, whom he valued so dearly, he could be deeply compassionate and caring, showing a surprising degree of sensitivity. Unlike many of his contemporaries he played no great part in industry affairs and would have baulked at the thought of pursuing the cult of personality that other so-called 'whisky barons' deployed so effectively to develop their personal and business brands. He was buried on 19 July at the New Cemetery in Kilmarnock, in the most modest of graves marked by a small, simple Celtic cross, his legacy to his family and fellow directors being the largest and most well-known Scotch whisky company in the world.

CHAPTER 4
MODERN TIMES

The sample room at Walker's Leadenhall Street offices – John Walker & Sons illustrated brochure by A. Barnard, 1894

'Ninety-nine men out of every 100 would prefer a blend.
 The other man would prefer an Islay, and the other
 99 would not look at it. The one man is accustomed to
 have a high flavour, but there is no doubt about it that
 a blend is not only milder but better for you than any
 individual distillery.'[1]

IF ALEXANDER WALKER was sometimes bewildered by the size of his whisky business, the scale of growth it experienced during the twenty years or so after his death would no doubt have seemed inconceivable to him, as would the value of the shares held mostly by his family, and the generous dividends they received. The loss of such a dominant figure in the firm created a vacuum in which long-serving senior managers jostled for position, but George emerged as the leading figure, assisted by his brother Alex. Under the stewardship of these two sons, who even at an early age blended a formidable mixture of production, commercial and marketing skills, the business retained its leadership of the Scotch whisky industry, seeing off close rivals such as John Dewar & Sons and James Buchanan & Co. Slow but steady growth was followed by an explosion of both sales and profits in the early 1890s. Fundamental to this achievement was the stubborn belief in the primacy of quality as the key ingredient for business success, and the need to guarantee that by the relentless investment in maturing whisky stocks, and in primary production. Quality touched every aspect of production, even when the firm was struggling to meet the demand for orders from both home and, increasingly, overseas markets, which accounted for around a third of sales value. And consumers were offered more choice by the introduction of a 'Special' and 'Extra Special' blend of Old Highland Whisky. 'Give quality and let it be its own advertisement', remained the watchword of the firm, which refused to follow the rush that many of its competitors made to increasingly extravagant and expensive advertising in both the home market and abroad.

With genuine cognac and brandy still in short supply as a result of *phylloxera*, the market in London and elsewhere was flooded with adulterated spirit, much of it from Hamburg. 'There is little doubt', wrote the *Brewer's Gazette*, 'that to all intents and purposes Scotch Whisky has killed brandy as a beverage in this country.'[2] Consumption of sherry had also nose-dived from its peak of fashionability in 1873 as a result of declining quality, and critically the loss of medical endorsements that had helped build its popularity.[3] And although leading brands such as Kinahan's ('Delicious and very wholesome ... universally recommended by the profession'), and Dunville's ('recommended by the medical profession in preference to French brandy') were heavily advertised, consumption of Irish whisky, 'which a few years ago attained such a high position in public favour', was also in decline. James Greenlees, one of the first Scotch whisky blenders in London, recalled that in 1871, when 'the bulk of whisky consumed in England was Irish ... we sold about three vats of Irish to one of Scotch'. But since the 1880s it had fallen foul of a familiar fate: 'The reason for the original dethronement of Irish Whisky', wrote Ridley's, 'is not far to seek. It was, undoubtedly, the flooding of the English market with spirits of inferior quality ...'[4]

> *The point on the circumference of the wheel of fortune where Scotch sits firm, can even hardly yet be said to have reached its perpendicular, while the place of Irish on the wheel, so far as the better class consumers are concerned, is hardly known ... we cannot think that Scotch is likely to be ousted from its supremacy for many a long day.*[5]

The importance of medical recommendation in Scotch achieving this position of supremacy was not lost on the *British Medical Journal*: 'The chief cause of the recent popularity of whisky is, no doubt, that the medical profession now very extensively recommend it when alcohol is required, as being, when fully matured by age, one of the best of all alcoholic stimulants.'[6]

Of course what had also driven the growth of Scotch was the blending of pot-still malt whiskies with patent-still grain whiskies, and the ability of the blending houses to cater for the tastes of consumers who were largely unused to, or as some would have it uneducated in, Scotch whisky. Also critical to this success was the increased availability of aged whiskies for the blenders of premium proprietary brands such as Walker's Old Highland to work with. This growing consumer preference for blended Scotch began in Scotland, where by 1890 'everybody who buys a glass of whisky knows perfectly well that he is buying a blended whisky ... and there is a lot of malt whisky of the highest quality that people would not drink'.[7] Grain whisky not only helped the blender create a product that suited the purchaser's pocket, but as James Greenlees explained it mellowed the tastes and flavours of the individual and often idiosyncratic single malts, and crucially helped integrate them. 'If you make a blend of say, five fine malt whiskies, without grain ... you can almost detect the different distilleries that they have come from, [but] if you put a very small quantity of grain spirit into your blend you at once marry them, and you cannot detect the difference in the slightest.'[8] As blended Scotch grew in popularity, so a number of vested interest groups became increasingly vociferous in their opposition to its success. None were more vocal than the self-styled experts in the wine and spirits trade, who clung to the elitist belief that it was only ignorance that prevented drinkers in London from embracing single malt whiskies, and continually expressed the hope that eventually at least 'the better sort' of middle-class consumers would see the light. By 1890 even as gruff and old-school a commentator as *Ridley's Wine and Trade Circular* had to admit defeat:

*Going back to a certain extent on . . . our views as expressed
in the past . . . We believe the lighter Lowlands, and the much
abused grain had much to do with the spread of the taste for
Scotch Whisky. It is since blending, aye, and blending with
grain, became the fashion, that it has taken the place in our
Trade it now occupies. We should feel inclined indeed to go
further than merely disputing the Highlander's assumption,
and to say that it is more the blends which have made the
reputation of Highlands than vice versa.*[9]

Whilst toddies were still popular, the increasingly fashionable way of
drinking Scotch was with soda water or seltzer, often 'long'. 'People
have taken more to drinking whisky with mineral waters than toddy,'
explained James Greenlees. This had implications for the way blends
were put together. 'Toddy was a much heavier whisky than the whisky
you drink with mineral waters. The blends have come now to be much
more suitable for mineral waters.'[10] The now fashionably rediscovered
'highball', mixing whisky with soda over ice, had been a common
enough drink since the 1870s.[11] Particularly enjoyed by travellers in
warmer climates, it was declared by the *Times of India* in 1884 to be the
'perfect drink'. 'Oh life to a man is his whisky and soda', declared the
first line of a popular temperance song.[12] Both the medical profession,
and for that matter proprietors of patent medicines, recommended
this beverage as a suitable, healthy drink. In 1889 a subsequently
much-repeated story alleged that the royal physician, Sir William
Jenner, had advised the Queen to give up claret and champagne, and
instead drink only Scotch whisky and Apollinaris mineral water, who
in their own advertising stressed the suitability of the brand as a mixer
with whisky.[13] But few were as explicit as Walker's in 1893, when Old

Highland Whisky made a uncharacteristic appearance in the press, advertised in the *Illustrated London News* in a joint promotion with Rosbach mineral water (whose agency Walker's held in New South Wales), promising customers a free 'small' bottle of whisky with their first order of Rosbach: 'Kilmarnock, or Old Highland Whisky, is a pure and well-matured spirit, and in combination with Rosbach water is a healthful and delicious beverage.'[14] And no doubt for relative whisky novices in London or the Home Counties, influenced as they might be by medical recommendation and the sovereign's drinking habits, diluting blended Scotch bottled at proof or '10 under', made the new drink far more palatable, in addition to 'healthful and delicious'.

That is not to deny, of course, that there wasn't still a small group of single-minded devotees ('the other man would prefer an Islay, and the other 99 would not look at it') for whom malt whiskies were still readily available. The four Clachan bars in central London claimed to be the only establishments in the city where 'all the finest Old Highland whiskies . . . are to be obtained in their natural purity', including Lagavulin, Caol Ila, Talisker, Glenlivet, Glendronach, Ardbeg and Long John of Ben Nevis.[15] Among the single malts listed by the Edinburgh Scotch Whisky Stores, off the Strand and 'opened principally to introduce to London what is rarely to be had, the very best brands of Scotch Whiskies', were Ben Nevis, Brackla, Cragganmore and Old Lochnagar.[16] The latter, advertised in London as early as 1861 as 'Royal Lochnagar Balmoral Whisky as supplied to Her Majesty and the nobility', had benefited enormously as a brand from the patronage of the Queen, who had first visited the distillery in 1848, granting it a royal warrant ('All the royal palaces solely supplied since 1848').[17] The Queen's regular visits to John Begg, and his to Balmoral, were fixtures of Court reporting in the national press, with the result that Lochnagar, bathing in the glow of regal endorsement, became one of the most prominent single malts on the market, and Begg could describe himself 'Her Majesty's loyal distiller'.[18] 'There is no whisky better known than Lochnagar,' wrote the *Wine and Spirit Trade Record* in 1898, noting that according to Gladstone, a connoisseur who knew how to drink his single malts, it 'made excellent toddy'.[19]

When Alexander Walker died in 1889, he left personal estate of £93,400, roughly the equivalent of £12 million today. Almost £70,000 of his estate represented his shares and balance with John Walker & Sons Ltd. His share in the partnership in William Rankin & Sons (with James Blair) was worth another £8,000. In addition to these and various small shareholdings and insurance policies, his other principal assets were Crosbie Tower in Troon, left in life-rent to his wife Isabella McKimmie, Piersland House in Kilmarnock, and Stoneygate Farm near Galston, next to Piersland Farm, which had been inherited by his wife. Walker made three substantial charitable donations in his will: £1,000 to Kilmarnock Infirmary, £250 to Kilmarnock Industrial School, and £250 to the Kilmarnock Charity Organisation Society. His estate was to be divided equally between his children, with the proviso that they should each receive a like portion of 250 shares in the business (equivalent to around £1 million each).[20] Four of Alexander's daughters were to marry over the next few years, while the youngest, Maggie, died in 1893. The result was that although all of Alexander's sons, with the exception of the youngest, James, were involved in the active management of the business, his married daughters and 'the brothers-in-law' exerted a significant influence on the future direction of the business in the twentieth century.

In the immediate aftermath of Alexander's death the critical issue seemed to be who of the surviving management of the business would take the dominant role. Blaikie, in London, held seniority on the basis of length of service. Blair, equally long in the trade, was the safe pair of hands in Kilmarnock. Jack, impulsive, with eight years in the firm, was in Australia struggling to make the Walker interests clearly felt in Mason Brothers. George, his father's 'principal assistant', was with Blaikie in London. Two tension points commanded their attention. The first, how the company could keep pace with the need for bonded storage and the demand for both bottled and bulk blends, which had apparently outstripped the facilities in the Strand, despite the continuous development that had taken place there during the decade. The second was the structure of the business, with Jack pressing since before his father's death for the formation of a public company, which would release cash to the existing shareholders and increase the firm's liquidity. The two points were obviously interlinked.

Moreover Jack, most keen for a public flotation, was in debt to his father (around £6,000 at the time of Alexander's death) and anxious to raise cash.[21] Blaikie, whose ill-judged financial speculations had more than once led Alexander Walker to contemplate his dismissal (and once prompted Blaikie to consider fleeing the country – as Walker explained: 'The reason for his proposing to go to San Francisco, was that he had made such an ass of himself that he was afraid to meet me'), also had significant personal debts to Walker, and to the business, and, as it turned out, elsewhere too.[22] He was therefore eager 'to have some cash or shares as I wish to wipe out my liability with the Bank etc.'. Jack's proposals to involve financiers, the bête noire of his father, were opposed by all: 'With regard to Jack's scheme for floating JW&S on a new basis. This has had our attention for a long time. The thing we cannot see ... is the intervention of a Financial Agent!'[23] Between banks and loans, ably arranged by the lawyer McCosh, the firm had managed to keep free of external influence. And the key decision-makers were neither the old manager directors nor the young family directors, but rather Alexander Walker's trustees, whose natural tendency was to

George Paterson Walker (on right) and a colleague in the Walker offices in Leadenhall Street, London, beneath a portrait of his father Alexander, 1894

err on the side of caution on behalf of the other brothers and sisters. Thomas Kennedy, of Kilmarnock's Glenfield Company and one of Alexander's closest friends, described the trustees as 'a stock broker, and banker and a Glasgow merchant who is a very sharp business man'.[24] After George Paterson Walker became chairman of the company in 1890 (aged only twenty-six), the matter was dropped until the capital of the private company was increased in 1903.

The issue of storage and production capacity was more intractable, and resulted in open conflict between Blaikie and Blair. Blair, in effect production director in Kilmarnock, had suggested that the one way to resolve the issue of bonded storage would be to use available space in the warehouses of local rivals William Wallace & Co., owners of 'The Real Mackay' brand. Wallace's had built a bonded warehouse in East George Street around the time of Walker's first expansion into the Strand, and were just completing additional bonded space in Titchfield Street, 'undertaken in the belief', thought Blaikie, 'that JW&S Ltd would require more warehouse room'. He was aghast at Blair's proposal, explaining that the late Alexander Walker was 'dead against encouraging Mackay'. Why not, he argued, use the bonded stores of William Lowrie in Glasgow (with whom Walker's had cordial relations), or use accommodation at Wallace's for stock belonging to James Rankin & Co.? It was all a matter of reputation: 'For the sake of our prestige in the Home Trade we must be able to say we bond ourselves & if we do go to an opponent, we are likely to be twitted as playing second fiddle to William Wallace.'[25] Blaikie and George Walker were also keen to use Lowrie for blending to take the strain off Kilmarnock: 'We are of opinion that sooner not later you will require to take advantage of Lowrie for blending ... the fact is in our opinion there will be no slackening of orders for months to come and the sooner this is recognised the better for ourselves.' Quality, argued Blaikie, was being compromised because of the pressure on the Strand:

> *Not a day passes but that we have complaints of the Old*
> *Highland! In our opinion the Whisky never was finer than*
> *now, but we cannot shut our eyes to the fact that the Whisky*
> *is not getting the time to wed and a rawness is palpable in*
> *consequence. This would be obviated by making use of, now and*
> *again, Lowrie's big vat.*

'We are having strong opposition,' he continued. 'Dewar, Perth, and others are presenting some capital whisky, well matured blends. It is not pleasant to lose orders.'[26] The result was another flurry of property acquisitions and building in the Strand, where a new cooperage had just been completed, which included taking over the old Crown Hotel to allow an extension to the existing bond.[27] By 1892 the company was able to report at its annual general meeting that the warehouse was complete (with 'the installation of electric light and power, and high pressure hydraulics, which will secure much greater safety and convenience') but that 'the rapid growth of the Home Trade has necessitated the acquiring of additional properties in Croft Street which are in the process of alteration'.[28]

In 1893 the normally publicity shy John Walker & Sons commissioned the father of whisky writing, Alfred Barnard, famed as author of *The Whisky Distilleries of the United Kingdom* (published in 1887), to produce a booklet describing the production facilities of the firm, which was then circulated all over the world. Barnard described the complex that had grown up around the Strand in characteristically glowing terms ('quite the most prominent object in the town'), but even allowing for his hyperbole what his readers saw was a best-in-class manufacturing operation, where the very latest in equipment and technology was deployed for the benefit of both efficiency and the health and safety of employees, who at this stage numbered around 170 'hands'. Department by department, from the 'bright and shining' boiler room, to bottle washing ('cleanliness next to quality here reigns supreme, and may be said to be the motto of the establishment'), to the bonded stores ('arrangements for the prevention of fire of every modern improvement are in evidence everywhere'), through bottling and packing ('exceptional solicitude is displayed in the brightness of the whisky and the cleanliness of the bottles'), to the cooperage and case-making departments ('containing the most improved machinery'), everything he described spoke of a perfectly thought through logistical triumph. As another visitor a couple of years later wrote, 'What struck me most was the almost military precision with which the system of division of labour is carried out.' Almost like some Chaplinesque *Modern Times*, 'The hands look as if driven by some great motor, each one timed exactly to keep others going.' Neatly uniformed staff, electric light throughout the building, departments all connected by telephone, and the promise that an order received in Kilmarnock could be in London the next day.[29] And yet despite this investment, growth of sales demanded further accommodation, partly delivered through the purchase of St George's Brewery on the Commercial Road in London's East End in 1901, which was to become an important adjunct to the bottling facilities in Kilmarnock.

The purchase and retention of whisky stocks would always be a matter of strategic importance for the Walker business, and the foundation of the quality upon which their success rested. As blenders like Alexander Walker had sought to perfect their blends, and achieve the Holy Grail of consistency between batches, so their demands for component whiskies became greater, in terms of variety, style and quality. For all the idiosyncrasies of individual whiskies, the industry thought of them in terms of regional style: Highland, Lowland, Islay, Campbeltown, and of course grains. As blends took hold both in London and England more generally, and in export markets, so an investment market developed for new and mature whiskies. 'It is an investment that is very much thought of,' said James Greenlees,

> and carried on to a very large extent in Scotland by gentlemen outside the trade altogether; there is a very large amount of money invested by the public; men who have money saved, instead of investing it in railways and other things, invest it in whisky; it is a very good and safe investment indeed.[30]

Whiskies were bought and sold like commodities, trade newspapers reported and prophesied on the state of the market for aged Highlands (normally going up) and Campbeltowns (normally going down), and distillers, rather than dealing direct with the end customers, more often than not found themselves dealing with ruthless speculators, and made annual journeys to Glasgow, Leith and London at the start of each distilling season to sell their wares in advance of costly production. The demand that began to grow for whisky investments led some distillers to behave in ways that reflected poorly on their reputations:

> The policy of notably one firm of Distillery proprietors has been much animadverted upon among the consuming dealers. The gentlemen in question own one very favourite brand, and are insisting upon double quantity being taken from their

*other two distilleries when this high-priced speculative brand
is purchased, i.e., a purchaser taking 10 hhds of the favourite
must take in all 20 hhds, of one or both of the other brands . . .
such a policy cannot ultimately benefit the authors of it, and we
think they will find the alienation of old consuming customers
scarcely compensated for, by the willingness of the speculative
buyer to submit to the conditions.*[31]

Blending houses had the choice of either buying on this cut-throat open
market as stocks were required, with all the risks and expense it could
bring, or investing heavily in new whiskies themselves to secure their
own stocks. Walker's, with the ability to deploy bank overdrafts and
steadily convert reserve funds into acquisitions, chose the latter. Their
purchase ledgers show that the company traded direct with many
distillers, including those from Campbeltown (Greenlees & Colville,
J. & A. Mitchell) and Islay (Mackie & Co.) that had always been staples
of their stock. Regular purchases were also made from individual
distilleries such as Bon Accord in Aberdeen (from whom Alexander had
purchased regularly), Moses Risk's Provanmill distillery in Glasgow, and
Bankier in Stirlingshire. Whisky brokers were increasingly important
in sourcing their acquisitions too, particularly Robertson & Baxter of
Glasgow, who might have accounted for as much as 40 per cent of all
their purchases in the 1880s and 1890s.[32] As we have seen, Alexander
Walker had a close (if occasionally brusque) relationship with the
company's principal, W. A. Robertson. When Alexander was in Glasgow
(which he frequently was) he conducted business from the Robertson
& Baxter offices in West Nile Street; of his sons, both George and Alex
were said to have benefited from the knowledge and the networks they
gained there.

Alex Walker joined the company in Kilmarnock in 1888 shortly before his nineteenth birthday, interrupting his training to be a lawyer with J. & J. McCosh of Dalry, the firm which had proved to be of such importance to his father.[33] In the short period before his father died he was immersed in the workings of the business both in Kilmarnock and London. But whilst Jack was almost entirely engaged in the commercial side of the business, and George straddled both sales, marketing and production, Alex was to spend his early years at work immersed in whisky. 'In looking at whiskies,' he said in 1908, 'which I have done continuously for 20 years, which is my province, I do practically nothing else but make up samples.'[34] As the company minute books reveal, he was almost obsessed with the critical issue of securing whisky stocks, and no doubt learned much from working with James Blair, his father's principal buyer. As the family reasserted their control over the management of the business in the early 1890s he was also responsible for a new departure, the acquisition of primary production through investments in distilleries. Alex had been appointed a director in 1890 following the death of his father, and as early as the following year was pressing his fellow directors on the necessity of these investments.

Alex was leading negotiations to purchase Glen Albyn distillery in Inverness in 1892 ('the Directors of the opinion that it will be of the great advantage to the business to secure the distillery'), when he became aware of the opportunity to purchase Cardow distillery in the heart of Speyside.[35] Licensed in 1824 and with a tradition before that of illicit distilling, Cardow was part of a farm of the same name owned by the Cumming family. Like many other distilleries it had found the initial transition from pre-industrial to industrial production challenging in terms of quality, but had eventually garnered a very high reputation for its whisky under the management of Elizabeth

Cardhu Distillery, c.1890

Cumming, daughter-in-law of the founder, John.[36] Elizabeth had totally rebuilt the distillery between 1884 and 1886 (selling off the exhausted and unwanted old stills with other equipment to William Grant in Dufftown for his new distillery there), and her whisky was described by Alfred Barnard, who visited the new distillery just as it was completed, as being of 'the thickest and richest description, and admirably suited for blending purposes . . . a single gallon of it is sufficient to cover ten gallons of plain spirit.'[37] Elizabeth had previously resisted approaches to sell the distillery, but possibly as a result of illness (she died less than twelve months after the sale) had decided to put it on the market in order to secure the future of her family. Negotiations were swiftly carried through in the summer of 1893, and in September the deal was concluded to purchase the distillery and farm for £20,500. A critical point was that Elizabeth's eldest son, John F. Cumming, was appointed a director of the company and received 100 shares, with the stipulation that he 'reside at Craig Ellachie or somewhere in the vicinity of the Distillery and to devote his whole time and attention to the management of the Distillery, and to furthering the business of the firm'.[38] After this success, Alex – now with the assistance of

Elizabeth Cumming of Cardhu, with her eldest grandson, c.1892

Cumming, who was to be in effect Walker's production director in the north – continued the search for other distilleries, and in the following year agreed to lease Annandale in the Borders, another recently rebuilt distillery, for a period of twenty years.[39]

Reckless speculation continued to have a destabilising effect on the industry, raising prices artificially and making it harder for companies like Walker's to build up their reserve of stocks. People with little understanding of the whisky business were drawn to the trade in the hope of earning substantial and relatively short-term profits, and adopted behaviours that were detrimental to the long-term health of the category. It also encouraged avaricious distillers to adopt dangerous levels of production, leaving large stocks of overpriced whisky maturing in warehouses. The first crack in this unsustainable edifice was the collapse of the Leith whisky firm Kidd, Eunson and Co., part of the Leith 'whisky ring', in 1887, which led to a rush of failures and a flood of whisky onto the market. For firms like Walker's this was much to their advantage, after years of suffering the effects of artificially high prices.[40] 'In consequence of what has been termed "the Whisky Crisis", the year has been an exceptionally favourable one for exporters and others,' said George Walker at the company's annual meeting in 1888, 'who like the Company, do not purchase speculatively, but only for the requirements of their business. Large quantities of Whiskies were thrown upon the market, and your Directors were enabled to make considerable purchase at prices which have favourably affected the balance.' Ridley's observed that 'Blenders with a good outlet never had such a time.'[41]

The general feeling in the trade was that the Kidd, Eunson failure was a salutary lesson to the industry which it would not quickly forget. However, the relentless thirst of Scotch whisky blenders for malt whiskies and the opportunities for easy profits only continued to promote unsustainable speculation on a scale previously undreamt of, both in distillery-building and stock-holding, and in the promotion and advertising of new brands. At the centre of a closely knit web of profiteers in both production and marketing were Pattison Brothers of Leith, whose spectacular and criminal fall from grace in 1899 was one of the principal drivers towards the consolidation that would take place in the industry between 1910 and 1925.[42] Their lavish approach to every aspect of their business was excoriated in a speech by Alex Walker months after the crash, as reported in the trade press:

> The so-called crisis in the Scotch Whisky trade was due to two causes – the failure of a large firm, and the over-production of Scotch Whisky. His view was that the first was a severe blow to a phase of the modern style of business, viz., advertise largely, and take the value of same out of quality (for, after all, it cannot be paid for otherwise), against the old, proper, and more honourable style of business – give quality and let it be its own advertisement.[43]

The proliferation of registered brands of blended Scotches on the home market, along with the surge of brewers' bulk whiskies offered for sale in public houses, and the range of prices between these tap whiskies and the very best proprietary offerings, made it difficult for Walker's to maintain their trade with only one offering, their Old Highland, or 'Kilmarnock Whisky'. As early as 1876, if not before, they were also selling a special whisky, 'Very Old Highland', at a price premium to the main brand.[44] Alexander Walker had worked hard to develop the new brand, Glencairn, which was positioned away from Old Highland both in terms of price (cheaper) and character; it was 'distinct', with 'a character of its own'. It was being sold in Australia by 1879 and was also sold in London (occasionally as the 'Royal Glencairn Blend').[45] No matter what its qualities, it was not destined for success.

All three of these brands were being sold in both bulk and bottles, and gallon jars.[46] Walker's used both square and round bottles for Old Highland initially. Business correspondence suggests that the square bottle was championed by the London office despite Alexander Walker's concerns with managing the returnable square bottle: 'If we had simply carried out the principle of a round bottle in a common case we would simply have sold a case of whisky and had nothing more to do with it, instead of having all the trouble of returned empty, half-broken, cases, broken bottles, and perhaps only half the number in each.' The squares were returned for reuse by Walker's, whereas rounds, it was argued, were more attractive to customers and not returned to Walker's: 'You will find that the wine merchant will try and buy whisky in bottles he can conveniently use for other purposes.' 'Father', wrote George, 'is altogether averse to this style of package & in the meantime won't entertain the idea at all.'[47] But the square bottle, although not the only one used in the world of Scotch whisky by 1880 (their Kilmarnock neighbours Rankin also used one at that time), clearly gave the brand more distinctiveness, particularly when combined with the slanted label, and aided its visibility in an increasingly crowded category in both home and export markets, and as such was more than worth the trouble it may have caused. When Rolfes Nobel in South Africa requested a higher quality of blend to deal with the threat of an Usher's whisky, Blaikie and George Walker agreed that 'our "special" is head and shoulders ahead' and suggested using 'Very Old Highland in a <u>Black Bottle</u> . . . with our ordinary "<u>Very Old</u>" Label printed across "<u>Special High Class</u>" in red ink!'[48]

During the last decade of the nineteenth century a third blend was added to the family of bottled whiskies, and they were renamed for sales purposes Old Highland, Special Old Highland, and Extra Special Old Highland. Priced in London at 3s. 6d., 4s. and 4s. 6d., they were being advertised by retailers in Australia under these names by 1894.[49] These three were also available in bulk along with three less expensive blends, Croft, Tun and Special Tun.[50] Increasingly the company wanted to distance the name John Walker from lower-priced whiskies in order to maintain its premium positioning, whilst at the same time meeting the needs of this particular, and profitable, segment of the market. The acquisition of Kilmarnock rivals Rankin's was one way of doing this – their whisky had been exported in square bottles as 'Rankin's Kilmarnock Whisky', but after Alexander Walker and James Blair took over the business their principal blend became the 'Dew of the Highlands'.[51] The company also had a long-standing relationship with Johnstone Sadler & Co. of London, and blended and bottled their brand Napier Johnstone, also in a square bottle (though quite distinct from the Walker square), which they sold on commission in Australia and South Africa. The brand was sold in India by Cutler Palmer & Co., and was subsequently acquired outright by Walker's as a secondary.[52] In 1898 they also acquired a substantial shareholding in the Glasgow firm of Slater, Rodger & Co., partly to take advantage of their surplus capacity for blending and bottling that couldn't be managed at Kilmarnock, but also to provide another route for putting secondary brands onto the market.[53] Bulk whisky continued to be problematic, and such was the appalling reputation of London tap whisky, much of it blended by the large brewery companies to be sold at the cheapest possible prices through their tied houses, that Walker's refused where possible to deal with them. They did nonetheless seek to extend their own influence with licensees by offering them loans and generous credit as a way of securing accounts.[54]

The strategy that Alex Walker embarked on, which would soon lead to Walker's long-standing claim to have the largest maturing stocks of malt whisky in the world, was driven by that same obsession for quality that had haunted his father. Alex was also driven by a concern for taste and flavour, and by the need for consistency, hard to achieve when the scale of the business was increasing at such a break-neck pace. But single malts, at the time so variable in quality from week to week and year to year, did not meet the public's needs: 'We have absolutely failed to sell pot still whisky by itself,' he said. His blends were carefully constructed with a view towards the changing public taste for less robust whiskies whilst maintaining the distinct taste and character of pot-still Scotch, and also to the way that the blends would be drunk. This process began at the distilleries, where when possible he intervened in the distillation to ensure the spirit that was produced would meet his needs when mature, and where he advocated direct-fired over steam-heated stills in order to retain flavour and character.[55] When blending, regional styles were vatted together as a first step, a practice followed by all leading blending houses. As James Greenlees explained,

> We blend malt whiskies, all pure malt made in different districts, and then we blend grains[;] we blend all Campbeltown, all Islay, all Glenlivet, all Lowland malt and all grain, and we use the proportion of each of these to get the whisky that we consider will suit the palate of the English public.[56]

Walker thus produced 'Highland', 'North Country' and 'Plain' vats of malts before blending these together with grains. He insisted on a high malt content (arguing that in his personal view a legal minimum proportion in a blend might be 50 per cent) and criticised those who went 'beyond the public taste' to offer blends that had lost the true character of Scotch whisky, which he believed was derived in pot-still flavours.[57] As we have seen it was also critical to have enough time to allow the blended whiskies to 'wed' before bottling. The interiors of Walker's sample room in Kilmarnock show just how complex the blending process had become, with shelves stacked with 'new-make' and mature samples as well as reference samples of previous blends. And ever present at the blender's table, a soda-water syphon to ensure that blends were tasted as they would be drunk by consumers. As drinking toddy fell victim to the fashion for Scotch and soda, so the style of blends were changed to suit the serve. Traditional toddy whiskies had a very pronounced and oily Islay character that was brought out with the warm water and sugar; the newer blends less so.[58] West Coast whiskies had always been prominent in Walker's purchases and still gave their blends the signature smoky flavours that marked their house style, but the new whiskies that Alex Walker produced were certainly blended for the whisky-and-soda age. This style was to some extent shared by other notable blends from the West of Scotland, such as Teacher's and White Horse, compared to the quite different lighter blends from the east such as Dewar's and Bell's 'Perth' whiskies, or Watson's of Dundee, with almost no smoky character. One of the reasons for the success of Scotch whisky in the late nineteenth century was the fact that between them, these and the numerous other brands of blends provided a range of tastes and flavours that suited almost every palate.

CHAPTER 5

THE TRIUMPH OF BLENDED SCOTCH WHISKY

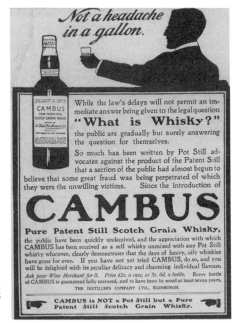

Cambus Single Grain Whisky, 'Not a headache in a gallon', 1906

'It is only by adaptation to modern taste and adoption of modern methods that Scotch Whisky will be enabled to retain its position.'[1]

AS A NEW CENTURY dawned on the Edwardian Age, the triumph of blended Scotch whisky might have seemed at first sight complete. In cities and towns throughout the kingdom brands such as Watson's, Buchanan's, White Horse and Usher's bellowed their names at consumers from enormous hand-painted advertising hoardings, from posters on the sides of buses and trams, and signs at railway stations. On London's Embankment, bewildered consumers were faced with a gigantic electric-lit Highlander, who, with kilt and sporran swinging in the wind, spent the night (and possibly the day) drinking from a thistle-shaped glass of Scotch.[2] In the weekly magazines, the *Illustrated London News* and the *Graphic*, brands like Old Uam Var and Robertson's vied for a share of voice with the bigger brands. High-class grocers and wine and spirits merchants boasted in provincial newspapers of their own bottlings of both blended and single Scotch whiskies, alongside their stocks of proprietary brands, whilst Lipton's were selling their 15-year-old Kiosk Liqueur Whisky ('The Cream of Scotch Whiskies') at discount prices. Shop windows large and small were filled with a cornucopia of attractively got-up whisky bottles and showcards. Ornate mirrors and elaborate signs declaring the virtues of one or other whisky brand decorated the walls of public houses the length and breadth of the country. And only a few years earlier, caged parrots had been employed to call out the name of one very particular brand in the capital's most stylish bars.[3] Remarkably the only thing missing from this cacophony was the largest and likely the most profitable blended Scotch company, John Walker & Sons, 'the diffident distiller'.[4]

Blended Scotch (like the Scottish diaspora) was to be found in every corner of the British Empire, as well as in bars and hotels from New York to San Francisco ('The Americans are inclined to turn liking into mania. As it was with the by cycle [sic], golf, buttons, so it was with Scotch Whisky, which suddenly, and without apparent cause, became a fashionable drink').[5] An advert in the *Singapore Free Press* declared: 'Scotch Whisky is the universal Beverage.'[6] Fashionable society and the establishment were apparently smitten. In the City of London, 'Men who formerly drank wine at lunch take whisky and Apollinaris or soda instead. In catering for this class quality is an indispensable necessity. Malt whiskies, either single or blended malts, are unsuitable here also, for as a rule these do not go well with minerals, and are besides usually too heavy for the purpose.'[7] In the West End's clubland, a whisky bottle and soda syphon ruled the table. At London's Carlton Hotel, and the 'leading smart "feeding grounds" of Society . . . one sees even the ladies preferring the Whisky and Soda to Champagne'. 'The society lady,' wrote an observer, 'without hesitation, takes whisky, and does not scorn to be helped from the bottle which is advertised in every paper.' 'Ladies', wrote another, 'take a great deal more wine than they used to at dinner, and they also indulge in frequent liquors and whisky and sodas.'[8] The *Sportsman* advised readers concerned that drinking Scotch might be a cause of obesity.[9] At the end-of-year prize-giving of the Gravesend Fancier's Society, bottles of Walker's 'Special Scotch Whisky' were liberally dispensed for the winning displays of pigeons and rabbits.[10] Polite society admired the adventures of war correspondent Lady Sarah Wilson, who greeted guests at her bomb-proof shelter in Mafeking in South Africa with Scotch and soda and cigarettes, and were horrified by the 'whisky famine' reported in Ladysmith.[11] The upright were scandalised by the long-running Chandos-Pole divorce case, where the principal indiscretions seem to have occurred whilst the accused parties were drinking whisky and soda (and smoking) 'until the early hours of the morning'.[12]

Street advertising in St Giles Circus, London, c.1910

Amongst the 'barber's accessories', 'clocks, barometers and telescopes', 'rubber goods', sherry, champagne and Australian brandy packed onto the American Ladies' Hospital Ship *Maine*, setting sail to offer respite for British troops in the Cape, were ten cases of Buchanan's Special Scotch Whisky. Another blender offered 2,000 bottles to the Lord Mayor of London's Equipment Fund for the London Imperial corps heading to the South African war.[13] During the summer at the seaside, whisky distillers were sponsoring brand-themed sandcastle-building competitions for children (one distiller in question said 'He did not think that wrong could be made by getting children to construct certain letters with shells').[14] At Bournemouth Theatre Royal and Opera House, families at the pantomime (*Little Red Riding Hood*, strangely enough) were dazzled by the spectacle of the courtyard, and later the 'gorgeous tableau' of the Grand Salon ('where festivities were the order of the day') at the 'Hotel de Whisky'.[15] Meanwhile, for insomniac readers of the *Norfolk News Sheet*, Dr W. Gordon Stables recommended Scotch whisky, to be taken only after food, in bed – 'the nightcap and the evening newspaper'.[16]

Despite the apparently complete cultural assimilation of Scotch whisky into British life at the start of the twentieth century, beneath the surface the industry was in turmoil. A deeply divisive dispute between the old whisky establishment, who were challenging the legitimacy and legal status of blended Scotch, and the massive enterprises that produced those blends, was headed for a very public denouement. And although the voice of John Walker & Sons was apparently almost absent from this clash, it was critical in shaping the future of their business in the twentieth century, and in the development of their brand. Indeed it's true to say that without the uncertainty created during this long-running dispute, which finally ended in 1909, 'Johnnie Walker' as the brand we know today might never have existed.

At first sight this was a simple dispute between the Highland malt distillers and the Lowland distillers of single grain whiskies. The one distilled a heavily flavoured spirit from malted barley in old-fashioned pot stills, the other a light and sweet spirit from a mixture of malted barley, maize and wheat in the patent still, invented, or perfected, only in 1832. Single malts may have had a constituency in the Highlands and among expatriates in London and a handful of self-styled connoisseurs (mostly in or related to the trade), but for the average drinker they were unapproachably fierce, phenolic, and frightfully strong. By mixing malt whisky with lighter and sweeter grain whiskies to produce a blend, Scotch was transformed.[17] It was the development of blended Scotch whisky by grocers and wine and spirit merchants in the early decades of the nineteenth century that had democratised Scotch, delivering a consistent product at an affordable price with an acceptable taste. The retail presence of single malts, never commercially well developed by the distillers themselves, and largely managed through wine and spirit merchants, had by comparison declined, much to the chagrin of the distillers, as the trade press lamented:

> It is small wonder that some Highland Distillers, whose brands have been in repute for years, should begin to be dissatisfied with the disappearance of their fine makes in the vats amid Lowland malt and grain spirit . . . it is nothing short of enraging to a Distiller from the North to be confronted with an 'old blended' or 'vatted Glenlivet' five years old at 5s per bulk gallon. He knows that there is not a really fine Highland whisky which can be bought at anything near the price, and the smug satisfaction of the Cockney merchant as he relates how much his customers like the blend he buys is a further bitter drop in the distillers' cup of humiliation.[18]

Nevertheless, the significant increases in the production of single malt whisky (from 13 million proof gallons in 1860 to 35 million at the turn of the century) and the almost catastrophic speculation that this created – from which the 'enraged' Highland distillers sought to profit as much as they could – was all driven by the growth of blends.

Looking back to an imagined Golden Age, the Highland distillers felt that their position of patriarchy within the Scotch industry had been usurped, either by the grain distillers, the blenders, or both. Their financial independence was compromised by the dominant position of urban blending houses, upon whom they were now critically dependant for business. Many of these upstart blenders had themselves invested in distilling capacity, which further reduced their influence. The pre-eminence of their product, the single malts that had been much vaunted by the trade press in the 1880s and early 1890s, was now undermined by the 'uneducated' consumer who continued to display a stubborn preference for the more palatable blends. A further irritant was that blended Scotch (mostly produced in the conurbations of Glasgow, Leith, Dundee and Kilmarnock, and increasingly in London) had, to a large degree, thrived by cloaking itself in the romantic, and royally fashionable, mantle of the Highlands:

> *The fact really is that the blenders used to be anxious to attach some romantic associations to their very prosaic proceedings at Glasgow and Leith, and gave names to, and designed labels for, their wares which had the savour of mountain flood, kilt and claymore, just as the idea of dancing lads and lassies under sunny skies lend poetry to the business of grape gathering.*[19]

At best, argued the Highland malt distillers, blenders were deceiving consumers by purporting by inference of name, or label, or showcard and advertisement, to be selling 'pure malt whisky' from the Highlands rather than a blend of malts and grains assembled in one of Scotland's great cities (and as such might be liable for prosecution under the Merchandise Marks Act, forerunner of today's Trades Description Act). At worst they were committing a blatant fraud by selling not a 'pure' product, but rather one that was adulterated by the addition of 'grain spirit', patent-still whisky which the Highland distillers demonised as being injurious to the health of the public. In this they were playing on long-standing consumer fears. In August 1887, the attention of the North of Scotland Malt Distillers Association had been particularly directed against the adulteration of whisky, and, in order to 'secure the public against that practice', the meeting had come to a resolution to apply to the Board of Trade to enforce the Adulteration Act of 1860. It was pointed out that this was a matter of the upmost importance, not only in the interests of the public, but in their own as distillers of malt whisky.[20]

These claims revived the long-running controversies around the adulteration of Chinese teas which had begun in the eighteenth century, and which were used to gain a commercial advantage by presenting 'adulteration' and 'blending' as one and the same thing, creating a doubt which has remained in the minds of some to the present day. The fact that it was widely known that English and German spirits and Irish whisky had been used to produce cheaper 'blended Scotch' for the tap in London pubs only served to strengthen the Highland distillers' case, and brought them allies in their cause from the public health and medical lobbies.

Threatened by the increasingly dominant position of the blenders and the grain whisky distillers, 'humiliated' by a concurrent loss of status, and emboldened by heightened public concern around adulteration of food and drink, the Highland malt distillers and their supporters focused the battle on which drink had the right to be called 'Scotch whisky' – malt, grain, and/or, a blend? There were other interested parties to this dispute, equally threatened by the disruptive presence of the proprietary blends, who were more than willing to join forces with the Highlanders. Despite their regular inability to satisfy the ever-increasing demands of the malt distillers, the often poor quality of their grain, and the fact that because of their failure to invest in drying technology it often came to market well after the distilling season began, Scottish farmers – particularly in Morayshire – were nonetheless demanding a monopoly on the supply of barley for the production of malt whisky. They and their landlords in the north (and possibly more generally in Scotland) feared that the continuing increase in the use by blenders of grain whisky, often distilled from imported wheat or maize, could lead to a serious loss of trade for their malted barley. Competition and costs might also, they feared, lead to malt distillers using cheaper, imported barley, rather than Scottish. In addition, they accused blenders of systematically reducing the quality of their brands to the point that the reputation of Scotch would be compromised, the category destroyed, and Scottish farmers and rural communities as a result impoverished. Blended whisky was also undermining the moral fibre of the Highlands and Highlanders:

> The bulk of the bad whisky which finds its way into the Highlands is manufactured in towns such as Glasgow and Dundee, and after being dignified with a name redolent of heather and peat, it is purveyed to the unsuspecting Highlanders and Lowlanders as the choicest product of the land of cakes. Not only is the Highland constitution undermined by the consumption of these abominable blends, but the good character of Scotch Whisky is taken away.[21]

The transformative impact of these disruptive proprietary brands spread far beyond either the Highlands, or Scotland. 'Thirty years ago', wrote Arthur J. Cox in *An enquiry into the present condition of the distributing branch of the wine and spirit trade* in 1895, 'there were no

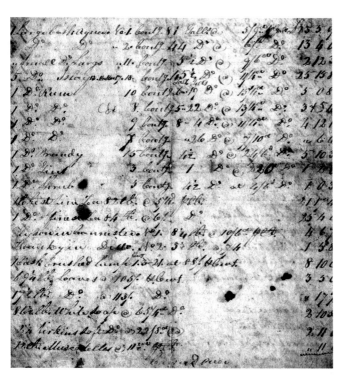

LEFT: The first surviving inventory of John Walker's shop, from 1825, including the whiskies

BELOW: Kilmarnock Cross, c. 1840

TOP LEFT: Alexander Walker, 1837–1889   TOP RIGHT: Showcard, c. 1880
ABOVE: The art of Toddyology

TOP: Bottling Operations at the Strand complex in Kilmarnock, c. 1894
ABOVE: The sample room at the Strand complex in Kilmarnock, c. 1894
Both images from the John Walker & Sons illustrated brochure by A. Barnard, 1894

TOP: John Walker & Sons showcard, c. 1882

ABOVE: Robertson's JRD blended Scotch Whisky,
a significant competitor to Walker's in the colonial export markets in 1894

OPPOSITE: A page from Sir Alexander Walker's blending notebook, early twentieth century

Very Old Highland

Grain.
P. Malt.
Campbln.
N. Country.

5 - 9 - 12 - 2 - 2 - 5

Grain.
Plain Malt.
Kirkliston
Campbelltown
N. Country

new OOll.

Grain
P Malt
Kirkliston
mg grain
Campbelltown

ABOVE: The Johnnie Walker advert that greeted the final report
of the Royal Commission on Whisky in 1909, by Tom Browne

ABOVE: The Underground', from Doris Zinkeisen's 'Poems' series, 1927-1928

George Paterson Walker
1864-1926

Sir Alexander Walker
1869-1950

Sir James Stevenson
1873-1926

RIGHT: John Walker
& Sons White Label of
1914 (withdrawn from
market in 1917) – Old
Highland Whisky was first
introduced in the 1860s

producer brands worth mentioning doing much injury to the trade of the country wine merchant[;] now they have increased in magnitude and multitude until they are overpowering us . . . The big brands are all powerful,' he continued, their success earned 'by superior value, by clever get-up of bottles, by persistent advertising, by regularity of quality'. As far as whisky was concerned, it was 'A fierce fight with the brands, as many of us are fighting now as men will do when driven from one position to another and are finding themselves cornered.'[22] The blenders, and the demand they had created for their brands, had taken away the small trader's own business and margins, and diminished their status and sense of self-worth.

> As the retailer is compelled to keep the article that is so advertised without regard to its commercial value . . . there is hardly a street in the town where these commodities may not be obtained – hence the wine and spirit merchant who as a judge of his business, can command the best markets and afford to allow his capital to remain idle until such time as his importations are matured for consumption, has much to battle against.[23]

It was not only the multiplicity of small independent businesses who were impacted by the brands. Firms like W. & A. Gilbey had positioned themselves as the merchant princes of the drinks trade, with an agency business that extended to over 3,000 retailers throughout the kingdom.[24] They distributed principally their own-label wines and spirits, and the often heavily advertised proprietary blends were a very serious competitive threat, their agents feeling compelled to stock them due to their popularity, despite the significantly lower

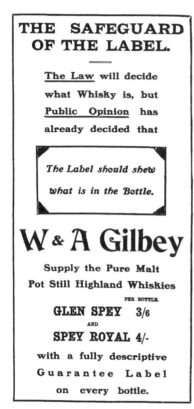

W & A Gilbey's 'Pure Malt' advertising
in the Times, 1906

profits they offered, at the expense of Gilbey's labels.[25] Gilbey's also had a growing interest in distilling, with three Speyside distilleries by 1904 and substantial stocks of malt whiskies which were hard to dispose of on the market at anything but a loss in the wake of the Pattison Crash in 1899. The failure of this large but exceptionally over-extended Leith blending house, noted for their extravagance in all things, had brought an abrupt end to the speculation in distilleries and whisky stocks that had accompanied the heady success of blends in the 1880s and 1890s. The two brothers at the centre of the business were tried for the frauds they had committed but the complex web of investments and investors that they had created in a relatively short period meant that few in the whisky trade were untouched by their firm's spectacular demise.[26]

Like others with a surfeit of stock, Gilbey's hoped to take advantage of the growing fashion for Scotch by selling their 'pure malts', supported by strong medical recommendation (mostly from *The Lancet*) and much anti-blend propaganda, to their 'discerning' upper-middle-class customers.[27] For firms like Gilbey's had built their businesses on 'the better sort of trade'. Their principal marketing activity had been the distribution of brochures and circulars to lists of customers – members of the Houses of Lords and Commons, the clergy, the magistrates of the United Kingdom, doctors, lawyers and members of the Stock Exchange. But the proprietary blends had not built their popularity on this consumer base of establishment 'connoisseurs'. They were aimed at the Mr Pooters of the late Victorian and Edwardian age, newly empowered consumers, 'the average citizen, who does not want to have his palate compelled to make too many suggestions'.

> It is all very well for enthusiasts, who consult only their
> personal likings, to say that there is nothing like malt.
> This observation has enough truth about it to win applause
> from the ignorant and approval from the prejudiced, but people
> are apt to forget that it is the millions of the middle class who
> have to be catered for, and not the few who can afford to drink
> malt whisky.[28]

'The blended Scotch Whisky drinkers', said one industry insider, 'are people who do not consume much Scotch whisky but like that little to be good, and when they buy a bottle they like to know they are getting a whisky upon which they can rely.'[29]

Together these groups of disenfranchised distillers, farmers and landowners, and retailers, made up a formidable and politically well-connected alliance who, for the last two decades of the nineteenth century lobbied for legislation that would strike a mortal blow at the commercial interests of grain whisky distillers and blenders. At the same time similar threats around the legitimacy of blended whisky were coming from two of the most important export markets for blended Scotch – the United States and Australia. The climax of the domestic conflict came in the early twentieth century, preceded by a highly coordinated flood of scurrilous newspaper articles in the *Daily Telegraph* and the *Evening Standard* attacking blended Scotch, followed by lengthy, vituperative correspondence from the rival parties.[30] Accompanying, if not paying for, the articles was heavy advertising from Gilbey's for their 'pure malts' Glen Spey and Spey Royal, and also from the caterers Joseph Lyons & Co., a late but by no means disinterested party to the battle, advertising their newly launched Throgmorton 'Pure Malt' whisky. 'Why should the public be careful to get an all-malt whisky?' asked one Throgmorton advertisement. 'Because a vast quantity of so-called whisky sold to the public is not whisky but merely raw unmalted grain spirit flavoured by artificial and sometimes harmful admixtures.' 'Questions have recently been asked in the House of Commons', said another, 'about blends which are only partially malt, plentifully mixed with cheap grain spirit.'[31] Lyons' showed all the aggression and understanding of advertising and public relations that they had deployed so effectively in their recent 'tobacco wars' where they had scored a decisive victory against dissident retailers and competitors. Their ambition was not only to sell their whisky through their Throgmorton and Trocadero restaurants in central London, but to take on the proprietary brands through a network of agents, as their cigarette business, Salmon & Gluckstein, had done so effectively. And, having just disposed of their tobacco business for a vast fortune, they had a treasure chest they could invest in Scotch.[32]

      This far-from-phoney war preceded attempts to introduce a Sale of Whisky bill through Parliament in 1905 that would have imposed strict labelling regulations on blenders to give, the promoters argued, the consumer greater 'transparency'. The bill had been drafted by Gilbey's, who had originally lobbied Lord Onslow at the Board of Agriculture for its introduction into Parliament. When he expressed pessimism about its chances of progressing, Alfred Gilbey took it to Sir Herbert Maxwell to promote in Parliament on their behalf.[33] 'We think', wrote the *Wine & Spirit Trade Record*, 'that a perusal of the Bill, discloses the fact that in their zeal for their own manufacture and for barley growers, the pot still distillers have overshot the mark in their not altogether disinterested attempt to protect the public.'[34] In the same year a show-trial took place in Islington, where a number of publicans and retailers were prosecuted under the Sale of Food and Drugs Act (1875) for selling 'blended Scotch whisky', an adulterated product 'not of the nature of the substance demanded'. Some thought the case was already lost in the eyes of the whisky-consuming public. Ridley's derided the attempts to bring the prosecution:

> All the strutting of the pipers, and all the squawk of the pipes, have ceased to enlist public attention, and [Gilbey's are now] making what used to be the weakest point in their estimation, trumps. A final stand is being made by Malt in the last ditch of the North London Police Court but the evidence as to the fact and repute and public favour to Patent Still as a dilutant, is as we write, being put so forcibly, that whatever the decision, the public mind and stomach will not be disconcerted.[35]

Even the most traditional distillers were silently adapting their processes to make spirit suitable for the modern age:

> From the heavy bodied highly pronounced and often unmatured whiskies of the early eighties, to the carefully

adjusted delicately flavoured older whiskies of today is a big step but it betokens a change in the taste of the public that is not confined to whisky alone. Even the Highland malt whiskies of today are lighter in body than those of a quarter of a century ago, and although one may occasionally come across veterans – both inside and outside the trade – who lament the change to the present order of things[,] is that really suitable for twentieth century conditions? 'New occasions teach new duties' and it is only by adaption to modern taste and adoption of modern methods that Scotch Whisky will be enabled to retain its position.[36]

Firms like Gilbey's, whilst being amongst the principal promoters and financiers of the anti-blend agitation, acknowledged privately that public taste was moving inexorably in the direction of lighter whiskies and blends. They also started to use barley from California at Strathmill and Knockando, as 'apart from the question of economy, the distillation from foreign barley was much lighter in character and of a less pronounced flavour and more suitable to the present taste'. Purifiers were introduced at Strathmill 'with a view to making a portion of the output of a lighter character'. They reduced the amount of peat used at Glen Spey, and when the character was still 'too pronounced to suit the present taste', they attempted to make 'the whisky slightly less distinct in character' by for example malting the barley more lightly. They even proposed 'omitting in future the sherry placed in the casks'.[37] In 1905 their agent in Australia wrote 'reiterating his disappointment that notwithstanding the large expense incurred in advertising[,] the efforts to popularise Strathmill Whisky in Australia had been so unproductive and urging that some steps be taken either to make the flavour more similar to those brands most popular there or to introduce a blend of malt and grain spirit'. The following year Alfred Gilbey told the board that 'The continued decline in the sale of all Malt Scotch Whiskies, particularly in London, notwithstanding the larger profit shown on their sale as compared to Proprietary Marks ... had convinced him that blended whiskies are now to the taste of the general public.'[38] However, when the Islington magistrate, Edward Snow Fordham, a noted prohibitionist, ruled in favour of the malt distillers' cause in February 1906, despite commentators from *The Times* to trade periodicals greeting the result with derision, Gilbey's and their fellow lobbyists again rushed, like moths to a flame, into print and advertising to promote their malts, and disparage grain whisky and blends.

For both grain distillers and blenders the very real likelihood that they would be prevented from describing their products as 'Scotch whisky' remained a matter of the greatest import. Nor could they be as confident as Ridley's that public opinion would remain in their favour. The malt lobby had managed the publication of a succession of high-profile newspaper articles that called into question, often in lurid language, the probity of blenders, and the quality, safety and origins of the ingredients they chose to use. As the Islington trial went to an inconclusive appeal – resulting in the establishment of a Royal Commission on Whisky and Other Potable Spirits in 1908 – the grain distillers, principally through the Distillers Company (a combine of seven grain-distilling businesses formed in 1877), and the individual blending houses moved into action to defend their reputation in the eyes of the public, and their businesses.[39] As one trade source commented:

When we consider the united selling value of the Pot and Patent Still Whisky annually manufactured in Scotland and Ireland, one gapes with astonishment that a decision so momentous in its effect on the money value in goods produced in one year, not to speak of the enormous value of the stocks which are in bond, should be at the mercy of any faddist among Medical Officers of any local body.[40]

As William H. Ross explained to the Distillers Company board in December 1906, 'To do nothing was to admit the justice of Mr Fordham's judgement . . . If the public confidence in blended whisky was to be retained it could only be done by showing them the wholesomeness and palatableness of that part of it that is manufactured in the patent still.'[41] The Distillers Company response was an extensive advertising campaign for Cambus grain whisky, with the memorable strapline: 'Not a headache in a gallon', and a proposed £4,000 plan for 'grain whisky propaganda' to appear in leading London newspapers, weeklies and Irish and Scottish titles.[42] As Ridley's noted,

Those who organised the Pure Malt campaign initially by means of statements in the Press, and concurrently by promotion of futile Bills in Parliament, all directed against 'Patent Still Spirits' as an article of consumption, must, we should think, regret their action now, as they contemplate the advertising columns in the daily newspapers with somewhat mixed feelings.[43]

The blending houses, who were happy to see the grain distillers lead the charge, were somewhat more circumspect in their response to the events of 1906. For the large advertisers like Dewar's and Buchanan's, or smaller brands like Robertson's and Watson's of Dundee, who had been investing heavily in print in the illustrated weekly and monthly magazines since the mid-1890s, as well as poster and other outdoor advertising, it was more or less business as usual, as they extolled the virtues of their brands whilst carefully avoiding the issue at stake. Dewar's had, however, commissioned the film producer Charles Urban to make a Bioscope called *What is Whisky?* describing the whisky-making and blending processes at Aberfeldy distillery and their premises in Perth in forensic detail. It opened at London's Alhambra on 11 December 1905, apparently 'altogether one of the most interesting turns of the evening'.[44]

The outcome of the Royal Commission was never in doubt. Despite the very public sparring still going on in the editorial, correspondence and advertising pages of the popular press over the virtues or otherwise of pot-still and patent-still whiskies, the commissioners found clearly the case for the latter. In conclusions echoing the findings of the *Parliamentary Report into British and Foreign Spirits* of almost thirty years earlier, they refused to limit the use of the term 'Scotch whisky' in the way the malt distillers and their very powerful allies had sought. 'Since whisky became a popular beverage in England,' said *The Times* in its leader on the Commission's report,

> *public taste has gone steadily in the direction of mild whiskies and the change is naturally unwelcome to those who have money invested in pot stills ... what the public wants is a wholesome spirit having the flavour it prefers and it gets such from a spirit from blenders who mix all sorts of pot-still and*

patent-still whisky in order to maintain brands of uniform character . . . how much flavour and what particular flavour whisky should have are questions of taste, and the blender who can appeal to the taste of the largest number will, other things being equal, have the largest business.[45]

Despite the clarity of the outcome there were some long-standing unanswered questions: 'The question is being asked,' said Ridley's, 'and has now been asked for some years, who is engineering, and who is inspiring the campaign in favour of Malt as against Blends of Malt and Grain Whisky?' 'It is a pity', said the *Wine & Spirit Trade Record*,

that the turmoil of the past two years, with the injury it has done to the whisky trade, was not prevented by a display of greater reasonableness on the part of those who, in the interests of the pot-still, connived at, if they did not actually instigate, the Islington prosecutions. Even at Islington the trouble has not ceased for local ratepayers are endeavouring to get the Board of Trade to inquire into the origins of the proceedings.[46]

CHAPTER 6
THE BIRTH OF 'JOHNNIE WALKER'

'The necessity for advertising to the consumer is instinctively realised by anyone who affixes a trade-mark or name, or indeed, any mark of identification, to his goods, to enable a trader or consumer easily and definitely to distinguish them.'[1]

An early (c.1908) sketch of the Striding Man by Tom Browne, with the words added 'Born 1820 Still Going Strong' and James Stevenson's initials

FOR JOHN WALKER & SONS of Kilmarnock, the crisis provoked by the 'What is whisky?' question was transformational, and their commercial response to the doubts being sown in the minds of consumers about the integrity of blended Scotch genuinely disruptive. It was led by a management team that mixed the impetuosity of youth with generations of knowledge and experience of the whisky trade. The company had been established some eighty or more years earlier, but had made its mark on the whisky business under the son of the founder, Alexander, and by the time of his death was probably the most profitable Scotch whisky business in the world.

Their business had been built on the back of Alexander's Old Highland Whisky brand, sold around the world both in bulk and in bottles, always with a distinctive small white label with gold lettering placed at a particular angle on the container. Alexander had taken 'OH' to London in the early 1870s before most other blenders had considered that opportunity, and to the thirsty colonial markets of Australia, New Zealand and South Africa. Success had been achieved despite the absence of clear branding and advertising, reflecting a firmly held belief of Alexander's that quality was what sold whisky. Although inside the firm the brand was known as 'OH', amongst customers and consumers it continued to have a number of names: 'Walker's whisky', 'Kilmarnock whisky', and sometimes 'Square-bottle whisky'. Variants were also added to meet demands from agents and consumers, notably a 'special whisky' known as 'Very Old Highland', which in turn developed by the late nineteenth century into three distinct qualities, 'Old Highland' (still the core of the range), 'Special Old Highland', and 'Extra Special Old Highland', each with its own distinctive colourway of white, red or black, which by early 1906 had been adopted as the shorthand names, 'White Label', 'Red Label' and 'Black Label'.[2] As the public clamour around the 'What is whisky?' debate grew, and the quality and even safety of blended Scotch was increasingly called into question, so Walker's went a step further in clarifying their offering to the public, and in underpinning their claims to quality.

In April 1906, at the height of the 'What is whisky?' controversy, the familiar White, Red and Black Label were launched, each in Walker's trademark square bottle, but each with declared ages of over five, over nine and over twelve years old, and ranging in cost from 3s. 6d. to 4s. 6d. a bottle.[3] Although their competitors, particularly Buchanan's, had a number of offerings, none of the other major owners of proprietary brands had the depth of whisky stocks to support a range of this coherence, breadth and branding segmented by age and price. The majority of the blending houses whose representatives gave evidence to the Royal Commission declined to support the introduction of a period of minimum 'bonding', or ageing, before whisky could be released onto the market. Alex Walker, however, in his contribution argued that not only should blends comprise a minimum of 50 per cent malt whisky, but also that there should be a minimum two-year ageing period before Scotch could be sold.[4] The equivalence of age with quality was clear in the evidence of all sides of the whisky debate, and Walker's chose to use their deep and unrivalled whisky stocks as a means of offering consumers concerned by the anti-blends propaganda reassurance about the quality of their whisky.

Despite the fact that they sat comfortably alongside, if not beyond, their main competitors by any relevant measure, Walker's had done relatively little to develop their brand in the minds of consumers. Indeed, for such 'a gigantic concern' (as surprised trade visitors from nearby Glasgow described it in 1896), the company maintained a public reticence that was strikingly at odds with, for example, that stylish doyen

John Walker & Sons 'Kilmarnock Whiskies',
1906

of the turf James Buchanan.[5] With titles, castles, country estates, art collections and extensive stables, the so-called 'whisky barons' knew how to spend the spectacular profits they had made during the 1890s. But for the 'thrawn' Walkers, arguably the most profitable of all of these companies, such conspicuous consumption was an anathema. This aversion to self-publicity and vulgar displays applied to the brand as well as the brand-owners. In what was, at the time, a rare public appearance, the young Alex Walker articulated the company's philosophy in a scathing indictment of the Pattison Crash of 1899, which was, he said, all due to lavish expenditure on advertising:

> *To the old-fashioned houses of the trade, who had done business*
> *for nearly a century on the latter lines, the advent of the houses*
> *of mushroom growth lavishly throwing money broadcast in*
> *advertisement ... was viewed with great alarm ... what a relief,*
> *therefore, it was when the bubble burst and the new-fashioned*
> *tactics were discredited. It was to be hoped the British public,*
> *who had been gulled long enough, would awaken to the fact*
> *that a largely over-advertised article could not be a good one.[6]*

An obsession with quality, and with what some, no doubt, regarded as an antiquated concern for 'honourable' business methods, were the very lifeblood of the Walker business. But this overriding belief that quality would speak for itself louder than any promotion meant that, whereas their rivals had been quick to adopt the new advertising techniques and opportunities of the 1890s, Walker's had steadfastly refused to, depending instead on old-fashioned salesmanship based on the product. The need to be seen and heard in the noisy debates of the 'What is whisky?' affair meant that this was no longer a sustainable position.

There was a further complication. With an unclear identity, and having chosen not to invest in what we would term today as 'brand building', the company had created a vacuum which was filled by their consumers. For in their mind, in popular culture, the Johnnie Walker (or rather, 'Johnny Walker') brand, and the idea of 'Johnny Walker as a living personality', had existed since the 1880s, if not before. The firm may have declared itself to the world as 'John Walker & Sons' in showcards and pub mirrors, and called its products 'Kilmarnock Whisky' (embossed on the punt of their early square bottles), but increasingly the brand, the whisky, was known in the minds of the trade and the public as simply 'Johnny Walker'.

> In these more materialistic days, the man is ignorant indeed who does not know that Johnnie Walker, the real Kilmarnock brand, has reached every part of the civilised world. Such a popular name, of course, is the popular designation that the 'man in the street' has given to a popular article.[7]

Retailers advertised Johnny Walker whiskies, newspapers suggested themes for Johnny Walker whisky advertisements, humourists featured Johnny Walker in their stories, and cartoonists celebrated Johnny Walker in print.[8] The 'Johnny Walker walk' was performed in London's music halls, the most popular entertainment of the day, by famed singer and comedian Charles Deane, whilst the 'up to date Scotch comedian with a number of catchy songs . . . Johnny Walker' was becoming increasingly popular on the London and provincial theatre circuit.[9] In 1893 at the 'Christmas treat' for South Stoneham workhouse near Southampton, the inmates enjoyed a supper of meat pies and beer while the hosts were refreshed by 'sundry bottles of Johnny Walker' in the boardroom; elsewhere 'the demon' Johnny Walker was conjured up at temperance meetings. Members of the Peckham Grove Conservative Club demanded Johnny Walker for the toast at their 1896 Christmas dinner.[10] Johnny Walker was known at almost every level of society, hard-of-hearing judges apparently being the exception. When a witness in the infamous Yarmouth murder trial of 1901 said the defendant (Herbert Bennett, accused of murdering his wife) asked for a 'Johnny Walker' shortly before committing his crime, 'The Lord Chief Justice did not recognise this term from the dictionary of Bacchus, and questioningly asked, "Gin and water?" at which there was laughter, and the witness explained the precise meaning of "Johnny Walker".'[11]

As Walker's whisky grew in fame and reputation, so Johnny Walker lived and breathed in popular culture and in the popular imagination, a powerful brand asset waiting to be unlocked. And yet the company refused to take advantage. James Stevenson, a Kilmarnock man who had been appointed a director of the company in 1908, explained why in 1909: 'We were not the originators of the word "Johnnie Walker". The public christened the brand, and for many years some of the directors objected strongly to it as being undignified.'[12]

Stevenson clearly did not share his fellow directors' reticence about using a popularisation of the name of the firm's founder in connection with its whisky. Neither George nor Alex Walker would have met their grandfather, but it's very likely that even during their father's lifetime 'Johnny Walker' was being used as a popular shorthand for the brand. As we have already seen, Alexander Walker was a man of very firm opinion, who would not have failed to let his sons know his view on the subject; in matters of business he very strictly referred throughout his correspondence to his firm as 'John Walker & Sons', and his brand as 'Old Highland', with no variation or vulgarisation. Moreover, George and Alex had sisters and brothers with shares in the business, all of whom would have had opinions on the subject. Their grandmother, Elizabeth, who outlived John by over thirty years and remained in the old family home in India Street in Kilmarnock till her death in 1890, was also no doubt a formidable figure with a formidable point of view, and exerted a

The first use of the name 'Johnnie Walker' in an official Walker advertisement, 1905

strong influence over her son till his death.[13] But Stevenson, albeit with strong connections to the family, was a modern man of business and appears to have been the first member of the firm to have dared to put 'Johnnie Walker' into print in a series of adverts he ran in Bristol when he was responsible for the Walker business in the Midlands of England. Two adverts ran throughout December offering a mixed case of White, Red and Black label for 12s. The first challenged readers to trial 'the Scotch Triumvirate' of John Walker & Sons; 'The question is often asked why is Scotch Whisky so popular? These whiskies supply the answer.' The second began: 'Popular articles acquire popular names' and continued: 'It is many years since the public designated the product of John Walker & Sons Ltd., Distillers, Kilmarnock, "Johnnie Walker", and to-day the name stands not only for Scotch whisky, but is associated with QUALITY consistent and uniform.' Both contained the claim that Walker's were the 'the largest holders of pure malt Scotch whisky in the trade', adding: 'No firm can give value unless they can hold large stocks.'[14]

When Walker's launched their first national advertising campaign in the spring of 1906, 'Johnnie Walker' was still absent. The small showcard-style advertisements in the national and provincial press and the illustrated weeklies featured simple images of either the Old Highland square bottle or label, and were headed 'Walker's Kilmarnock Whiskies', with the repeated claim about holding the largest stocks of malt whisky, 'a guarantee of quality, age, and uniformity'.[15] The following year saw the inclusion of an almost diffident 'the popular Johnnie Walker' into the copy, and the specific claim to hold 'over 3½ million gallons of maturing whisky'.[16] By this time the company, possibly inspired by James Stevenson, who was becoming increasingly influential, had employed the advertising agents R. C. Empson to work on their account, the result being the short-lived 'I recommend Johnnie Walker' campaign. If the family members had agreed reluctantly to use the popular name, they had clearly only done so under duress, so these illustrated advertisements (printed both in colour and black and white), which were also used as point-of-sale for display in shops and bars, were very respectful to the memory of their grandfather. They purported to show a portrait of an amiable, if not slightly confused, old man in a periwig, standing at a dark shop-counter almost reluctantly holding a bottle of Walker whisky, with White, Red and Black Label lined up in front of him. 'The secret of its popularity

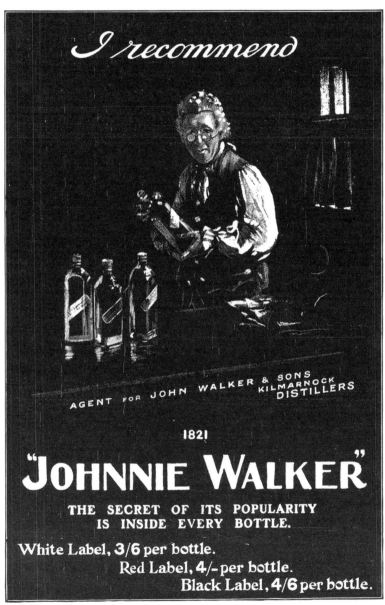

The first (and short-lived) attempt to bring 'Johnnie Walker' to life, in 1907

is inside every bottle' were the words as if from his lips.[17] Rarely could an advert have been so timid, so lacklustre, so less in tune with the vibrancy of a new age, and so ill-equipped to enter the febrile debate that had engulfed Scotch whisky.

These might well have been the words of Paul E. Derrick on his first meeting with James Stevenson. Derrick, an advertising professional since the mid-1880s, had first come to London from the United States on behalf of his client, the Quaker Oats Company, whose business he had obtained in 1894. He set up an office in London in 1900, and seeing the opportunities for advertising agencies there, moved permanently to the capital in 1905. Although he had not originated the idea of the figure of a Quaker to represent the famous oatmeal brand, he was the man credited with bringing it to the fore in the form we would recognise today on packs, on posters, in the press, and even on the White Cliffs of Dover to welcome returning troops from South Africa. He had also created the hugely successful, but now forgotten, Gold Dust Twins to promote a washing powder brand in the United States. Derrick's aggressive approach to advertising, summed up in his personal catchphrase, 'Do it Better!', was explained in his book, *How to Reduce Selling Costs*, a manifesto aimed at the reluctant manufacturer that demonstrated the economy and value that thoughtful and fully integrated advertising campaigns offered. He condemned 'men who do not have a definite, well-planned, well-considered and courageously undertaken scheme of advertising' as 'dabblers'. Advertising had to be both highly original and ruthlessly efficient to deliver value to the business. At the heart of his thinking was the consumer, and the brand. What the consumer wanted, he argued, was to know that 'The maker of those goods has sufficient confidence to put his name or mark upon them … and that his guarantee of quality follows the goods wherever they go.' The guarantee of quality was 'the creative force in advertising that develops a state of value apart from the price'.[18] In advertising, he said, 'Ideas are paramount ... the mastery of mind over mind is the real purpose of advertising':

> *The display of mere words and commonplace phrases is an expensive and rudimentary form of advertising. In its highest form advertising is the vivid presentation of a living message that creates favourable public action by a resistless appeal to purchase, and adds to the popular value of the article advertised by creating around it an atmosphere of distinction.*[19]

In developing trademark advertising, 'the addition of some distinct associated figure is desirable':

> *It should be of such a nature as to make it possible to use either the name or design separately, as will at times be desirable. Distinctly human, animal, or purely imaginary figures are always interesting, and, if they possess easily recognised and remembered characteristics, are most desirable. Such marks permit of a variety of presentation, thus obviating monotony in advertising. They are storage batteries for all the accumulative sales force that permits advertising to accomplish a constantly descending percentage in sales costs.*[20]

Not only did these views attract business from the Quaker Oats Co. and John Walker & Sons; within a few years his client list included Remington typewriters, Wrigley's chewing gum, Bols gin and liqueurs, Tootal ties, Horlicks, Homepride and (also from Kilmarnock) Saxone shoes.

There are a number of legends and deeply cherished stories surrounding the development of the Johnnie Walker 'Striding Man' in which Derrick does not feature, but his role and the discipline of thought he brought to bear in bringing Johnnie Walker to life were critical. He much later claimed that he brought an almost fully developed idea to Walker's, but it is not entirely clear if he sought out the Walker business or if they went in search of him. Either way, by early 1908 Empson had lost the Walker account, and Stevenson and Derrick, assisted by Roy Sommerville (who later ran the advertising department at *Punch*) and creative and copywriter Horace Barnes, were working on the campaign.[21] As Stevenson recalled in an interview with advertising trade magazine *Printers' Ink*, there were to be some clear guidelines that the work should follow. The first was that it should stand out from, and disrupt, a crowded and clichéd category where the common theme was 'bibulous-looking gentry rubbing shoulders with smugglers and kilted Highland chieftains'. The second was that it would never show anyone drinking, and nor, in outdoor posters, would it use the word 'whisky'. Both, it was agreed, tended to cheapen the reputation of the brand and also could unnecessarily antagonise the considerable and vocal lobby campaigning for greater restrictions on the sale of alcohol, if not for total prohibition. Third, in giving character to this 'Johnnie Walker' already so loved by the public, they had to capture the sense of energy that the name so clearly evoked: 'As vitality was the keynote of their business they concluded that it was desirable to typify that force in the creation of a vigorous personality.' There was also the matter of trust; given that the integrity and quality of blended Scotch whisky had so recently been called into very public question, this 'Johnnie Walker' had to command the full confidence of his public. And he had to have the ability to transcend his Georgian origins and outfit in order to maintain a relevance to his audience – he had to be a timeless, and classless traveller, as at home in the present as the past, as easy with paupers as with prelates. And last but not least, he had to accomplish all of this with good humour and good cheer.[22]

Derrick certainly had all the copywriting skills he needed in Barnes and others at the agency; however his choice of artist was critical, and in recruiting Tom Browne, probably the foremost comic illustrator of his day, he found the perfect person to bring the brief to life in pen and ink: 'Tom Browne is an artist popular in a very literal sense of the word. He belongs to the people, he is of them. He understands them, they him: sympathy is mutual.' His pedigree, from the famous cartoon characters Weary Willie and Tired Tim, who were to occupy the front page of the *Illustrated Chips* halfpenny magazine from their creation in 1894 to the closure of the magazine in 1953, to his illustrations for popular books such as *The Night Side of London* (a gritty exploration of the city that never slept) and the fantasy *The World that Never Was* (in which he brought to life a number of well-known advertising figures, including the Quaker Oats Man and Force cereal's 'Sunny Jim'), was impeccable.[23]

In his developmental sketches for the Johnnie Walker figure, Browne began with the 'bibulous-looking gentry' who were discounted in the brief, and worked through to a highly energetic and now familiar figure striding purposely forward with top hat, monocle and cane, and a small dog.[24] There were other walking characters around, such as Sunny Jim, who with a tailcoat, hat, cane and spectacles had paced across the Force cereal packets and advertisements since 1901, or the heavily bearded Waukenphast walking figure ('Five Miles an Hour Easy'), who first appeared with tailcoat, hat and cane as a trademark for the boot and shoe brand in 1883.[25] However, the character that

Browne created certainly was unique and had immediate effect
once it appeared in posters in London and elsewhere. It was 'a
carefully drawn figure of a man – a genial, humorous, glad-I'm-alive
man – who gives at once personality and a character to the abstract
name of Johnnie Walker'. *Advertising World* saw him as 'the hurried
pedestrian who, with a charming old-world courtesy, raises his
hat to you in a salutation as you pass him by. This fine old English
gentleman is certainly one of the happiest figures ever invented for an
advertiser's purposes. He is a triumphant vindication of the use of the
pictorial advertisement.'[26]

By the middle of 1908, as the Royal Commission was still
taking evidence from expert witnesses on both sides of the dispute,
the first brightly coloured posters featuring Tom Browne's figure were
appearing on 'thousands' of hoardings in cities around the United
Kingdom. The famous 'Born 1820 – Still Going Strong' logo would follow
a little later. One brilliantly designed work showed the Johnnie Walker
figure stepping out from the poster to join his admirers on the pavement
below. These were followed by print adverts in November ('Even experts
disagree') in both London and the provinces, and full-page adverts in
titles like the *Tatler* at Christmas. In these the Johnnie Walker figure was
accompanied by his case-carrying page boy, who also made appearances
in some of the 'sporting prints' that Browne produced, these latter
being so popular that they were put on sale as 'art prints' shortly after
Tom Browne's death in 1910.[27] Under the heading 'The history of Scotch
whisky is the history of Walker', they also advertised a free illustrated
book, *The History of a Small Scotch*, promising readers 'that you'll know
more about the production of Scotch than the man who doesn't'.[28]
In the days before cinema, radio broadcasts and television, regularly
changing posters and print advertisements played an important role

in popular culture, the subject of both office and tea-table talk then as social media posts might be today.

> *The identification of a familiar character or figure with a particular commodity is one of the best known forms of modern advertising. It has everything to recommend it. The character is created. It appears on hoardings, at railway stations, or in the columns of the daily Press. By this means the public becomes quickly familiarised with the character, and if there is any originality, any touch of grotesqueness or individuality in the pictorial design it is discussed in clubs, at dinner tables or at the various places men and women do congregate. Before long the name of the character passes into the current coin of daily speech; and by this time half at least of the battle of the advertiser is won.*[29]

The Royal Commission prepared its final report the following year. As its interim findings had made clear, its conclusions would forever legitimise the blending of single malt and single grain whiskies, and the use of the descriptor 'Scotch whisky' for blends. In the press the Johnnie Walker figure appeared triumphantly through a dense swirling mist with the caption, 'Out of the fog of uncertainty in whisky Johnnie Walker leads the way – every step from barley to buyer is carefully taken.' Only a year later, *Printers' Ink* could claim that 'There is hardly a country in the world where Johnnie Walker is not now a household word – all after only two years' work.'[30]

An often-repeated story tells that the Johnnie Walker figure was sketched on a menu over a lunch between Tom Browne, James Stevenson and Alex Walker at London's Savoy Hotel ('Born 1820 – Still Going Strong' was added as an afterthought); another that it was dreamt

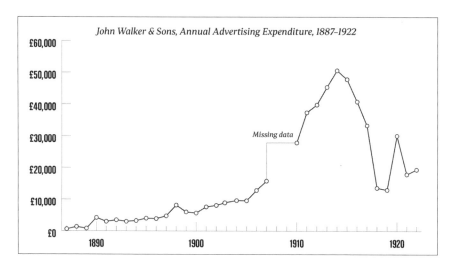

John Walker & Sons, Annual Advertising Expenditure, 1887–1922

up in Walker's office by Alex Walker and Browne.[31] There may well have been a lunch or meeting somewhere, at some point in the process, but these versions ignore the work of Stevenson and Paul Derrick's agency, who with Tom Browne rewrote the semiotics of whisky advertising at a stroke. The advertising press admired the evident clarity and consistency of thought in Walker's advertising which, they said, made their principal competitors' campaigns, for all the outstanding graphical and artistic quality, look confused, ill-considered, and frankly somewhat Victorian.

> *The strength of the 'Johnnie Walker' advertising has always been even more in the ideas behind it than in the admirable manner in which they were rendered. Other advertisers, especially those in a similar line of business, would do well to think of a subject-matter for their advertising equally inspiring and interesting.*[32]

The big stride forward that Walker's took in 1908 would never be surpassed by its rivals. It was not just a new advertising campaign, or the creation of a much-loved advertising figure, it was the birth of the brand we know today. Trademarks were registered, shoulder labels were changed on bottles, tissue wraps and packing cases were redesigned, new point-of-sale was commissioned. Johnnie Walker, in its unique hand-drawn font, was everywhere. 'Now we never use any other name,' said Stevenson, 'I do not suppose there are many people in England or the Colonies to whom it is not familiar.'[33] The impact on business performance was transformational and lasting. As we shall see, in the inter-war years the idea of Johnnie Walker permeated almost every aspect of society both in the United Kingdom and in export markets, and in many respects transcended the Scotch category. In a review of 'Man-made figures that have conquered markets' in *Advertising World* in 1924, Fernand A. Marteau would not apologise for choosing Johnnie Walker as the first among his peers, none of which have lasted the one hundred years since so well. 'Could anyone imagine our hoardings, our tubes, our magazines, bereft of his cheery smile and invigorating personality. He has become more than an advertising figure. He is an institution.'[34]

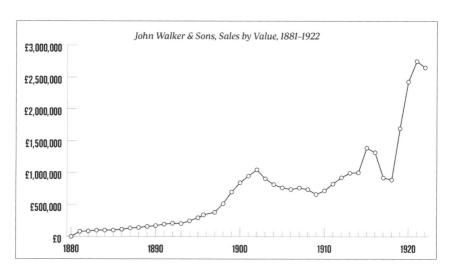

John Walker & Sons, Sales by Value, 1881–1922

CHAPTER 7
THE SCOTCH WHISKY TRIUMVIRATE

'They have been described as the Scotch Whisky Triumvirate and when we consider it is estimated that there are about 5,000 distinct brands of Scotch whisky on sale in England it will be apparent that to warrant that designation a high and consistent standard of quality must be maintained.'[1]

John Walker & Sons, Old Highland, Special and Extra Special Whiskies, c.1905

THE FIFTEEN YEARS from 1895 to the start of the Great War witnessed an astonishing growth in both the sales, and even more so the profitability, of the Walker business as the world emerged from the Long Depression. Whilst the home trade still accounted for over two-thirds of the total business, exports continued to grow in both the traditional colonial markets and, increasingly, the United States. George Walker, a somewhat distant figure who avoided the limelight almost as much as some of his principal competitors coveted it, was firmly in control of the business, with his own management team in place. None would be more important than James Stevenson, who had masterminded the development of the 'Johnnie Walker' brand and the associated advertising developed by Paul Derrick. Increasingly familiar in trade circles as all firms sought to protect their interests against threats from government and the temperance movement, Stevenson rose to become probably the most politically influential man in the whisky trade and the architect of regulations that still govern Scotch whisky today. In 1905 Stevenson had coined the phrase 'the Scotch Triumvirate' to describe Walker's White, Red and Black Label whiskies. The phrase could have been equally well applied to Stevenson, George Paterson Walker and his brother Alex, or to the three companies who by then led the Scotch whisky industry, Dewar's, Buchanan's, and John Walker & Sons.

James Hodge, the amply rewarded and sometimes troublesome 'head traveller' in London, had died in 1895.[2] This was followed a year later by the deaths of John Kilgour and John Blaikie, leaving George Walker as the most senior member of the firm. In place of Hodge, George Hunter, from New York, was brought in to introduce some American sales techniques to the 'travellers'; his responsibilities also included dealing with agents, setting up new agencies, and travelling overseas when required. Sharply turned out in frock coats and top hats, these men were at the coalface of the business, and were well rewarded for their endeavours. Two years later, Hunter was made a director of the company to ease the burden on George, who was making increasingly frequent overseas trips.[3] The company had also made appointments to cover sales in the north of England and Birmingham, where their representative proved to be a sorry failure. In 1897 he was replaced by James Stevenson, son of Archibald Stevenson, who had managed the Walker shop (grandly described as an 'Italian warehouse') in Portland Street, Kilmarnock. James had joined Walker's as a teenager

Walker's London salesforce, led by the American George Hunter, c.1900

after a short spell at W. P. Lowrie in Glasgow, working as a clerk in Kilmarnock before the move to Birmingham. Within three years he had transformed that part of the business, had a staff of eight, and was among the top five earners in the firm. When George Hunter was asked to resign in 1907 (with a handsome cheque of £1,000), 'as it is desirable that a younger man brought up in the Trade should occupy his position', Stevenson was promoted to London and became a director very shortly after. His was a prodigious talent, and his contribution to the business, and to Scotch whisky, would be extraordinary.[4]

In Kilmarnock, Alex Walker was the senior manager, still assisted by James Blair. In 1894 Robert Cattanach had been taken on, 'the ultimate object being that after sufficient experience the present Directors will do all in their power to have him appointed to the position of Director'.[5] Cattanach was appointed a director with responsibility for the home trade in 1902, along with the younger brother of George and Alex, Thomas Hood Walker. Thomas seems to have joined the firm in around 1899 in his early twenties, having already spent some time in South Africa where he may have been associated with the British South Africa Company, as well as representing the Walker business there. In 1895 he enlisted as a trooper in the force that was responsible for the failed Jameson Raid in the Transvaal. He was also said to have served with British forces and was decorated in 1896, before returning to Scotland.[6]

One of George Walker's first overseas trips as chairman was to South Africa, which under the Rolfes Nobel agency had become the firm's most important export market. Its rapid growth, fuelled by both diamonds and gold, had provoked intense competition with established brands like Usher's. Rolfes Nobel were approached by rivals seeking agents, and sought permission from Walker's to distribute a Distillers Company blend. 'This coming, as it does now, on the back of our large expenditure for advertising', wrote George, 'is to me a bit disappointing. I don't so much fear the DCL whiskies, but the transference of part of your energies to pushing a brand equal in price.' Nonetheless permission was granted on the condition that Rolfes increased their sales from 8,000 to 12,000 cases. 'I do not wish to presume', added George, 'and give you advice yet knowing the Scotch Whisky Trade fairly well, I think it is inevitable that JW&S is a much better brand than DCL's.'[7] The company were also negotiating to produce and sell the Royal Scottish brand, a secondary blend, in the Cape. All of these matters needed George's personal attention. At the same time Jack was travelling to New Zealand to manage the fall-out from the termination of the long-standing agency with Bernard Lewis and the 'serious decline' in sales there.[8]

To the continued frustration of his colleagues in London and Kilmarnock, Jack Walker had failed to have any impact on the performance of Mason Brothers in Sydney. Mason's general financial position continued to deteriorate, as did the whisky side of their business, while expenses (particularly for advertising) increased. The personal and familial relationships that had been so important in setting up the company were in tatters. In 1890 Walker's decided to terminate the agency agreement with Mason's and in their place Jack was tasked to set up a new company in Sydney.[9] Mason Brothers Ltd were put into liquidation in 1892. Conditions for business were testing, with a major banking crisis and trade depression in 1893. Yet to all outward appearances the Walker business in Sydney was flourishing; brands such as Special and Extra Special were being regularly advertised by prominent hotels and bars, Jack had established agencies for beer and (Rosbach) mineral water, was exporting small parcels of cased goods to Samoa, Tonga and Fiji, and late in 1896 the firm had announced a sponsorship of the Inter Colonial Sailing Competition.[10] However when George Walker travelled to Australia in June 1896 to visit all of Walker's agents there, he discovered that not only was his brother's business trading insolvently with significant debtors (the largest being John Walker & Sons), but also that Jack had succumbed to illness – possibly a recurrence of his earlier problems – and had been committed to an asylum (where he died in December of that year). In a very short space of time George took control of affairs, paid off all the trade creditors, put Jack's former manager John Soutter in charge of the business, and the New Zealand agency into the hands of Alfred Kernot. Showing considerable nerve in the face of adversity, George was also able to conduct an interview with the *Sportsman* newspaper at the end of the trip, explaining that he had found 'everything highly satisfactory'. By 1898 George Walker could report that the business had recovered sufficiently to pay off the outstanding debt on the accounts incurred by Jack.[11]

The United States was much slower than these colonial markets to develop a taste for Scotch whisky, despite the publicity given to it by some competitors which made the American market appear far more important than it was. In reality Scotch in the USA is a twentieth-century story. That's not to say that small parcels weren't being exported from Scotland in the early nineteenth (or for that matter eighteenth) centuries using well-established trade routes. Nor that there weren't thirsty Scots anxious for a taste of the old country. Casks of 'Scotch Whisky' were often advertised for sale in newspapers in the 1820s; in 1833 one dealer was advertising 'Mountain Dew, Old Scotch Malt whisky from Glenlivet Scotland, more than ten years old'. Whisky from James Stewart's Saucel distillery (possibly malt, possibly grain) was being sold in New Orleans in the 1860s, as was Mackay's Islay whisky, along with puncheons of Ramsay's whisky. And, of course, the Americans were not short of recipes to manufacture or compound their own 'scotch whiskies', often blended with genuine imported spirit to deliver an authentic character. It was estimated that around two-thirds or more of all the whisky (Scotch and Irish) imported into the United States went through the port of New York, and data from there shows how relatively slow growth was during the nineteenth century. In 1879, 49,500 gallons were imported 'in wood', along with just over 2,200 12-bottle cases. In 1890 the figures were 37,500 gallons and 14,500 cases. At the turn of the century the totals stood at 54,100 gallons and 82,800; by 1910 it was 52,087 gallons and almost 150,000 cases. A number of things are clear from this. In normal circumstances the demand for cask whisky (often destined for use in admixed products) was at best static; it was bottled, branded Scotch that was driving growth, particularly from the late 1890s. In the 1880s a consumer preference for American whisky certainly slackened growth, but by 1900 one trade commentator noted, 'It can safely be asserted that the question as to whether Scotch Whisky is a fad on the other side of the water is now definitely settled in the negative.'[12] Some degree of connoisseurship was also developing in the market: 'There are few spirits regarding which more discrimination is displayed in selection than in Scotch whisky, and American people in this direction have reached a point where they are fully capable of analysing the merits of the goods shipped there.'[13] In 1904 Ridley's could declare:

> *There is no branch of the importing business that has shown more activity during the past year than has been displayed by the Importers of Scotch whiskies. The demand has been increased considerably, not only in the cities of the first class,*

> *but Scotch whisky has found its way into the less populated sections of the country. Even at the South, which is commonly supposed to be wedded to Corn Whisky, Scotch is gaining ground, and in cities like New Orleans there are now displayed in the cafés and restaurants almost all the leading and popular brands. They are not only displayed, but they are liberally consumed.*[14]

'Scotch Whiskies', Ridley's wrote in 1905, 'are now consumed in nearly all parts of the States, and from present indications the demand will grow, the spirit being to the liking of the tastes of many Americans. The keen competition and rivalry between brands is astonishing, and second only to that displayed in the Champagne trade.'[15] Make no mistake, this was a luxury product for the discerning middle classes with leading retailers adopting distinctly different strategies: while New York grocer's Park & Tilford listed fifty-four brands of 'well known Scotches', in 1909 Macy's listed only one, Mortlach single malt, in five grades, supplied by John Walker & Son. Advertising was an essential tool for the distillers. As Ridley's noted, 'There is perhaps no article more extensively advertised than Whisky, and taking into consideration the many brands there are represented in the States, there is an active campaign carried on all the time, thus keeping Scotch and Irish whiskies constantly before the public'. Commenting on the growth of Scotch in the States, the *Wine & Spirit Trade Record* wrote, 'It is quite apparent that many consumers who formerly purchased a bottle of wine with their meals are today taking a highball or other drink containing whisky instead.'[16] But in order to change consumer habits the guarantee of quality was even more important.[17]

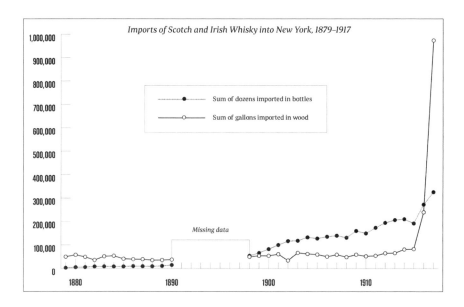

Imports of Scotch and Irish Whisky into New York, 1879–1917

It's not clear exactly when Walker's went into the United States, but in 1883 they determined they should 'cultivate the American market more than we have been doing'. An introduction to one of the partners of the wine and spirit broker Williams & Humbert in London that year marked the start of a relationship that lasted till the onset of Prohibition.[18] They were also looking to develop a market in Canada, and eventually appointed a sole agent for British Colombia in 1887 (minimum sale '100 cases').[19] The 'celebrated John Walker Kilmarnock Scotch whisky' was being sold in Louisville, the bourbon capital of the USA, by 1894, and in Pittsburgh too. In Baltimore drinkers were recommended to try Kilmarnock whisky in 'milk punch, cocktail, or high ball'. Extra Special and Old Highland were on sale in New York.[20] However, the United States market does not appear to have been a priority until the start of the twentieth century, when James Stevenson and Alex Walker began to visit with some frequency and a real sense of urgency can be seen in the dealings with business there. The Williams & Humbert agency was extended for another ten years in 1909; by 1910 the company was spending £2,000 on advertising there, surpassed only by Melbourne and Sydney (£4,000), and had sent out an additional salesman from London to push sales in New York. In 1912 Walker's agreed to invest £8,000 a year in the US for three years to develop the business and appoint an additional representative to drive sales. Stevenson was tasked to develop an advertising campaign for them 'on the lines which have proved successful in other markets'. On the verge of the outbreak of war, Williams & Humbert were offered a five-year extension to their agency if they could guarantee sales of over 45,000 cases a year.[21]

One of the principal barriers to growing both the Scotch category and individual brands in the United States was the long-standing issue of counterfeit. This was not only an issue for Scotch but was pervasive in the expanding world of luxury wines and spirits, with prominent cognac and liqueur brands, and numerous champagnes falling victim to impersonation all over the world.[22] As the popularity of Scotch grew in the nineteenth century so it too fell victim to these crimes, as many brands discovered:

> *Counterfeiting and infringement of reputable brands is again on the rampage . . . a glaring instance . . . is the counterfeiting of King William IV, Scotch Whisky of John Gillon & Co., Leith. So exact is the imitation of the label that it is a perfect counterfeit. The quality of the counterfeit goods is so execrable that it may be ranked as positively poisonous. The source of the counterfeiting is Chicago.[23]*

This wasn't only a problem in the USA. Colonial export markets were plagued by fakes and the constant problem of product adulteration; in fact wherever Scotch sailed, so substitution followed. As we have seen in the home trade, adulteration or substitution was likely to occur even in the most respectable accounts. One way to deter this practice was through prosecution under local trading laws (in the UK, the Merchandise Marks Act); in 1891 Walker's brought what was believed to be the first case in law against a publican, in London, for fraudulent use of their name. 'We trust', said *Harper's Weekly*, 'this case may be a warning to other offenders in a similar way and may be a means of checking an evil which is growing.'[24] When he was managing the Midlands sales region, James Stevenson persuaded Walker's to pursue this policy with considerable vigour, often employing agents (normally retired police officers) to help catch offenders.[25] Some suggested that the larger Scotch whisky brands should combine to act against something that was so damaging to the category's reputation, and in 1908 Walker's became founder members of the 'Whisky Section' of the Incorporated Society for Industries, a broadly based group offering legal protection to brand owners from soap to Scotch, against adulteration and adulterators.[26]

Even though it involved greater expense, and more cost for the consumer, bottled whisky offered drinkers more confidence: 'I have a fear', wrote the first Alexander Walker, 'that the sale of our whisky will fall off in the colonies from the fact that people got tired of paying for bottles corks & cases[;] still it is there [sic] only surety of getting the genuine article.' Finessing packaging was another route to greater protection. As early as 1884 Walker's were developing special capsules (the branded lead seals over the driven corks that closed the bottles) to prevent bottles being reused: 'We are of opinion that the more delicate the capsule can be made, as long as the "get up" on the bottle is not destroyed, the better protection we will have against the capsule being used again to represent a whisky that is not ours, as it will be used only once, and useless afterwards.'[27] The hanging, lead-weighted strip on the Walker closure was part of an ingenious get-up that ensured that, once opened, capsules could not be reused. Such ingenuity proved insufficient to deter the most determined faker; prior to the adoption of more comprehensive controls and measures, it was not unknown for authentic packaging components to be shipped overseas from the UK for use by counterfeiters, and skilled forgers could copy nearly any packaging component at the time.[28]

By the last decade of the nineteenth century the Holy Grail at the time for those seeking to prevent the sale of adulterated spirits was the 'perfect' non-refillable bottle, the quest for which occupied the minds of many, particularly in the United States. It seemed as if a fortune beyond the dreams of avarice awaited the inventor who could create such a bottle, and the speculators who could put it into production. These dreams of riches were fuelled by widely circulating stories of a million-dollar bounty on offer from a Kentucky distiller. But, as the American press delighted in reporting, the road to success was littered with disappointment, madness and suicide, and an increasing scepticism that the hallowed objective would ever be achieved. Amidst all the attendant frenzy of attempted invention it seems that few had read a widely distributed circular from a Canadian distiller as early as 1897 offering 'no encouragement whatever to inventors' working on non-refillable bottles, condemning them as impracticable, expensive, and confusing to consumers, 'as any such device would manifestly be of no service unless the public were thoroughly familiarized therewith', necessitating 'very heavy advertising expenditure'. Ten years later, after numerous frauds and false promises, the same company repeated these views even more trenchantly, condemning the idea of a 'practical' non-refillable bottle as 'an impossibility'.[29]

Despite the discouragement, at the end of 1908 the 'NR Capsule Syndicate' in London invited journalists to a demonstration of its new non-refillable fitment, that 'looks as if it were going to deal a death blow at the substitution of inferior whiskies for well-known brands'. Based on patents by T. Heffernan and H. C. Braunn, the company claimed that 'the capsule is far and away the best remedy yet discovered for the great evil which distillers and blenders have had to put up with', urging producers to adopt it as soon as possible. To gain further publicity for the device, which they claimed could be fitted to any bottle (using their patent 'spinning' machine), they opened a showroom in Shaftesbury Avenue.[30] James Stevenson began conversations with the syndicate the following year, and by 1910 had persuaded Walker's to invest in the new business, providing they could gain control over the patents. Walker's made an initial investment whilst 'experiments . . . were being made with the NR Capsule with a view to its adoption', principally to meet objections made by Stevenson to the cost of the device – 'under no circumstances could the price of the fitment exceed 12/– per gross' – and the process of attaching it to bottles, leading to the development of an entirely new fitment. The company also began to advertise its patent.[31] George Paterson Walker joined NR's board, and attempts were made to encourage their principal competitors, Buchanan's and Dewar's, to join them. Despite his other increasing duties Stevenson was deeply committed to the development process, persuading the Walker board to invest in another 4,750 shares early in 1912, when it was also decided that the focus for the fitments should be Red and Black Label.[32] By April the product was being tested on the home market, with advertising and brochures explaining how to pour with the new fitment (a relatively simple valve device that allowed liquid to leave the bottle, but prevented it being filled), and 'certain defects which only experience with the goods actually on sale could bring to notice, were being dealt with'. Despite the fact that markets were keen to take the new product, it was decided to hold back exports until the teething troubles had been addressed. However, by the end of the year the new bottle had been launched in Australia with a blitz of advertising, the manager there reporting 'that it was highly desirable that the attentions of the Company should be devoted to the furtherance and the perfecting of such a preventative for refilling, as in his view such would achieve results of considerable importance to the Company's benefit'.[33] And while the fitment was still not perfect it was, in Stevenson's view, easier to apply than a cork, and if not 'scientifically non-refillable' certainly robust enough to give consumers the assurance they needed. Walker's would not have invested had they not thought it 'a practicable commercial device'.[34]

Robert Brown, a London-based blending company, were persuaded to make use of the fitment at its launch.[35] However, in the United States other distillers and patentees had brought fitments to some degree of perfection, notably the Wilson Distilling Company from Baltimore, who had first, and very briefly, advertised a non-refillable bottle for their rye whisky in 1910.[36] Like Walker's they launched again in early 1912, but only a year later were involved in talks with Stevenson to merge the two fitment-making subsidiaries, with the result that the Anglo-American Patent Bottle Company was formed in 1913, with Walker committing another £5,000 to the capital required. With powerful advertising produced by Paul Derrick in the UK trade press, the new company argued 'that no manufacturer whose goods are sold in a bottle and who suffers from refilling and adulteration can afford not to investigate the merits of the NR non-refillable fitment'. At the start of 1913, Walker's had also launched their new bottle in the United States with another major advertising campaign from Paul Derrick's agency ('a worthy successor to many excellent advertisements of the same delectable liquid that have preceded it', said *Advertising World*), and efforts were redoubled in Australia (where 'The *Australian Wine and Spirit News* attributes to the non-refillable bottle a great deal of the increased success with which the firm has met in that colony'), and Argentina. By 1914, White Horse, Usher's and others had adopted the non-refillable closure, and although a shortage of aluminium made it impossible to produce during the First World War, this new concept, championed and financed by Stevenson and Walker's had a profound impact on the category at the time.[37]

At the same time as leading the development of the non-refillable bottle and the advertising campaign to support it, James Stevenson was also attempting to resolve the intractable issue of securing bottle supplies to meet the apparently unstoppable demand the company faced. The availability of quality glass was clearly essential to the growth of the Scotch category, but the development of technology in glass-making had been held back by the imposition of excise duties in the United Kingdom until 1845, and slow development thereafter. By the 1880s Walker's were certainly sourcing glass from Bagley & Co. in Yorkshire, and by the early twentieth century it was coming from nearby John Lumb & Co., in Castleford, by which time the requirement for bottles stood at around 1.5 million per annum.[38] Supplies were erratic, bottle size was variable, and quality sometimes wanting, as Alex Walker frequently complained; and the production of square bottles was particularly testing for manufacturers.[39] The slow adoption of new technology and fiercely protective working practices were all brakes on improvement, but new machinery, particularly the Owens automatic bottle-making machine (invented in the United Sates in 1903), offered blenders and bottlers consistently sized bottles, in theory at cheaper prices. A group of English glass manufacturers had acquired patents for the Owens machine in the United Kingdom, and, given the specificity of their requirements, Walker's needed to avoid falling into the grasp of a bottle-making cartel at all costs.[40] Their strategy was to invest in Lumb & Co. and offer them guaranteed production, a similar deal to one that Lumb had with the beer and stout bottlers Read Brothers. At the end of 1910 Walker's committed £8,000 for the construction of a new furnace, but twelve months later decided to buy a third of Lumb's shares for £9,000 instead. In 1913 they loaned Lumb £6,000, around a third of the cost of acquiring patents for new equipment that would make their thirty-eight Simpson Bradshaw machines fully automatic. The following year Stevenson reported that 'supplies of the Company's bottles have now been assured' following a buy-out of Read's contract, allowing Walker's to exploit the additional capacity to build up contingency stocks of bottles in Kilmarnock. As the likelihood of war strengthened, it was agreed that the contingency stock should be matched by an equivalent stock held at Castleford, and in 1915 Walker's began the process of taking over the entire Lumb business.[41] Despite these successes the imperative to maintain an independent supply of top-quality glass would shape strategic thinking for the next two decades.

Between 1895 and 1905 the value of sales for John Walker & Sons had increased threefold (they had peaked at just over £1 million in 1902, but then fallen back to £765,000), and profits had soared from £25,000 to £132,000.[42] Trading conditions in the first decade of the

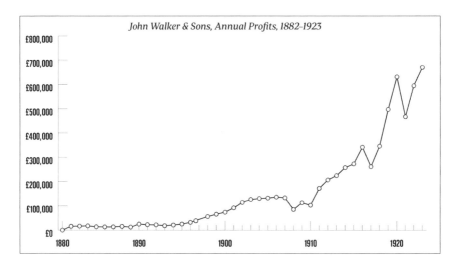

twentieth century were challenging. The fall in the cost of whiskies on the open market disadvantaged Walker's, whose stoic policy of persistent investment in stocks meant that the costs of the whiskies they were selling were sometimes higher than competitors'. In addition there was a steady decline in the consumption of spirits in the United Kingdom between 1900 and the outbreak of war.[43] Although the US market was increasing steadily, sales in established colonial markets were faltering and there was an increased urgency to review and consolidate long-standing agency agreements in markets such as India, and to expand the business into new territories. John MacQueen had been appointed to manage exports in 1909 following the death of Robert Cattanach, and market visits by him, fellow directors and senior managers increased significantly.[44] Most damaging of all to the business was the duty increase in Lloyd George's so-called 'People's Budget' of 1909, which increased the duty on a gallon of whisky from 11s. to 14s. 9d. Walker's, along with their main competitors, increased the price of their brands by 6s. a case, which took the price of a standard brand like Walker's White Label (Old Highland) up to 4s. a bottle.[45] The dent on the sales and profits of Walker's and the whole whisky trade was severe, leading some to fear that the increased duty could only lead to a diminution of quality through the use of cheaper whiskies, which would in turn destroy Scotch's reputation.[46] However, given the well-known temperance sentiments of the chancellor, some thought this budget only the beginning, and a greater concern was the fear of prohibition that began to stalk the Scotch whisky industry like a sinister shadow in the night.

The downturn in trade and the increased costs of doing business (particularly in export markets) had led Dewar's and Buchanan's to begin discussions about a possible merger of interests early in 1909, and they invited a wary James Stevenson to join the talks on behalf of John Walker & Sons.[47] Lloyd George's budget only served to exacerbate the situation. Price Waterhouse were employed as honest brokers in the negotiations, and given access to the profit and loss accounts of the three firms. Buchanan's were seemingly most keen to press ahead with an agreement, with Dewar's taking the view that James Buchanan was keen to remove both his money and himself from active involvement in the business. Tommy Dewar and his elder brother John viewed themselves as being in the strongest position.[48] Walker's were definitely on the back foot in the initial discussions, as attempts to determine how the profits of a new venture could be split three ways were to be based on an average of the previous five years of profits, as adjusted by Waterhouse. A few poor years for Walker's put them at a distinct disadvantage; Waterhouse indicated to Walker's that: 'It has been pointed out to me that the circumstances of trade during the last five years have been such as to affect the holders of large stocks prejudicially, and that consequently the above figures may not represent so fairly as they otherwise might, the true earnings power of the several businesses concerned.' Walker's pressed for a longer run of profits to be taken into account, but with little success.[49]

Although aligned on the impossibility of accepting a proposal based on five years' profits, the senior Walker directors could not entirely agree themselves on the most desirable outcome. Alex Walker insisted that the Distillers Company Ltd (DCL) should be part of any solution, whilst his brother and James Stevenson thought it 'unsuitable and impracticable'.[50] At a meeting of the principals of the three firms, a committee was set up of James Stevenson, A. J. Cameron (John Dewar & Co.) and William Harrison (Buchanan & Co.). But the meeting was not easy. As for involving the DCL, Walker's doubted 'the wisdom of these brands being identified in the public mind with grain whisky and plain spirit – in short that the public might be taught that they could get whisky for their stomach or spirit for their motor out of the same concern', and were fearful that the DCL's poor reputation in export markets could damage sales.[51] Even as potential for a compromise was explored, George Walker was very open of the difficulty with the members of the family, and those other significant shareholders who needed to be persuaded that the deal was in their best interests.[52] And it was felt that the other parties underestimated the position of the Walker's business and the value their directors would bring to the combined venture.[53]

By October 1910 there appeared to have been a change of mood from Kilmarnock. George Walker, still the senior member of the firm, was more amenable to the proposals, and appeared to be contemplating an early retiral in the event of a satisfactory agreement. The government's budget seemed to have had a greater impact on Walker's than the others, and had possibly influenced their change of thinking.[54] Despite the encouraging position, talks seemed to have stalled and Price Waterhouse were once more deputed to look at the most recent balance sheet; when they reported back in 1911, it showed an extraordinary increase in Walker's sales for the previous year, both in the home and export trade. Walker's were now exceptionally advantaged in any division of profits and their rivals began to despair of any deal being done.[55]

Early in 1914 Stevenson came forward with a startling new proposal based on the belief that 'the majority of the economies likely to be effected by a combination are largely connected with the production end of the business', and suggesting the creation of a jointly owned company that would control distilleries and inventory. In addition, reflecting concerns that Walker's were already dealing with, he proposed that, as 'bottles, casks, cases are all costing increasingly more all the time, and in our opinion such advance in price is not unconnected with combinations in the trades from who we buy . . . mutual defence in this direction would, we feel sure, be a highly desirable arrangement'. Moreover, Dewar's and Buchanan's were told, it was clear that as far as the Walker shareholders were concerned, this was a mandatory first step towards any further degree of amalgamation or profit-sharing.[56] The adviser from Price Waterhouse was convinced that such a favourable opportunity to conclude the deal was unlikely to repeat itself. But despite favourable arguments, the discussions were brought to an abrupt end, leaving Buchanan and Dewar to combine interests in the Scotch Whisky Brands Company Ltd in 1915.[57]

There is no doubt that the dramatically improving business performance of Walker's, whose profits soared between 1910 and 1914 from £100,000 to £250,000 (about £11.8 million and £29 million today), changed the dynamics of these merger discussions. And although some factors contrived to improve the performance of many whisky businesses at the time, the one clear difference between Walker's and their competitors was the remarkable brand and advertising campaign they had launched in 1908 with the creation of 'Johnnie Walker', and which was then taken all over the world with a relentlessness and discipline that was worthy of the very best modern marketing. Advertising expenditure, including outdoor posters, print, showcards and 'novelties', had increased from around £5,000 in 1900 to almost £28,000 ten years later as the new Johnnie Walker campaign was getting into its stride. At the outbreak of war annual investment stood at £50,000.[58] The power of mass communication in building these new brands was very clear to both brand-owners and, as we have seen, their critics. Arthur Bramall, who had led the original Islington prosecutions against blended Scotch in 1905, complained bitterly of its influence.[59]

Advertising was both expensive and complex, particularly in export markets:

> *Advertising to maintain a foreign market is a much more elaborate business than may be supposed, and covers expenditure in many odd ways. For instance, the temporary wood hoardings of a new building in New York are profusely filled, not by printed posters, but often by hand-painted advertisements. Again, everybody carries in his pocket some knick-knack or other having reference to the goods . . . there is also constant demand for large parcels of miniature samples, a mode of advertising universally approved by shippers so long as these are honestly given away free, but they are not always so.[60]*

For Walker's the difficulties of coming late to advertising were offset by the benefits of the ruthlessly 'scientific' approach adopted by Paul Derrick, which saw no opportunity lost both to promote the brand name and to provide consumers with 'reasons why' to buy in print advertising. Advertising, said Derrick, was simply 'the first step in making a sale'.[61]

There were nevertheless shared messages that the leading blending houses sought to deliver to existing and potential drinkers, to a greater or lesser degree of success. Principally they sought to legitimise the reputation of what was in effect still a 'new' product in the eyes of consumers, particularly in the context of a very public and well-coordinated establishment campaign to traduce the reputation of blended Scotch. The way to do this was to create an imagined past, to craft an ingenious narrative through time that made blended Scotch appear as old as the ancients. A narrative successfully created around age also had the benefit of boosting product credentials, of both teaching consumers (rightly or wrongly) that age was a principal determinant in the quality of a blend, and of implying, through these historical associations, that the product in the bottle was indeed 'whisky of great age' without having to go to the length of putting an age statement on a label. None were better in delivering this point than Dewar's. Two examples may suffice, the first being 'The Whisky of His Forefathers', a campaign based around a painting commissioned from Matthew Hewerdine in 1894 which was used in posters, print and, most famously, in possibly the earliest film advertisement for any product. The picture showed a kilted man sitting with a bottle of Dewar's at a table, whilst his ancestors stepped out of the past from paintings hung on the wall behind to reach for a glass of their 'favourite' whisky.[62] The second, and more audacious still, was inspired by Tommy Dewar's visit to Giza as part of his famous world 'ramble', and the Edwardian fascination with Egyptian archaeology. It was a series of posters and print advertisements published from 1904 showing images of bottles of Dewar's, surrounded by hieroglyphs and ancient Egyptians, on fragments of excavated stones and unearthed antiquities.[63] The message couldn't have been clearer. Current marketing theory explains this advertising idea from over a hundred years ago thus: 'An important means by which new ventures gain legitimacy is by engaging in actions that convey associations with reputed entities. Such actions affect stakeholder confidence in new ventures, in particular in their ability to introduce products successfully.'[64]

The genius of Walker's 'Striding Man' character was that he was a timeless traveller who could shift effortlessly between the past and the present in a single stride. Derrick's copywriters provided the backdrop for this in a succession of themed historical print campaigns which were introduced following the death of the cartoonist and illustrator Tom Browne, whose work was used retrospectively for much of 1910 (he had died in May of that year). Typically these were published in weeklies such as the *Sphere*, the *Graphic*, *Illustrated London News* and the *Tatler* with solidly respectable middle-class readerships. Browne's duties as illustrator were taken over by Bernard Partridge, who drew the 'Fashions come, fashions go' series, and was in turn followed in 1912 by Leonard Ravel Hill with 'The modern cry', which put the Striding Man on the thoroughfares of London celebrating the street cries of the past, and was followed by 'Old English Song'. The historical metaphor in these print advertisements was reinforced by consistent messaging around the age and range of products and by the promise of 'guaranteed same quality throughout the world', in addition, of course, to the perennial 'Born 1820 – Still

Going Strong'. The strength of the 'Johnnie Walker' advertising, wrote *Advertising World*, was in its relentless clarity of thinking.[65] Leo Cheney started work on Johnnie Walker in 1914 with a campaign that focused on Black Label, drawn in a more contemporary spirit, and then took the Striding Man to war.[66]

The Walker poster campaigns (so little of which have survived in any form), which were sometimes linked to the print work but sometimes completely original, were often both humorous and topical: 'Served without a fault since 1820' was the strapline for a tennis-playing poster launched to coincide with the All England Championship in July 1914. They continued to avoid any explicit references to Scotch. 'The firm does not believe in putting out any advertisement which, in the words of their managing director, "could incite the populace to booze".'[67] It was, rather, all about building familiarity, and an affinity between the consumer and the character of 'Johnnie Walker' himself, a relationship that transcended whisky: 'It is not so much his beaver hat, his cravat, his ruffles, his breeches, his eyeglass, or other signs and tokens of the later Georgian era, that compel attention; it is rather the geniality that he radiates. Here is an atmosphere of *bonhomie* about him, and through *bonhomie* you may easily win your way to the heart of a man of the world.'[68] As the Striding Man played cricket, tennis, golf or billiards on huge poster sites throughout London, major cities around the United Kingdom, and in Australia and the United States, so he built up a trusting and trusted relationship with a much broader group of the population than that found in the illustrated newspapers: 'He loves posters, does the man in the street. The Bovril blanket gives him a warm feeling on these days of early Spring. He smiles at the sweet innocence of the Soap girl who graces the busiest thoroughfares, naked and unashamed. Johnnie Walker embodies all the best qualities of a representative Englishman . . . this poster makes him laugh, and that poster makes him think.'[69]

Neither advertising nor anything else would survive four years of war without severe disruption. Salaried and weekly paid staff joined the forces as soon as war was declared, initially being granted extended leave of absence, with wages being guaranteed or partly guaranteed, till their return.[70] Walker's provided John Lumb & Co. with additional capital to allow them to build up reserves of bottles at the start of the war. Shortages of raw materials dictated that the company had to adopt black-metal glass bottles, first for the increasing US market, and then for Red Label throughout the world. Wood, metal closures and corks were also in short supply.[71] Distilling continued at Annandale and Cardow in 1914 and 1915, albeit on a much-reduced scale. The decision was taken as the 1915 distilling season progressed to retain all new-make from both distilleries, and both Alex Walker and production director John Cumming were charged with obtaining stocks of barley (home-grown or imported) on the open market wherever they could, and before they were commandeered by the government. Output at malt-whisky distilleries was reduced to 70 per cent of normal production in 1916 (assuming distilleries could obtain barley to distil), and the following year it was prohibited, the production of grain whisky having already stopped.[72] Walker's did significantly increase their distilling capacity during this period by the acquisition of a third share in Coleburn and Clynelish distilleries, and in the Dailuaine-Talisker Distillery Co.; in both instances their partners in these investments included the Distillers Company Ltd.[73]

Against this background Walker's sales continued to climb in the first years of the war, falling back in 1917, the only wartime year in which profits declined. Demand was buoyant in the home market, but the appetite from export markets for Scotch, particularly the USA, was insatiable, and the imminent threat of a shortage only served to exacerbate the pressures this created for companies like Walker's. The exportation of bottled whisky (Scotch and Irish) into New York increased from some 200,000 cases in 1914 to almost 350,000 in 1917. But bulk imports, which had remained fairly static, increased from 81,000 gallons in 1914 to just under 1 million in 1917, as US government restrictions on both the distillation and sale of spirits were put into place, and some sort of permanent prohibition seemed ever more likely.[74]

Whilst their principal rivals had difficulties in the United States before the war, opening lavish New York offices with much publicity and then closing with somewhat less coverage, the Walker business, managed by Williams & Humbert, had continued to grow.[75] Part of the reason for this success was undoubtedly the new branding and advertising, and also the impact of the non-refillable bottle. In 1916 Williams & Humbert's contract was renegotiated to a minimum shipment of 6,000 cases per month, but they were shipping 7,000, and with annual sales to the USA approaching 100,000 cases, Alex Walker and Stevenson began to investigate what the possibilities might be for bottling there, given problems with materials and labour in Kilmarnock and London.[76]

The other issue to be dealt with was whisky stocks, particularly as demand was increasing for both Red and Black Label, blends with higher ratios of older malt whisky to grain, despite price increases caused by government regulations. Before the outbreak of war, Alex Walker had argued that the company should seek the finance to invest an additional £100,000 in stocks of mature whisky, but buying became harder as prices rose dramatically.[77] Husbanding stocks became the most important issue; the sale of cheaper bulk blends was stopped and White Label was withdrawn from a number of markets ('It was figuratively trading at a loss to sell the White Label quality at all,' said Alex Walker), although George Walker's proposal to take it out of the home trade was deemed too extreme. Eventually it was agreed in June 1917 to gradually withdraw White Label and 'establish Red Label as our standard brand'.[78] Alex Walker had 'strongly emphasised the acute seriousness of the Scotch Whisky stocks and pointed out that if the present rate of output continued the position would eventually resolve itself in businesses being closed down purely for the lack of supplies'. Cautious and expensive buying brought stocks up to over 8 million gallons ('larger than they had ever been'), but it was still necessary to introduce allocations in mid-1916, despite the concerns that this could damage the goodwill of the company and the position of its brands, restricting output to 52,000 cases a month, or some 620,000 cases a year.[79] Government intervention setting strict limits on the amount of whisky that could be released for the UK market, the entry of the United States into the war, and a total ban on Scotch whisky exports in January 1918, took the matter out of the company's hands.

One of the unanticipated consequences of the war was the appointment of James Stevenson to the Ministry of Munitions by Lloyd George in 1915. Stevenson, who was playing an increasingly active role in trade affairs, had been prominent in industry delegations to Lloyd George when Chancellor of the Exchequer to protest over the 'People's Budget', and had spoken publicly and uncompromisingly on the matter, condemning the 'humbugging interference of a Temperance minority', and a budget 'conceived in malice, born in spite and matured in vindictiveness'.[80] However, this apparent antipathy disguised some degree of mutual respect, perhaps forged over the golf course at Walton Heath, and having only been at the ministry for a matter of weeks, Lloyd George appointed him to a group of 'push and go' men, 'handpicked and not easily influenced by the Whitehall machine', to transform the war effort.[81] Stevenson was appointed Director of Area Organisation, responsible for establishing the structures that linked groups of sometimes recalcitrant local munitions manufacturers to central government.[82] In 1917, having been made a baronet, he became vice-chairman of the Ministry of Munitions Advisory Committee and was also advisor to the Director of National Service amongst a long list of other responsibilities; when Churchill took control of the ministry in July 1917, he and Stevenson forged a close and lasting bond. 'Every week', said Churchill later, he 'used to say to Sir James Stevenson the staff must be got down by 200 or 300, and every week at the end it showed a rise of 700 or 800'; Churchill quickly came to regard 'Jimmy' as his 'right hand man', and took him after the war to the War Office and then the Colonial Office, despite pleas from George Walker to release him from government service to help a firm 'who were faced with many reconstruction problems of their own'.[83]

The board minutes of John Walker & Sons don't suggest that Stevenson's responsibilities with his fellow directors for the strategic leadership of the business were in any way diminished by his wartime responsibilities. However, there were changes to the board. Thomas Hood Walker, the South African adventurer and younger brother of George and Alex, had died in 1910 and was replaced by Adam Cairns Smith, a Kilmarnock solicitor and scion of the printing family of the same name who had produced Walker's first labels. James Blair retired the following year after thirty-six years in the business. (He died in 1912 and was buried next to the Walker family plot in the New Cemetery.) The two remaining Walkers on the board, George and Alex, along with Stevenson and John Cumming, were joint managing directors. In 1918 John MacQueen was appointed export director, Archibald Stevenson (James's younger brother) home-trade director, and Arthur Hogarth production director in Kilmarnock, with responsibilities from bonded warehouses to blending.[84] In February 1917 Alex Walker too joined the Ministry of Munitions, having been appointed to a committee to advise on the rationing of raw materials to non-essential industries.[85]

One of the continuing frustrations for the company, and the industry as a whole, were the regulations imposed by the Central Liquor Control Board in 1916 and 1917 to reduce the strength at which whisky could be retailed. Scotch was mostly sold at proof or 10 under proof, 57% and 51% abv. The trade was vehemently opposed to strength reduction, arguing that they would rather have constraints on the amount of whisky that could be sold than its character. Alex Walker was prominent in the negotiations with government on the matter, and although he had supported moderate reductions in strength in discussions with the Walker board, his delegation argued that excessive dilution of whisky

> would entirely alter its character and if forced to reduce one's high-class blend to 35 under proof would, to many brands, mean ruin. Years of labour in making a reputation would be wasted, for every whisky has its particular characteristic, but when diluted to a large extent, this would not be recognisable, and thus the article would fall to the common level; after all, a drink is only acceptable because it has flavour.[86]

Despite their arguments, step by step the board continued to reduce the permitted strength, finally arriving at '30 up', or 40% abv, in February 1917. Like the minimum age of three years old, this minimum strength of Scotch has since become a fundamental part of its legal definition. As if Scotch had not suffered enough from the wartime government (which, it should be noted, was ordering vast quantities of blends through the Navy and Army Canteens for the use of commissioned and non-commissioned officers), Bonar Law's budget of 1918 more than doubled the duty on a gallon of Scotch, and introduced controlled pricing of spirits which saw the price of a bottle of Red Label, now the principal focus of the Walker business, go from 4s. at the start of the war to 9s. 'The Chancellor of the Exchequer', wrote Ridley's, 'appears to have had advisers who could only think of one section – the Brand owner. The dealer or middleman is to be crushed out by controlled prices, and great hardships will be occasioned to the struggling local wine-merchant and distributor.'[87]

By this time James Stevenson was very much at the centre of political affairs, something he evidently relished. Perhaps his most critical intervention on behalf of the whisky industry was in 1915, when he developed the proposal for Lloyd George that became the Immature Spirits Act of 1915, restricting the sale of spirits under three years old. In order to reduce excessive consumption of alcohol, particularly in munitions-producing districts, the chancellor, a keen advocate of temperance, was considering a variety of possible options, some extreme. It was 'an undoubted fact', said Stevenson, 'that the Government in the Spring of 1915 had made up their minds to enforce total prohibition of spirits for the period of the war'. At a meeting in April at the Treasury, Stevenson argued the case for the maintenance of distillation, not least because of its importance in munitions production, and the necessity of having yeast supplies for the production of breads. His alternative, to introduce a minimum three-year bonding period for whisky which became enshrined in law (and forms a critical part of today's definition of Scotch whisky), was the best possible outcome for companies such as Walker's, selling premium brands, with extensive stock-holdings of mature whiskies. It also helped remove from the market much of the low-quality tap whisky which had always dented the quality credentials of Scotch. 'I wonder if you remember the days', wrote former deputy chairman of the Inland Revenue, Laurence Guillemard, to Stevenson in 1921,

> *when we had a battle royal over Immature Spirits. You defeated me hip and thigh and induced our present Prime Minister to pass a bill which I, as Chairman of Customs and Excise, opposed. I as the vanquished, retain a very pleasant memory of the fray. I should like to think that you as victor feel the same.*[88]

As one trade journal wrote admiringly, Stevenson had become politically the most powerful man in the industry.[89]

CHAPTER 8
CARRY ON

'We shall continue to carry on the old firm on the traditions and policy of the past, and Johnnie Walker will still be individual in his attitude and service to his good friends in the trade.'[1]

Johnnie Walker Goes Everywhere (Sir Bernard Partridge), 1921

AS THE FIRST WORLD WAR ended, John Walker & Sons was still a family firm; by the start of the Second World War it appeared to be destined to be a firm without the family. In 1940 Alex Walker retired from the business, leaving an industry that had been structurally transformed in the years since the Armistice. In the early 1920s the last act of the Pattison Crash was played out as the Scotch industry was drawn into ever-closer consolidation, partly a result of the long hangover that had afflicted the industry since the events of 1899. In addition, the impact of the war and almost four years' lost production on stocks and on prices sent the Walker home-trade business (and that of their competitors) into a decline from which it would not recover until the 1950s.

By 1940 export sales surpassed home for the first time and would go on to become the dominant force in the Walker business. The United States, only seven years after the end of Prohibition, was Walker's largest and most valuable export market, accounting for half of all overseas business. Ironically the 'great social and economic experiment, noble in motive and far-reaching in purpose', had only served to cement the reputation of Scotch for quality in the minds of American consumers. The United States remains one of the brand's most important markets, a business built on foundations laid, and reputations made, in the first decades of the twentieth century.

Whilst sales at home may have declined, the popularity of the brand and its place in the nation's popular culture had not. Tom Browne's roguish and vibrant figure had evolved into a part of British life, a national treasure as much loved as 'the Master' Jack Hobbs – the Surrey and England batsman widely considered to be one of the greatest cricketers of all time – or the 'saloon-bar Priapus' Max Miller, the hugely popular, risqué vaudevillian and probably the best stand-up comic of the inter-war years. The creative drive that had characterised the launch of Paul Derrick's campaign continued into the thirties, when the combination of the Depression and a new generation of drinkers with cinemas and dance-halls to tempt them away from pubs and bars demanded that the advertising returned to focus on the brand's (and the category's) intrinsic values of quality and consistency. The brand's association with sport, particularly golf and cricket, became increasingly important as a means of reaching out to these newer consumers.

Within two years of the end of the First World War, Chancellor Austen Chamberlain more than doubled the duty on a gallon of Scotch, from Bonar Law's 30s. per proof gallon to 72s. 6d., taking the price of a bottle to 12s. 6d. In just ten years the price of a bottle of Red Label had tripled. In addition, home sales were restricted to 75 per cent of any given customer's orders in 1916. Exports of Scotch, which had been prohibited in January 1918, were by 1919 allowed, but restricted at the same level as the home trade. Whilst some blenders looked to introduce whiskies at 'pre-war' strength, the duty increases made a compelling argument to retain a standard 40% abv for the majority of brands. The government also attempted to restrict blenders to marketing one brand only. Ridley's feared all these regulations 'still further safeguard the interests of the large proprietary firms'. They were also concerned that the unique character of particular brands, and the choice available to consumers, could be threatened by too much regulation:

> Before control was instituted, scope was given for the blenders making the most of their stocks of Highland Malts, to give variety to their different proprietary brands, and so, thereby, being able to cater for different tastes among the public. It is not a thing to be desired in any trade, or at any time, to do away with individuality.[2]

In addition to managing the demand for cased stock from existing domestic customers, not helped by continued difficulties in the supply of bottles and other raw materials, Walker's were having to refuse to take on new business 'owing to the greatly increased demand for our goods and the consequent abnormal pressure on our output'.[3] In order to focus on the more profitable cased business, Walker's restricted the sale of bulk to almost all markets, except where duty structures made it a more favourable way of doing business. To try and keep the inventory in good shape Alex Walker was authorised to purchase 'a moderate quantity' of stock at the end of 1918, but more ambitious acquisitions would follow as the industry began to follow an inexorable path to consolidation.[4] Despite these difficulties the value of sales more than doubled between 1918 and 1920, and stood at £2,652,090 in 1922. Profits rose from £345,885 to £594,621.[5]

In 1920 the company celebrated Alex Walker's knighthood, awarded in recognition of his government service (particularly after the war in the disposal of surplus munitions), George Paterson Walker's thirty years as chairman (commissioning a portrait 'by one of the leading portrait painters of the day'), and their centenary. In January the public were encouraged to join the Johnnie Walker character in a journey around the world – marking the fact that it was now being sold in over 120 markets – illustrated in a 'travel series' of over thirty cartoons drawn by Leo Cheney, from a first stop at Gibraltar ('I know my reputation is as steadfast as a rock') to North and East Africa, China, South-east Asia, India, the Caribbean, Latin America, South Africa, New Zealand and Canada. Now firmly in the grip of Prohibition after the Volstead Act of the previous year, the United States was omitted from the series. 'Guaranteed same quality all over the world' was the simple 'reason to believe' claim.[6] The series was printed in illustrated

From George III. to George V.
———One hundred years long
Born 1820—Still going strong.

Leo Cheney's Around the World series in 1920 celebrated the global reach of the Johnnie Walker brand

weeklies over a two-year period, following which they were collected
into a photographic travelogue, *Around the World*, dedicated to the
agents of Johnnie Walker throughout the globe 'whose support has
so materially contributed to the unique position obtained by this
famous product of Scotland'. In March 1920, a bowing Johnnie Walker,

hat raised, thanked the world for their felicitations with the words, 'Thanks, same tae ye'.[7] Commenting on the campaign, *Advertising World* said: 'It places Johnnie Walker quite definitely among the two or three outstanding personalities that have left their impress on the public mind today. And it has associated him with nothing that is not uncommonly pleasant and jovial.'[8] In 1921 a Bernard Partridge poster, 'Goes everywhere', showing the Johnnie Walker character boarding an ocean liner called the *New Century*, was produced for hoardings, the London Underground and showcards. 'The appearance of a new poster for Johnnie Walker whisky has a significance of considerable importance,' said the trade press.[9] The drawing was used as the frontispiece for *Around the World*: it was, to say the least, a particularly bold, optimistic and almost defiant statement to make to a world still in the grip of post-war anxiety and austerity.

By 1920 the two principal shareholders in the business were George and Alex Walker, both of whom held a little over 2,000 shares each. Of the 18,000 shares issued, the family accounted for more than 14,000. The remainder were held by banks (3,000) and current and former employees.[10] The anniversary, at a time of unthought-of profitability, was clearly an opportunity for the directors and shareholders to put something back into the business. For employees, by way of 'some special recognition for the staff who have been connected with the company for a number of years and have by loyal service contributed to its success', the directors established a Centenary Pension Fund for salaried staff, and issued a Centenary bonus of half annual wages for those not included in the scheme.[11] On 28 December there was a celebration in Kilmarnock for staff and 'friends' of the company in the Art Galleries and Agricultural Halls, a 'sumptuous supper', speeches, a concert and dancing, 'a function such as we have never seen in Kilmarnock'. 'The beauty of the scene was such as had rarely been equalled and never eclipsed in the town,' wrote the *Kilmarnock Herald*. It also noted that 'with their usual innate modesty the firm did not desire to have a great deal made of their celebration'. No doubt fully aware that communities all over Ayrshire were still planning and building memorials to the victims of the war, reports on the anniversary in the local press were deliberately muted, and there were none of the new pension scheme.[12]

If the home trade for Scotch was depressed, demand for exports from all over the world continued to grow, despite disruptions in important markets and the supply of raw materials, and the general difficulties of shipping freight in the aftermath of the Armistice. The only difficulty the industry had was in meeting the demand, particularly after the imposition of the 1915 Immature Spirits Act.[13] Walker's had specific problems with agencies. Having learned in 1914 that 'the public' in South Africa 'were establishing a boycott, purely for patriotic reasons, owing to the German nationality of the Company's agents', the company paid compensation to Rolfes Nobel and declared the market open.[14] Disagreements also broke out with Williams & Humbert over alleged short shipments of cases to the USA before the introduction of wartime restrictions in 1917, which, according to Walker's, was totally unjust 'in view of the efforts we had put forth to meet the demand for the USA at the expense of more important markets'. Agreement was reached in June 1918 that Walker would make up the shipments, as well as resuming the regular monthly quantity once the wartime restrictions were lifted, with the prescient qualification that 'In the event of adverse legislation or commandeering of our stock, we would not be able to carry out the arrangement.' The fluctuating government restrictions on exports, and those imposed

Bootleggers went to extraordinary lengths to smuggle whisky during Prohibition

by the newly formed Whisky Association on the quality and price of whiskies that could be exported (in force until 1926) appeared to be no barrier to the surge in exports.[15] At the start of 1920 Walker's imposed a cap on their annual production of 1.3 million gallons, of which 1 million were for 'London and export'.

Ridley's reported in 1920 that 'the demand from overseas markets is remarkably active, and as a matter of fact exporters are experiencing difficulty in supplying all their agents' orders. The importance to the trade of this export demand is realised when it is kept in mind that neither age nor price are vital considerations as a rule.' The demand, it was clear, was driven by the United States. A few years later Ridley's observed: 'The export trade figures make a wonderfully good showing but it would be foolish to close one's eyes to the fact that the improvement recorded is very largely attributable to increased shipments to the Scheduled Area and that the old-established markets are doing no more than holding their own.'[16]

Regardless of the continuing arguments around the lasting effects of the Prohibition period on drinking behaviour in the United States, one simple fact is beyond contradiction. At repeal, after thirteen years of 'dry America', Scotch whisky emerged with the reputation of being *the* premier luxury imported spirit. Moreover, it was to confirm Johnnie Walker's standing as the leading Scotch brand in the world. Whilst ceasing any trade with the United States, Walker's had continued to sell mostly cased and sometimes bulk stock to large, increasingly consolidated companies based in various ports in Canada, to the French territory of Saint-Pierre, and to the Bahamas and other parts of the Caribbean. They distanced themselves completely from any complicity in the activities of 'rum runners' and 'bootleggers' in the United States. When Sir Alexander Walker welcomed a delegation of 'dry goods warehousemen' from the United States and Canada to Kilmarnock in 1921, where they were fêted at a grand dinner and reception, he was reported to have said that 'America had always been one of the greatest customers for their products, and when Prohibition came along, he had thought that that avenue of trade would be closed.'[17]

Despite the overwhelming demand, a combination of the long-term effects of the Pattison Crash, the gradual reduction and then cessation of distilling in Scotland (particularly in the case of grain whisky), Stevenson's 1915 Immature Spirits Act, the huge increase in the domestic price of Scotch, and a strongly held fear that some form of state control of the alcohol-beverage business in the United Kingdom was inevitable, resulted in a whisky market in turmoil. Another problem was an unforeseen consequence of Prohibition, namely the dumping of significant quantities of cheap American spirit onto the English market that was starved of Scotch. Much of this was finding its way into lower-priced blends of 'Scotch', leading the Whisky Association (which then represented both Scotch and Irish distillers) to advertise about this particular 'evil of Prohibition', telling consumers that 'definite guarantees that whisky offered for sale is wholly Scotch or Irish should be obtained, and no foreign whisky should be accepted'.[18] There were also complaints of cheap Irish whisky being used in Scotch blends that were being sold by the gallon for less than a price of a bottle of Red Label: 'Much dissatisfaction is felt with the action of certain traders in substituting American and other imported spirits for Scotch Whisky in blends sold as genuine "Scotch". Even the use of the products of the Irish Distillers in such circumstances is indefensible.' It was, said Ridley's, 'by no means altogether satisfactory to see the different spirits losing their respective nationalities in this way. Time was when the nationality was rigidly preserved, a fact which played no small part in elevating the Scotch Whisky Trade to the pinnacle of prosperity to which it eventually attained.'[19] In 1920, when Sir Alexander Walker was trying to sell off stocks of Irish whisky, Stevenson strongly pointed out, for the record, that 'it ought to made clear that the Company had at no time blended Irish Whisky with its own whisky, nor had it any intention of doing so'.[20]

In the same year, Ridley's complained that the Scotch industry 'seems to be going from bad to worse, when we find company after company "fleeing from the wrath to come" after their directors have made their sufficiency, and have had their heads crowned with honours for what they have done or did in the Great War'. Fearing an even greater concentration of power and influence in the hands of the large blenders, it continued: 'Since the year began three more well-known distilling and blending companies have taken advantage of the conditions of trade, following the restrictions on spirits, to get out of a much abused industry with little or no consideration for their clients who helped them along on evil days when they could hardly make ends meet.' The directors and partners of Usher's, Bulloch Lade and Robert Thorne & Son had all decided it was time to capitalise on the value of their stocks and exit the business (Usher's and Bulloch Lade being acquired by the DCL). 'Third generational entrepreneurial decline', age and ill-health, the fear of state control, and quite simply the huge sums that could be made for aged stocks from those with the money and access to the North American market, were all driving factors towards consolidation.[21]

As early as 1918 Samuel Greenlees, one of the first blenders at scale to move his operations to Glasgow, gave up business 'owing to the unsatisfactory state of his health'; a fifth of his whisky stocks would eventually end up with Walker's.[22] In 1920 Walker's bought 350,000 gallons of whisky from Thomas Kennedy, another well-known Glasgow blender.[23] The following year, in combination with Watson's of Dundee, William Lowrie and the DCL, they acquired Kennedy's remaining stocks as he closed his business down. In October 1922 Walker's acquired the whisky stocks of Ainslie, Baillie & Co. of Leith, astonishment being expressed at their paying 'as high as 45s. per original proof gallon for even a Highland malt whisky bonded in 1915'. Then in June 1923, in partnership with Buchanan Dewar, Walker's purchased the business and stocks of James Watson & Co. of Dundee, put at over 5 million gallons, of which 'a comparatively small proportion is old whisky'.[24] At the same time despite these and other purchases the company was attempting to expand its footprint in distilling, already increased during the war with the acquisition of major shareholdings in Clynelish and Dailuaine-Talisker. In 1923 they agreed a deal with Dr Cowie of Dufftown to acquire Mortlach distillery, associated properties and its whisky stocks; valued at almost £76,000, the whisky was worth more than the distillery.[25] However, with Sir Alexander and production director A. J. Hogarth developing detailed forecasts based principally on stocks for Red Label, allocations still had to be put in place: overall the stock available for sale stood at 2 million gallons a year, with 1.8 allocated to London and export, and some degree of tension between the board over how restrictions should be worked in the home trade.[26]

At the 1919 Annual General Meeting the directors had warned that the need to raise capital to allow the company to recover the stock position it had held at the start of the war – which had been badly eroded by three years of very heavy business – was critical. The company also jealously guarded its claim to have the largest stocks of malt whisky in the world. Although generous to its relatively small circle of shareholders, the company was conservative (or 'old fashioned') in matters of finance. Rather than look to financiers (with all the cost and lack of independence that could bring), they preferred to build up substantial reserves from profits to meet capital needs. In addition, they accepted private loans, and encouraged 'thrifty' employees to make deposits with the firm (although Alex Walker had negotiated an informal agreement with the Distillers Company during the war to accept loans for stock purchases in the last resort). In 1920 the capital of the company was increased to £1,260,000 by the issue of 42,000 shares of £20 each among existing shareholders by capitalising £840,000 of undivided profits held in reserve funds.[27] In 1923, after lengthy deliberations, a more fundamental reorganisation took place in terms of both finance and management when the business converted to a public limited liability company. At this point George Paterson Walker, after over thirty years as chairman, John Cumming and Archibald Stevenson retired from the board, receiving generous 'compensation'. Sir Alexander Walker, Sir James Stevenson, A. J. Hogarth, the lawyer Francis Redfern and Adam Cairns Smith remained directors, and were joined by G. P. Walker's son, G. Gordon Walker. The capital was increased to £4.76 million through the issue of debenture shares worth £2 million and preference shares to the value of £1.5 million; ordinary shares to the value of £1.26 million were divided between existing shareholders.[28] Rumours in the trade suggested that Walker's wanted the additional capital in order to purchase 'a well-known distillery company in the West of Scotland owning four or five distilleries', Walker's responding that it was simply to allow for 'certain impending family arrangements'.[29] The 'well-known distillery company' was White Horse Distillers, who like Walker were desperate for capital and whisky stocks. 'The whole question', wrote Peter Mackie, 'is one of stocks and the financing of the same ... There is no doubt that we could do double the trade today had we bigger stocks.'[30]

Regardless of Walker's intentions, the Distillers Company was still engaged in discussions with all of the 'big three' around the increasing consolidation of the industry, the division of available whisky stocks from those wishing to sell up, and the fate of competitor brands.[31] 'The policy of absorption in the Whisky trade', said Ridley's,

> has had the effect of diverting the demand more and more to the leading and widely advertised brands. Evidence of this can be found in the fact that there are at least one or two big firms who, either cannot supply their existing customers in full, or are compelled for the time being to refuse to take on new customers.

In addition the disposition of the consumer is more and more to confine his attention to the well-known brands with which he gets what amounts to a guarantee of quality.[32]

These discussions inevitably led to a revival of the idea of an amalgamation, similar to the one discussed before the war, but this time including the Distillers Company, something that Walker's had argued for in the past. James Stevenson made the proposal in November 1924, and despite some residual antipathy among the key players, a strong disagreement between William Ross (of Distillers), Stevenson and the Dewars over the location of the new company (Stevenson and Dewar strongly favouring London with its ready access to capital markets), and concerns from Walker's over some of the personal financial arrangements, the deal was agreed by February 1925.[33] Both Stevenson and Alex Walker were determined that John Walker & Sons, and Johnnie Walker, would retain their individuality within this loosely defined combine.

The formation of the new company was hardly a surprise, 'as with the disappearance of so many important distributing firms and the growth in importance of the big three and the subsidiaries of the Distillers Company Limited some sort of combination for protection against excessive competition that might have been instituted as a result of the slump in consumption was rendered likely'. 'The individual companies', said Ridley's, 'will continue to conduct their business on the same individual lines as formerly.'[34] At the Annual General Meeting of John Walker & Sons in the following August, Alex Walker (now Sir Alexander) was very clear about the future direction of his business:

*The figures show that the Company maintains its preeminent
position in the trade and that the popularity of its whisky is
higher than ever. It will be our endeavour to further entrench
ourselves in public favour. While we are satisfied that our
quality cannot be surpassed, by research and methodical care
we are continually improving the product of our distilleries. Our
stocks are now much greater than at any period of our history,
so that we can continue to ensure uniformity in the age and
style of our blends. The change which has taken place in the
ownership of the ordinary shares of the company will make no
difference to the conduct of the business. We shall continue to
carry on the old firm on the traditions and policy of the past,
and Johnnie Walker will still be individual in his attitude and
service to his good friends in the trade.*[35]

The constituent companies of the new concern were all given equal
representation on its main board, with Sir Alexander Walker, Lord
Stevenson and A. J. Hogarth representing Walker. Stevenson and
Walker were also placed on the Home and Export Committee, and the
Distilling and Blending Committee. Joining them as required were
Francis Redfern, Alexander Adams, Ronnie Cumming and Edward
Grahame Johnstone. Adams had joined Walker in Birmingham, working
with Stevenson, and had moved to London in 1908 where he managed
the London office, becoming a director in 1926. Ronnie Cumming, son
of John Cumming, joined in Kilmarnock in 1921, but quickly found his
way to London, where he became export manager in 1925. Grahame
Johnstone, Lord Stevenson's step-son, had joined the company in
London shortly after the outbreak of war, but in 1917 volunteered for the
Royal Naval Air Service, winning the Distinguished Service Cross 'for

the pluck and determination shown by him in engaging enemy aircraft' whilst flying Sopwith Camels. He became a director in 1926 and was responsible for advertising, among other things, where he was joined by Laurence Jay as advertising manager in 1928.

What quickly became apparent in the attempts to achieve some degree of integration between the new companies was the gulf that existed between the senior managers of the Distillers Company on the one hand, and Walker's (and to a lesser extent Buchanan and Dewar's) on the other, on their understanding of brands. The Distillers Company had come relatively late to blending, and their brands (for the most part restricted to the export trade) were relatively staid, in all respects, compared to Walker's. Distillers was a whisky-making company for whom brands were an adjunct; for Stevenson and Walker brands were the life blood of their business. This difference was to become most apparent in disputes over advertising strategy and investment, and the approach to the sale of cheaper Scotches and their relationships to the main, 'standard' brands. Stevenson and Sir Alexander Walker were at the forefront of making the case for individual brand advertising over the group or category approach advocated by Distillers. In 1926 William Ross complained that 'in his view, the fusion of the interests had not – as far as advertising was concerned – resulted in the benefit anticipated of economy of administration and expenditure . . . Advertising', he continued, 'was conducted on the lines of the various brands being quite separate concerns to the public and that the time had now come to show that we were a combination.' He would allow 'each firm to advertise their own individuality as before – subject to supervision which can be decided upon in order to produce the desired result with economy'. Sir Alexander objected vehemently to this, arguing that 'individualism was "essential"'. 'In his opinion the public did not bother or were unaware that the various leading brands were amalgamated.'[36]

Ross persisted in promoting a scheme of combined advertising prepared by the DCL incumbent agency, MacQueens. This was rejected by the sub-committee set up to consider the matter, who argued that 'a more intensive policy should be adopted rather than a policy of curtailment'.[37] The example of combined advertising by British sherry shippers was promoted as a positive example to follow, but Sir Alexander and others may also have had in their minds the unsuccessful 'Veritor' campaign for Irish whisky that ran intermittently between 1911 and 1912, never to reappear.[38] Paul Derrick's agency – which the newly merged business had seriously considered purchasing to act on behalf of all the brands – was brought in to develop a generic scheme, which when originally proposed was focused on themes relating to Scotch education, although this was eventually much watered down.[39] The campaign ran through November 1926 to March 1927, with a series of eight somewhat eclectic executions, some illustrated by cartoonist Wilmot Lunt, and tied very loosely together with the mystifying slogan, 'The safest and best drink in any climate'. Subjects ranged from 'Cheers the Heart of Man', 'Dutch Courage', to 'Also the Americans' and '3,500,00 Gallons Lost Annually'. The adverts, which carried no attribution and no branding, were weak and unremarkable compared to 'An Axe to Grind', and 'Mind your P's and Q's', the latest full-page 'Old Sayings' adverts from Johnnie Walker in the illustrated press. Perhaps in working with Derrick, Johnstone and Sir Alexander had contrived to sabotage Ross's idea, which they clearly disliked so much. Either way, these ran in the London and regional press, but to what impact is unclear. Certainly, although complaints continued about the level of advertising expenditure from both Ross and Thomas Herd (Ross's second-in-command at the DCL, and his eventual successor), the subject of generic advertisement appeared to fall from the agenda very quickly. It would take a global depression to bring it back.[40]

Sir Alexander Walker was equally uncompromising when it came to the matter of selling secondary brands, which became increasingly pressing from 1927 as markets demanded lower prices for brands in order to meet competition from firms such as Teacher's and Train & McIntyre. He was clear that while the business should not be refused, it should in no way be allowed to detract from the reputation of Johnnie Walker. Walker's had used subsidiaries such as Slater, Rodger & Co. and Napier Johnstone to deal with this trade before the war, building up a substantial business in India.[41] However, the key issue for Walker was the distance that should be kept from this market and the standard brands such as Red Label. When the matter was again debated in early 1928, Walker explained 'that there is a certain demand for this cheap cased whisky and that Slater Rodger had always done this class of trade, they feeling that they do not interfere in any way with the trade of the high class brands . . . if outside firms are doing this trade an effort should be made to secure it within the group, and this could be done without danger to chief brands.'[42] He was 'firmly of the opinion that the competition from outsiders should be tackled. These outsiders start at the bottom with their [low priced] brands and after having got in with them they introduce the better brands. As far as Slater Rodger were concerned this was and always had been their business,' not Johnnie Walker's.[43] In effect this meant that he ensured that Walker's name never appeared on a quotation, an invoice, a cask or a case, let alone a label, of anything that was sold below the standard brand price.

During these early years of the new combine, despite the fact that they were notionally all 'on the same side', the various representatives of the constituent companies were more like boxers in a ring in the early stages of a bout, defending their own territory implacably but keenly trying to seek out the weaknesses of their opponents and judge the extent of their reach. As the surviving committee minutes show, Lord Stevenson was as active as Walker on behalf of the Kilmarnock firm; he'd been at the forefront of the negotiations to bring the 'big amalgamation' about and was punctilious in attending to his other responsibilities as a director of John Walker & Sons. And yet he had never severed his close ties with government or Winston Churchill, and was effectively doing two jobs, either of which would have been overwhelming in its demand and intensity. After giving up his role in the Ministry of Munitions he became Churchill's commercial advisor at the Colonial Office: 'I am counting absolutely on Stevenson going to the Lords and acting as business adviser to the Colonial Office,' Churchill wrote to David Lloyd George; 'he is essential to my making a success of this business, or rather the business part of this business.'[44] He also served as chairman of the Rubber Investigation Committee, where he formulated, according to Churchill, 'that scheme of conservation that has finally rescued this important British industry from destruction and has proved of inestimable advantage to the State', and as vice chairman of the Advisory Council on Civil Aviation, where some credited him as the father of commercial air traffic in the United Kingdom. Stevenson and Churchill shared a special sort of intimacy among men: 'It is true to say that the Chancellor of the Exchequer has no greater champion than Lord Stevenson and Winston has proclaimed publicly that he considered Lord Stevenson possessed of one of the best brains in Britain,' wrote one anonymous observer.[45] Certainly, Stevenson was dedicated to Churchill. 'Don't forget, if at any time I can assist you I am yours to command,' he wrote to him in March 1925, adding, 'So far you have made only one mistake; you don't take me into your confidence politically. Give me a trial, that is all I ask!'[46]

Early in 1923 Stevenson had been asked to take control of the planning and execution of the British Empire Exhibition, a piece of national boosterism aimed at reasserting the reputation of Britain both within the Empire and beyond, and intended as a stimulus to post-war trade. Weak leadership and an unwieldy exhibition board had brought the event to the verge of chaos, or, as the *Kilmarnock Standard* reported, 'It seemed to be getting into a tangle ... With much reluctance he accepted a task already seriously compromised.' Yet by a mixture of tact, diplomacy, drive and determination he delivered a huge success (in terms of visitors, if not financially), which left as its legacy to the nation, Wembley

Stadium – a small part of which still sits in the homes of many Scottish football supporters.[47] His elevation to the peerage was in acknowledgement of this, his coat of arms, like Kilmarnock's, having two squirrels as supporters. His motto, simply 'Carry On'. 'His immense efforts to compel success in this field', said Churchill, 'occupied and exhausted the closing years of his life.'[48] Not entirely so; in addition to his work for Walker's and the government, in 1923 Stevenson had taken on a directorship of Crosse

Baron Stevenson of Holmbury, whose motto was 'Carry On', 1924

& Blackwell, who also 'seemed to be getting into a tangle', to aid with
the reconstruction of the company, invited to help because of 'all he has
to do with sales and propaganda, together with his personal knowledge
of overseas markets throughout the world. He led the reorganisation
of their overseas agencies, and they adopted, under his "immediate
control" . . . a progressive advertising policy for all of our companies.'[49]
Stevenson and managing director J. C. Goff, whom he had known through
Goff's involvement in the NAFFI when it was set up in 1920, produced
two deeply critical reports ('We have been like divers who have gone
to the bottom of the sea and who have examined the wreck') on the
structure and management of the company, and its failure to exploit
the manufacturing economies offered by combination. The work was
intense. As Stevenson told Crosse & Blackwell's Annual Meeting in 1924,
'If he had known what he was letting himself in for nothing would have
induced him to accept it [*Cheers*].'[50] 'I am off abroad today for greatly
needed rest,' he wrote in December 1924, as he planned to extend the
running of the Empire Exhibition into a second year in order to try and
recoup some of the huge outlay spent on it.[51] Throughout 1925 he oversaw
the exhibition and played a major role in setting up the 'amalgamated'
Distillers Company and bedding-in its new organisation. He was also
deeply involved in managing personal relationships and business affairs
with some of Walker's most important, and intractable, customers in
Canada. He was meeting with them as late as May 1926, before the very
short illness that led to his death, from arteriosclerosis, on 10 June 1926.[52]

Here was a shopkeeper's boy from Kilmarnock who had
achieved remarkable success in both the business and political spheres,
its first son to be elevated to the peerage. He had been the moving
force behind the creation of the world's biggest Scotch whisky brand,
and through his political influence had done much to shape the future

course of the Scotch industry. 'With the passing of Lord Stevenson', wrote one collaborator, 'advertising has lost a great genius.' A man who wrote crime thrillers in his spare time, and enjoyed the occasional round of golf, a 'hard headed keen business genius' and a 'loveable romantic schoolboy', by all accounts his greatest gift was to be liked by almost everyone.[53] He had married twice, first Jessie Hogarth in 1897, who died in 1917; and then Stella Fraser in 1918, but left no children, his title becoming extinct. 'It is the language of bald truth to say', wrote Churchill, 'that in ten years of public service for honour alone he wore out and consumed the whole exceptional strength of his mind and body.'[54] Following his death, friends organised the Stevenson Memorial Trust (chaired by Churchill), partly to provide educational scholarships, and also to fund a memorial – four altar pieces designed by Sir Edwin Lutyens – to be placed in St Paul's Cathedral.[55] However, fate stalked this man who was always cautious about the possible offence that speaking publicly about Scotch might cause. When the Dean and Chapter of St Paul's discovered his connections with whisky they demurred, leading one of his friends to write in frustration to Edward Marsh, Churchill's private secretary:[56]

> *Why do governments make deaf and debilitated diehards into deans and canons? . . . can't Winston make some of these doddering canons bishops and get them out of the way? One of these old men had the hardihood to ask me if I thought that it was right that a whiskey [sic] merchant should have a memorial in the cathedral where Nelson is buried. I told him that Nelson was much fonder of whiskey than Stevenson.*[57]

The memorial was presented to the cathedral by Winston Churchill on 12 July 1928.[58]

A WELL BALANCED TRIO

Sir Bernard Partridge's 'Fashions come, and fashions go' series, 1911

JOHNNIE WALKER : " What ! Are you trying to pass the age test ? "

ENTHUSIASTIC FRIEND : " No. Unfortunately I cannot do that as easily as you, but I am going to make a bare-faced attempt to join the National Guard."

JOHN WALKER & SONS, LTD., SCOTCH WHISKY DISTILLERS, KILMARNOCK.

ABOVE: Leo Cheney marched the Striding Man through the various branches of the Empire's armed forces, both at home and abroad, during the First World War, 1915

OPPOSITE: 1920 – John Walker & Sons centenary advertisement

From George the Third
To George the Fifth
One hundred years long
Born 1820. Still going strong

"Thanks! same tae ye"

Sir James Stevenson &
Sir Winston Churchill, 1924

Sir Alexander Walker in retirement

Good work ... Good whisky

JOHNNIE
WALKER

Born 1820 — still going strong

ABOVE: Johnnie Walker planning post-war reconstruction in London, by Clive Upton, 1946
– The 'Good Work' series was published in illustrated weeklies such as *The Sphere*

Thank you

JOHNNIE WALKER

—there's no better drink than

the smooth round whisky

in the square bottle

Born 1820—still going strong

TOP: Johnnie Walker in Japan, 1950s
ABOVE: Johnnie Walker delivery vans in Venezuela, c. 1950
OPPOSITE: 'Thank you Johnnie Walker', 1952

'Keep Walking' campaign in New York, 2019

The core Johnnie Walker range, 2019

CHAPTER 9
'GOOD WORK, GOOD WHISKY'

'A Scotch Presbyterian constitutionally unable to smile' — Sir Alexander Walker (of himself)

The Walker family, and business, had a long-standing connection with golf: H M Bateman's certificate for the Johnnie Walker 'Hole in one' competition, 1927

FOLLOWING THE DEATH of Stevenson, Sir Alexander Walker was left as the last of the third generation to manage the business. But he didn't go quickly – as we shall see, he only finally stood down as chairman of the company in 1940, during which time he remained deeply involved in the management of the business despite his many other responsibilities within the Distillers Company. He was also to be the last of the family to play any direct role in the management of the company. He was in some respects a character of contradictions. On the one hand he appeared to revel in that 'thrawnness' that he had clearly inherited from his father and shared with his brother George. Tall and gaunt, he once joked at his own expense that he was 'the ugliest, sour-visaged, hard-mouthed devil to deal with'. On another occasion he described himself as 'a Scotch Presbyterian constitutionally unable to smile'. 'Sir Alexander', said one admirer, 'has no great liking for fulsome flattery, he much prefers criticism . . . he revels in replying in that quiet incisive way he has, and showing that the critic is all wrong, and has not a leg to stand on.'[1] He rarely contributed to the various blending committees without, as the minute-taker carefully recorded, being 'strongly' or 'firmly' of an opinion. But like his father too, this fierce exterior cloaked a warmth of heart and generosity that made him a foremost benefactor of both Kilmarnock and his adopted home of Troon. He was responsible for the administration of the War Relief Fund in Kilmarnock and, as was observed, seldom did applicants 'go away empty handed', even if the relief came from the pocket of Sir Alexander himself. 'Every good scheme', said the provost of Kilmarnock in a speech in 1920, 'that has the interest of the people in view has his hearty and sympathetic support – housing, town planning, child welfare, sanatoria, education etc. – and amongst all these he has found time to promote and encourage art and music and all that is good and beautiful.'[2]

Sir Alexander was a utopian, an idealist who very genuinely sought to use his influence to promote better ways for society to be managed for the good of all. But he sometimes appears to have lacked the ability to bring these ideals to fruition in a meaningful way. The comment that 'he could not and will not put down my scheme, and that he will simply "talk" but will do nothing to crystallise the idea, though he is anxious enough to see it adopted,' may well have been true.[3] Like many of his day he began to look to the Continent (where he travelled widely on business) for inspiration, urging, for example, members of the Scottish licensed trade to go to Switzerland or Germany (at his expense) to better improve their understanding of levels of service that could be offered to customers.[4] But his solutions to the troubles of the inter-war years were to be found in individualism rather than collectivism, as he told the Junior Imperialist League of Kilmarnock: 'The world today was as badly in need of true leaders as it ever had been,' a view he shared with Churchill, whom he admired as a potential model leader for the future.[5]

George Paterson Walker died in October 1926 in London after a short illness. He was buried in Putney near his house, the elegant yet understated Celtic cross that marks his grave belying both his impact on the Walker business and the fortune just shy of £1 million that he left to his wife and two children. Somewhat forgotten in the folklore of the company (possibly as a result of the very dominant personality of his younger brother), George nonetheless played a vital role at perilous points in the firm's history. From being his father's 'right-hand man' in Kilmarnock whilst still a teenager, to running the London business and making personal interventions in both Australia and South Africa to ensure the future of these two critical export markets, his hands clearly shaped the huge growth the firm enjoyed between 1890 and the 1920s.[6] Moreover, his refusal to put the company at the mercy of capital markets by floating publicly, and to reject the overtures of Messrs Buchanan and Dewar before the war, ensured substantial profits for his fellow directors, shareholders, and the family. And though one suspects he may have been the principal director who objected to the popularisation of his grandfather's name in connection with the brand, he clearly saw the talent and imagination that James Stevenson brought to the business, and not only ensured his rapid promotion but gave him the latitude to appoint Paul Derrick and bring the Johnnie Walker brand to life. George's son, George Gordon Walker, had joined the firm in 1923, but remains something of an anonymous figure. Somewhat uncharacteristically for a Walker, he had a widely reported society wedding in 1922 when he married Madge Thiel from Sydney, although the partnership did not last long.[7] He married again in 1927, but had already resigned as a director earlier that year, citing 'ill health'.[8] James

Sir Ronnie Cumming, 1900–1982

Borland Walker, George and Alex's youngest brother, though a substantial shareholder, had never taken an active role in the company. He had fought as a young man in the South African War, between 1899 and 1902. He ended as a squadron commander in the Cavalry Brigade and returned to Kilmarnock after three years as a war hero.[9] He became a captain in the Bedfordshire Yeomanry in 1913, with whom he served during the First World War, being promoted to lieutenant colonel.[10] Subsequent to this he became an underwriter at Lloyd's, and also took to the turf, becoming a successful breeder of racehorses near Newmarket and an important member of the Jockey Club. The longest surviving son of Alexander Walker, he died in 1958.[11]

Sir Alexander Walker remained managing director of John Walker and Sons until 1936, with some exceptionally talented younger members of the board, notably Ronnie Cumming and Edward Grahame Johnstone. Johnstone was possibly an awkward fit on the board; a well-educated cricket-loving Home Counties socialite didn't necessarily sit well alongside Kilmarnock men. Nevertheless, he had already travelled widely on behalf of the business before taking on sole responsibility for advertising following the death of his step-father. The following year (1927) he married the artist Doris Zinkeisen, already well known for her exhibits at the Royal Academy and her theatrical costume and scenery designs for a range of major London productions.[12] The two of them were to become regulars in the society pages, not only because of Doris's paintings or her equally glamorous artist sister Anna, but also for their association with the Pytchley Hunt in Northamptonshire, where they lived at Thornby Manor. In later years they were just as well known for their twin daughters, who became eminent artists in their own right.[13] It's possible Johnstone and Zinkeisen met through Paul Derrick's agency, or perhaps Johnstone introduced Zinkeisen to Derrick; either way she was commissioned to produce a series of designs for Walker's that would run throughout 1927 and 1928. In doing so, she replaced the incumbent Leo Cheney, who had worked on the brand since 1914, and who, possibly already unwell, died in March 1928. To the modern eye Doris Zinkeisen's designs are ground-breaking, and the advertising world was full of admiration. After almost twenty years, said *Advertising World*, the Johnnie Walker campaigns had run out of steam: 'Johnnie had run the whole gamut and his further journeyings were somewhat limited by the advertising activities of his competitors.' The advertising challenge was 'to do something, somehow, that no one else has done, in a manner entirely new, and yet he has to be recognisably "Johnnie"'. They said in essence what almost every advertiser is saying every day. The executions were planned as a series of twenty-four striking and witty parodies of Georgian cartoons in the style of Rowlandson set in contemporary locations from the Stock Exchange, via the Underground, to the seaside, or from the boxing ring, via an all-night coffee stall, to the dogs. This 'bold move' on the part of Walker's was welcomed as a brilliant example of how 'an old advertiser has solved the problem of being new'.[14]

It could well be that not everyone on the board shared this view; the Zinkeisen campaign came to an abrupt end early in 1928 to be replaced by a clever but more conventional series that deconstructed the different elements of the Johnnie Walker character's costume, from hat to boots. Various poster and print executions followed that 'heroed' the Johnnie Walker character, including the visually powerful 'Seeing Double' ('Even people who cannot read . . . would understand this story at once'), followed in 1930 by Alan Macnab's cleverly drawn print adverts showing Johnnie Walker witnessing scenes of historical innovation and enterprise.[15] Some of the earlier pieces by Tom Browne and others were also being recycled in the press. By this time Paul Derrick was in effect semi-retired ('Johnnie Walker is, I believe, my most spectacular achievement'); his agency had amalgamated with Crawford's in 1929, and he was spending more time in the United States, where he returned permanently in 1934.[16] A new campaign, 'He said to me', illustrated in his characteristic style by Edward Ardizzone, was launched in May of that year and fell foul of Sir Alexander Walker, who advocated 'the re-introduction of a selection from the old Tom Browne and Cheney drawings together, if possible, with any new sketches on similar lines', and – something particularly supported by Alfred Adams – that 'the "Bottle" should be given prominence in future advertising'. Although recorded as 'unanimously approved', both Johnstone and Cumming argued, without success at the meeting, that the Ardizzone campaign should be seen through to its natural end.[17] Instead in January 1935 it was continued with a new illustrator, returning to the style of Leo Cheney, with a bottle prominently displayed at the foot of the page, and then in executions that bore the hallmark of being designed by a client's committee, with the illustration framed by sheaves of barley. Clearly the relationship with the Derrick agency, despite the talent within the larger Crawford organisation, was coming to an end, and it was no surprise when the Walker business was put out to tender in January 1936, pitching Derrick's against the American agency Erwin, Wasey & Co., and S. H. Benson, who held amongst others the accounts of Guinness, Lipton's, and Colman's Mustard. Benson's got the business.[18]

Advertising allowances continued to be a source of squabbles and dissension among the leading brand companies within the Distillers Company, the only point of agreement being that they did not support any attempt to reduce spending, particularly as economic conditions worsened and sales dropped during the Great Depression.[19] The need for a generic campaign had again been raised in 1930, with Walker's Francis Redfern suggesting 'advertising the value and merits of whisky as a beverage'; he also argued that support should be given towards the publication of the *Savoy Cocktail Book*, and 'pointed out that if we could convert the public to drinking whisky cocktails it might be a good thing'.[20] Although the idea was scotched, there clearly was a sense of unease that unbridled creativity in advertising might have come at the expense of basic category messaging, the argument being

> *that certain types of advertisements were insufficient to attract the public and ... there appeared to be a general feeling that a really good 'write-up' embodying all the advantages, benefits etc. of Scotch whisky, would assist in stimulating renewed interest. It was admitted this method of publicity had been given effect to previously, but it was pointed out we were now dealing with a new generation.*[21]

Investment remained high during the 1930s, Walker's annual spending rarely less than £215,000, and sometimes as high as £290,000. As the decade progressed Walker sales on the home market continued to fall, and as Benson's got into their stride there was a distinct change in the feel of Walker's advertising. The Johnnie Walker character had gradually been losing the sharply defined facial features that had marked Tom Browne's original drawings and became less cartoon-like and more human (almost photographic) in appearance, and more overtly masculine. And although the advertising lost none of its approachability and humour, nor its originality of design, it did begin to focus more explicitly on product truths, explaining to this 'new generation' of drinkers not just the specialness of Johnnie Walker, but also the importance of age and maturation, and the skill behind blending whiskies. Walker advertising also found its way round the world quicker than any of its competitors'; on 16 October 1934 the company was the first to send an advertisement by 'wireless telegraphy', which 'was despatched at 7.00 am from this country and received in Melbourne clear and ready for instant reproduction barely fifteen minutes later'.[22]

Advertising had also played a critical role in the introduction in 1928 of a cork stopper to replace the driven cork used on Red and Black Label, and to score a point over competitors. Teacher's had been the first brand to introduce a cork stopper as far back as 1913, and White Horse had introduced a revolutionary (though not entirely efficient) screw cap in 1927.[23] The various companies within the DCL had been looking at alternative closures for some time and had decided on the metal 'Kork-N-Seal' lever-cap closure once issues around leakages in transit had been resolved.[24] In May 1928 Dewar's announced the change in the pages of the national press and the illustrated weeklies, Buchanan's following shortly afterwards. 'Under the air-tight seal of the new cap . . . every bottle comes to you in perfect condition'; 'This new fitment facilitates opening and resealing and is the most perfect fitment on the market,' claimed the advertisements.[25] Walker's however took a different view, wanting to preserve the premium reputation of their brand, and, as Redfern explained, assert their individuality. So without any consultation they launched a milled-top cork stopper in September, supported by a campaign developed by Grahame Johnstone and Derrick's at their mischievous best. In trying to meet customer requests for an easy-to-open bottle, they explained to readers of *The Times*, 'we have been experimenting on closures of every conceivable type. But so far we have found nothing better than cork . . . If there ever comes a better kind of stopper', they added, 'our customers shall have it.' 'The new Johnnie Walker stopper's a corker!' ran the strapline on many of the announcements.[26] The Kork-N-Seal company complained bitterly that the Walker advertisements were damaging to their reputation, whilst competitors such as Buchanan protested that 'the advertisements were so worded as to be detrimental to the fitments adopted by the companies other than Messrs Walker'. Redfern responded to these complaints with a lawyerly insouciance, observing that the claims made for the lever-cap closure were equally derogatory towards cork, and that 'advertising which tended to diminish the idea of a "combine" or which would have the effect of increasing the individuality of the various firms was good for any of the brands'.[27] Walker's continued their campaign unabashed, adding in December a widely published pastiche of 'This is the house that Jack built': 'This is the corkscrew that's lost its berth displaced by the top that's milled all round that is now on the cork of proven worth that is stuck in the bottle world-renowned containing the whisky for Christmas.'[28]

Johnstone's brief extended beyond advertising to the ill-defined world of 'publicity'. In some respects this was not a difficult assignment, as from its inception the Johnnie Walker character had been a publicity engine beyond compare. 'The other day in the Underground', wrote a correspondent to the *Illustrated London News* in 1920,

> *I met an old friend whom I have known for many years. Raising his hat with a true regency flourish he told me that it was his hundredth birthday and that he 'was still going strong' . . . on looking again at the advert I noticed a remarkable scarcity of letterpress that is usually scrawled across our vison in these tube posters and it struck me as little short of marvellous that any firm should produce an advertisement showing neither their name, the name of the goods, nor even a picture of them, but so well known is this figure that public recognition is instantaneous.*[29]

If the name 'Johnny Walker' had been adopted before the brand name was formally created, then Tom Browne's cartoon persona was embraced wholesale by the British public. Perhaps Master Lyonel Clark was the first person to have a photograph of himself published in the press wearing a 'Johnnie Walker' costume at a fancy-dress party at the Mansion House in January 1910.[30] He was certainly not the last. 'One unexpected result', said James Stevenson, speaking of the new campaign just after its inception, 'is a large increase in the business of theatrical costumiers. We have received over 5,000 applications for the costumes . . . but as we are not running a costume business we cannot supply them.' Throughout the 1920s and 1930s not a carnival parade, fancy-dress party or other public event seemed to pass without the Johnnie Walker character being present. And by the 1920s the firm *were* lending out costumes to consumers, at least selectively.[31] They had also at least one vintage car which toured major events, accompanied by 'Johnnie Walker', much to the delight of the crowds. Statues of the figure were sent to licensees and grocers for public display, a tempting target for the light-fingered. Rarely did a humorous after-dinner speech go by, particularly at retiral functions, when the phrase 'like Johnnie Walker, still going strong' wasn't coined to much laughter. And advertisers of all stripes were keen to jump on the bandwagon, such as the 'genuine' London Greyhound Investment Syndicate which offered unlikely returns to investors with the slogan: 'Like Johnnie Walker – still running'.[32] There was even an unlooked-for synergy with that other walking figure that the United Kingdom had taken to its heart in the 1920s, the cartoon character Felix the Cat. Created in 1919, the perpetually ambulatory feline was celebrated in 1923 with the song 'Felix Kept On Walking'. 'Why Keep on Walking?' soon read an advertisement for Raleigh bicycles, and shortly afterwards Felix was pictured in comic postcards clutching a bottle of Red Label with the warning words in his ears, 'Felix, remember you've got to keep steady on your pins.'[33] The droll 'Scotch comedian' Johnny Walker, sometimes with his 'mascot', entertained music-hall audiences throughout the kingdom and in the United States in the twenties and thirties, as did American matinée idol Johnnie Walker as he transitioned with some difficulty from silent to talking films.[34] Elsewhere on the stage, veteran vaudevillian Sam Mayo sang his Johnnie Walker song 'in the spirit that we all like', and Hollywood scriptwriter Harry M. Vernon saw a performance of his thriller, *The Case of Johnny Walker*, performed at London's Coliseum theatre.[35] To say that this brand had deeply embedded itself in popular culture is at best something of an understatement.

Despite the growing popularity of cinema, 'popular culture' for many in the inter-war years started and ended with sport, both highbrow and low. Tom Browne had Johnnie Walker playing golf in some of his earliest drawings, and the family affection for the sport (Sir Alexander Walker, like his father, built himself a house at Troon within a stone's throw of the now world-famous golf club that his father had helped to establish) almost demanded a tie to the brand. In 1926 Walker's formalised their 'Hole-in-One' programme, offering a bottle of Red Label to any player who had a verified shot, bombarding golf clubs throughout the country with publicity materials. To their surprise they gave out 779 bottles in the first year, and 1,457 in the second, leading one commentator to observe that 'Holing out in one is more common in golf than might be expected.'[36] But the scheme fell foul of the English Golfing Union, who felt it compromised the amateur status of players; following some considerable public debate, Grahame Johnstone withdrew the programme in April 1933 in order to meet 'the general wishes of the golfing public'.[37]

Johnstone was on better ground with cricket, which was both his personal passion and had been linked to Johnnie Walker since the Tom Browne '1820 Not Out' advert published in the summer of 1909, which showed the Johnnie Walker character leaving the pitch (undefeated) with his spliced cricket bat under his arm. This was one of 'a number of errors (spliced bats were not introduced until much later than 1820) that were made on purpose', said James Stevenson; 'we wanted to get our poster talked about, and we did.'[38] Johnstone rubbed shoulders with the giants of the sport both socially and on the cricket pitch; he personally entertained visiting Test touring teams. His assistant, L. S. Lay, was also a cricketing enthusiast. The idea that they developed captured the minds of the British public; it was a startling yet simple innovation that brought live Test match cricket to 'hundreds of thousands of people' throughout the country for the first time, and its backdrop was the most controversial series of Tests between England and Australia in the history of the game.

'The Johnnie Walker Scoreboard' brought the domestic Ashes series of 1930 and 1934 to life in major cities and seaside resorts in the United Kingdom in real time. This was years before the now famous and familiar ball-by-ball commentary was introduced on BBC radio in England; before that there had only been some experimental 'live' radio broadcasts in Australia, and the first television broadcasts of cricket were six years away.[39] Using direct telephone lines from each Test match ground and an ingenious construction that detailed the disposition of both batting and fielding sides, a scoreboard with a simulated pitch in the centre (worked by five operators) showed the trajectory of the ball after each delivery, how and by whom it was fielded, and how many runs had been scored or wickets taken.[40] It had been trialled by Walker's at the Sydney 1928–29 series, and now Johnstone brought it over to

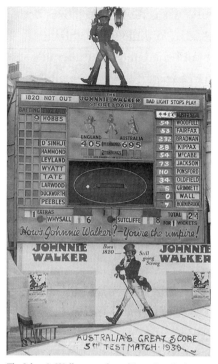

The Johnnie Walker scoreboard in action during the Ashes in 1930, postcard image by A.W. Wardell, 1930

England, personally supervising its installation in each location.[41] One captivated spectator wrote of the excitement as over 5,000 spectators watched 'Jackson and Bradman running halfway up the pitch, just meet, and then hurriedly return', applauding 'just as if they were on the field'.[42] In Brighton thousands of spectators stood for hours 'watching at second hand, as it were, the fortunes of the Test match', and when it came to the decisive final match of the series the sea-front around the scoreboard was brought to a standstill, such were the size of the crowds, as was also the case in the centre of Nottingham and elsewhere.[43] Advertisements ran throughout the summer, some including telegram-style copy – 'Enormous crowds here saw all the thrills of the test matches on ball by ball scoreboard STOP men COMMA women breathless with excitement'.[44]

When the scoreboard returned to twelve seaside resorts for the Ashes series in 1934, excitement was fuelled by the intervening 'Bodyline' series in Australia during the winter of 1932–33. The *Cricketer* could hardly suppress its delight: 'Until television really emerges from laboratories I do not think that there can possibly be invented a better method of watching distant cricket than was provided during these test matches by these scoreboards . . . The difference between fast and slow', continued the mesmerised correspondent, 'and even googly bowling can be indicated by the manner in which the ball is manipulated' by the trained operators, 'who must be able dramatically to interpret cricket'.[45] At a time of declining sales in the domestic market and increasing economic uncertainty this was an innovative campaign that combined the disruptiveness that was so typical of Walker's advertising with some of the core values of the brand and its living embodiment, particularly inclusiveness and generosity of heart. With cricket so deeply rooted in the popular culture of the day, both at home and in Australia (where trade was at an all-time low), it's hard to think of a more impactful brand-building activity.

Equally innovative had been the company's attempts to secure the supply of high-quality bottles from John Lumb & Co. through the development of its own automatic bottle-making machine, free from the influence of the bottle-making 'combine' or the excessive licensing costs required to operate machines such as the Owens automatic. Charge of this project, which had begun as far back as 1916 when Lumb's were authorised to spend up to £10,000 on developing a machine in the United States, had been given to Francis Redfern. In 1919 the company secured patents for the design of a machine from Robert Hall, like Redfern a Birmingham native, which was to form the basis of the new machine. This was to be part of a drastic programme of upgrades at the glassworks required to 'bring the manufacturing methods abreast of modern progress', at a cost of over £40,000 ('It was useless to spend money in patching up a plant which when patched up could not compete with modern plants').[46] Some of the barriers presented by the war and its aftermath were overcome when both the Ministry of Reconstruction and the Ministry of Munitions decided that the construction of the machine was 'a matter of national importance', and cleared the way for the necessary permits to be issued for materials. Redfern also had to manage the intransigence of the unions towards the introduction of the new automatic machine. By 1920 the first machine was in operation in Castleford, allowing the company to adopt 'one standard or universal square bottle' with a standard filling level for the first time, which had a significant impact on the efficiency of the whole packaging process. The machine, which was widely considered to be superior to the Owens, was praised by a delegation from the Society of Glass Technology who visited Lumb's in November 1924 to see it 'very successfully manufacturing the square quart bottles used for Johnny Walker whisky', commenting on its 'perfectly smooth and noiseless running'.[47] By this time Redfern was already developing plans to increase the machine's output, and Walker's had sold patents for the manufacture by Metropolitan Vickers of two machines to Mitsubishi Shoji Kaisha Ltd.[48] Development of the upgraded machine would take some years and it was not in use until 1934, by which time Lumb's had been merged with three other glass-makers to form the British Bottle Company. However Walker's remained convinced of the superior quality of the square quarts produced by the Redfern-Hall machine. Not only that, but it allowed them to experiment in 1933 with the introduction of light-weight glass in the home (20oz bottles) and export (18 and 16oz) markets.[49]

As part of the plans to capitalise on the investment made in the automatic bottle-making machine, Redfern travelled to the United States in 1928 at the height of Prohibition to try and interest American glass-makers in buying patents. His memoir of the visit paints the picture of a country where liquor flowed freely. 'It was the custom', he said, 'to consume cocktails innumerable before the meal. In fact, there was so much superirrigation before the meal that the meal itself became a mere act of supererogation.'[50] As far as Walker and the rest of the industry were concerned, the early days of Prohibition where entrepreneurial consignors put together ad-hoc shipments of Scotch, dispatched on hastily purchased or hired vessels to rest outside territorial waters, from whence the supercargo would make (often cash) sales to bootleggers, were over.[51] Walker's did everything they could to prevent their brands falling into the hands of these adventurers, particularly by stopping under-bond supplies to customers in the Irish Free State which frequently ended up on the other side of the Atlantic. Maintaining respectability was key, so they were also exceptionally cautious about dealing with new or unknown customers. Men like Captain Cecil Attfield were keen to obtain parcels of Scotch for shipment to Amsterdam and beyond, but his reputation made him a *persona non grata*.[52] Attfield had been found guilty of gun-running in 1924 and subsequently imprisoned for non-payment of a substantial fine, although he argued the incarceration was for 'political reasons'. In 1926, whilst trying to raise funds to purchase parcels of whisky, partly by taking a commission on the sale of surplus naval ships to 'foreign powers', he found himself entangled in a spying scandal about the theft of top-secret submarine plans. And having been declined supply from Johnnie Walker for his shipments to 'Amsterdam', he was later arrested in Egypt for possession of hashish, claiming in his defence that he was working for American intelligence.[53]

Of continuing great concern was the issue of counterfeit in the United States and elsewhere. There are numerous accounts of the extent to which both domestic and particularly 'imported' brands were subject to falsification during Prohibition. Stevenson reported in 1925 that he had been informed that three Chicago firms were 'supplying the capsules, labels, etc. for the rebottling of Whiskies . . . and other high-priced goods imported which are diluted with four or five times the quantity of denatured spirit'.[54] Johnnie Walker Red and Black Label were regular victims of counterfeit in Canada, the bottles being 'taken across the border for American consumption'. Sometimes these fakes were produced on an industrial scale, from the printing and production of labels and capsules to the filling of bottles and shipping of cases.[55] When Redfern was in Pittsburgh he saw people making 'the Johnnie Walker square bottle, putting "John Walker & Sons, Kilmarnock" on the bottom of the bottle and even reproducing our mould numbers'.[56] Nor should it be supposed that these were poor imitations; some of the counterfeiters were perfectionists. 'I was enjoying myself by making up the most perfect package,' said one. Eric Sherbrooke Walker, an Oxford-educated war veteran who turned to 'rum running' in the early 1920s, regretted not having been able to introduce ('as one would a pupil to a master') Sir Alexander Walker to 'Izzy', 'a manufacturer of, dealer in, retailer of, and specialist in Johnnie Walker . . . for there is much that Izzy could teach him about making whisky' which enables him 'to accomplish in one day what nature and Sir Alexander take years to do'.[57]

As it became clear that Prohibition was coming to an end, Walker's were fêted by potential suitors for their business in the United States after repeal. Early in June 1932 the first of what were to be numerous approaches from potential USA distributors was received. Sam Bronfman and Joseph Reinfeld, who would both be important DCL customers after Prohibition, travelled to Scotland chasing exclusive distributor rights for Walker and the other Distillers

Company brands. They were also approached through an intermediary by a syndicate of 'bootleggers from New York' offering to sell 100,000 cases of Walker, and the same of each of the other main brands, in an eighteen-month period once the laws were changed. They were asked to put down their proposal in writing.[58] At the same time, liquor company Schenley's Lew Rosenstiel travelled to the United Kingdom to 'become acquainted with various old well-established Houses of high reputation', advertising his distribution businesses in the trade press, as did former Cincinnati whisky-broker Sid Klein, 'always a colourful figure in the industry'.[59] 'Applications for agencies', said the *DCL Gazette*, 'literally poured in from all parts of the USA.' At the moment of repeal there was considerable confusion and in London misinformation around the position of would-be importers and the likely regulations that would be put in force with respect to bottle sizes, labelling and the like. Sir Alexander Walker acted unilaterally on behalf of his brand, and as 'the various reports he had received are so conflicting and contradictory' determined to send Grahame Johnstone and Ronnie Cumming out to New York 'to gather information and to ascertain the organisation and standing of the different firms who have applied for Walker's agency'. They were there for some months, returning in August having pin-pointed Canada Dry Ginger Ale, Inc., as one of their two preferred distributors for the post-Prohibition period.[60] Reporting on the still-fluid situation, they were 'most emphatic that goods should be on the spot early as in their opinion the brand should be in the market with an organisation behind them so that they can be distributed at once on Repeal'. In pursuit of this, Cumming set about trying to send cases to Canada for transhipment as soon as was legal, although he was frustrated in this by import and export regulations, and the continuing uncertainty over bottles and labelling.[61] In October

1933 a ten-man deputation from the Distillers Company travelled out to New York and set up shop at the Waldorf Astoria for a fortnight, interviewing potential distributors, many of whom had been involved in one or other end of the transhipment business during Prohibition. However, Johnstone and Cumming had clearly already done their deal with Canada Dry, and it was announced in December that 'This famous Scotch Whisky will again be available to American connoisseurs who have not forgotten the once familiar red-coated figure of Johnnie Walker, born 1820, still going strong.'[62]

At first sight a ginger ale company might have seemed like an odd choice for Johnnie Walker, but Canada Dry had risen to astonishing prominence in the United States in a very short period of time and demonstrated with their soft drinks a mastery in the art of advertising and brand building. Originally formed in Canada in the early part of the century, the business had opened a branch in New York in 1920; in 1923 it was acquired by entrepreneur P. D. Saylor and an aggressive advertising campaign began the following year. There were four, or perhaps five, things you needed to know about the 'Champagne of Ginger Ales'. It was a natural product that easily associated itself with the great outdoors of Canada and the United States. It was safe, recommended by doctors and used in hospitals. It was made to a secret recipe ('known only by three men'), from 'genuine Jamaica ginger' and tasted 'like a mellow old wine'. It was stylish, to be found only in the finest restaurants and hotel bars, yachting and country clubs, drunk by the right sort of person. Fifth, and finally, 'it mixes so delightfully with other beverages'.[63] Canada Dry was relatively late to an already highly competitive market that included brands like Harvard Ginger Ale ('aged and mellowed'), Schultz's ('Don't ruin wine and whiskies by adding impure or unreliable mineral water'), Beech Nut ('a smooth full-bodied winey flavour') and Cliquot Club ('Who will take the place of him whom Volstead killed?').[64] Despite the popularity of other soft drinks, ginger ale was the drink de jour of Prohibition America, and the ginger-ale highball was the whisky serve of choice.[65] In New York during Prohibition it was not unusual in a bar to ask for ginger ale. 'The bartender inquires "imported or domestic?" If the customer wants imported ginger ale and he's the right kind of customer he gets a regulation pre-Prohibition highball.'[66] 'Camouflaged ginger-ale highballs' were readily available in the city, sometimes pre-mixed and served from ginger-ale bottles. In Harlem in the 'joss houses of jazz and shrines of syncopation an order for ginger ale brings forth ginger ale plus'. Drinks of ginger ale 'seemed to have a wonderful effect on one and all', wrote a visitor to Broadway's Garden Club. Presidential election night in November 1920 was celebrated through 'a thick Scotch mist', when 'inspired ginger ale seemed to be the principal beverage'. When Lady Mountbatten and entertainer Sophie Tucker were seen 'around the town drinking ginger ale together', everyone knew what was really in their glasses.[67] And for those bars or restaurants that had no alcohol to serve the 'set-up', glasses, ginger ale and ice on the table for those with a pint or quart bottle to hand was a very profitable line of business. Hotels offered the same to arriving guests.[68] As Francis Redfern discovered on his Prohibition travels, buying a bottle of Scotch in an American hotel was not a hard thing to do. As the end of Prohibition dawned so some feared for the businesses that had flourished under its yoke, but the (anonymous) head of one of the largest soft-drinks companies remained 'perfectly calm'. He was convinced, 'We are a nation of highball drinkers and will continue to guzzle set-ups.'[69]

The growth of the Canada Dry brand during Prohibition had been quite staggering, reflecting both the huge increase in demand for non-alcoholic beverages between 1919 and 1933, and the exceptional marketing skills that they brought to the category. In 1927 the company reported profits of $2.3 million, compared to $1.7 million in 1926 and $1.2 million in 1925. In 1926 it sold 1,360,000 (12-bottle) cases. Saylor had an ambition to sell over 7 million.[70] In 1929 one financial column advised investors: 'If you are dry . . . buy some Associated Dry Goods. If you are wet Canada Dry Ginger isn't bad.'[71] The Wall Street Crash certainly put a brake on the firm's meteoric rise, but as the end of Prohibition approached and brought with it new opportunities, they set up a division to specialise in the sale of imported liquors which would exploit its extensive distribution network. In addition to investing in the Hupfel Brewing Company, they obtained agencies for Johnnie Walker, Holloway's gin, Cinzano, Sandeman's, and domestic rye and bourbon whiskies sold under their own labels.[72] For Walker's this was to be a marriage made in heaven, particularly after the first few uncertain years of post-Prohibition import quotas and high duties had passed. Post-Prohibition sales started slowly, but had reached almost 200,000 cases by 1936–37, supported by the largest campaign for the brand the country had ever seen, with 'newspaper advertising in 72 cities, colour pages in 16 magazines and painted outdoor signs in metropolitan centers'.[73] Cumming had returned to New York in the summer of 1935 and came back arguing for a significant increase in investment in the brand: he 'was strongly of the opinion that we must continue to spend money now, the only alternative being to give up'.[74] By the start of the Second World War the figure stood at over 350,000 cases, almost half of all Walker's exports from the UK, and over 20 per cent of the company's entire sales.

Walker's Australian business, once the jewel in the crown of their export trade, had been in serious decline since the First World War

when disruptions to supplies forced 'an entire revision of policy which
... must be based on the principle of conserving our good will ... so that
whenever conditions become more normal we shall have a sound basis
on which to build future business'.[75] However, continued allocations and
price increases stunted recovery, although as the Sydney office wrote
in 1923, 'Poor performance' could also be attributed to the withdrawal
of the non-refillable capsule. Increased advertising investment failed
to stem the decline; Dewar's, Buchanan's and White Horse all grew at
Walker's expense, as did secondary brands such as Ainslie's and Peter
Dawson.[76] The situation was not helped by the long-standing issue of
preferential tariffs for domestic whiskies in Australia, which eventually
led DCL to invest in a distillery at Corio outside Melbourne, opened in
1929, to produce both Australian whisky and gin.[77] Whilst this may have
given DCL a share in the local market it did nothing for Walker's, whose
sales slumped to a mere 18,000 cases in 1930–31. Loss of public favour
of this sort was very hard for a brand to recover and it would take thirty
years before they recovered in any meaningful sense. Walker's did,
however, expand and consolidate distribution in Europe, Asia, Africa
and Latin America, although the 'Rest of the World' failed to keep pace
with case sales in the United States. In 1932, Johnnie Walker Swing was
launched in some export markets where sales of Red Label had been
in decline. Sir Alexander Walker explained that 'the word "Swing" was
derived from the fact that the bottle in which the brand was to be put
up was one which was so shaped as actually to swing or rock'. The style
of the whisky, which was developed by Kilmarnock blender Bernard
Lewis, was distinctly different from either Red or Black Label.[78]

New territories for Scotch brought new problems, many to do with
the protection of the definition and reputation of Scotch. In 1931 Sir

Alexander was outraged when he learned that a South American government had given a monopoly on the manufacture of spirits to a local producer, and subsequently received a letter from his agent there urging him to give the local company 'Messrs Walker's brand to manufacture'. Walker personally intervened with the Foreign Office, with the result that the concession was withdrawn.[79] In the absence of a clear legal definition for Scotch and the sort of worldwide protection it now enjoys, it was not uncommon, nor generally unlawful, for domestic spirits producers around the world to describe their products as 'Scotch Whisky' on their labels. As an example, in 1930 Walker's and the other DCL brand-owning companies became increasingly concerned about the sale in Asian markets of locally produced 'Scotch Whisky'. The recently formed Whisky Association took the issue on, as did the Federation of British Industries, and complaints were lodged in London, whilst Redfern was instructed to oppose trademark registrations wherever they were lodged. Lawyers advised that Asian consumers of whisky 'seem to be well aware of the famous trademarks like Johnnie Walker', and that 'there seem to be very few who might purchase [the whisky] as genuine Scotch whisky'. The Asian response was that it may not be right to call any kind of whisky 'Scotch', but that in their view it certainly deserved this appellation; they went on to explain the lengths they had gone to replicate the production process in every way, for example by dispatching their expert to Scotland to study the art of distilling. There was, they argued, no intent to deceive.

The issue lingered on, with Walker's still arguing that the labelling might cause confusion, while the other side maintained a different opinion. Johnstone travelled to Asia in 1933 to meet with government representatives, and in London Redfern was lobbying the

Board of Trade. The matter was finally brought to closure with the passing of relevant local laws.

What issues in Asia, Germany, France and Latin America raised with the production of local whiskies, and the sales description of admixes of Scotch and foreign spirit – was the weakness of the legal definition of Scotch. Another long-standing and unresolved issue was the persistence of what had been 'traditional practice' in the nineteenth century in the cheaper end of the market, namely the blending of Scotch and Irish whiskies for sale under the descriptor 'Scotch Whisky', which had become particularly prevalent 'during the shortage period in post-war years'.[80] It was suggested as early as May 1930 'that steps be taken to have this defined under the Food and Drugs Act in this Country and as far as possible in every country through the world'. One particular concern was that it would be impossible 'to fight any Countries abroad until our own Country had defined our Scotch commodity. The aim is to secure a definition to the effect that Scotch Whisky is Whisky produced in Scotland.'[81] The Finance Act of 1933 contained the stipulation that any spirit described as Scotch whisky had to be distilled in Scotland and bonded for at least three years, although Sir Alexander Walker complained that unscrupulous competitors were still evading the law and competing unfairly.[82] The huge demand from the United States after repeal of Prohibition brought the dangers faced by blending Irish with Scotch whisky, and Scotch with American spirit to the fore again, and Sir Alexander Walker played a leading role in the lobbying of the Secretary of State for Scotland and the Board of Trade on the issue in 1937 and 1938.[83] These efforts led to a test case being brought by the Board of Trade against Henderson & Turnbull in Glasgow in December 1938 for selling 'Scotch whisky' which contained 33 per cent Scotch and 67 per cent Irish whisky. Harold Howie Laing, a senior blender at

Johnnie Walker, gave evidence that 'Scotch whisky should come from nowhere but Scotland', and denied that 'Scotch' had become a generic term. The trial resulted in a judgement in January 1939 affirming that 'Scotch' could only be made from spirit distilled in Scotland.[84]

Home-trade sales for Johnnie Walker declined steadily during the 1920s and 1930s as the combination of exceptionally high duties, stock shortages and increasingly difficult economic conditions stifled consumer demand. By the outbreak of the Second World War sales were just shy of 550,000 cases, a 50 per cent decline since 1924. Nonetheless, the business continued to invest in brand-building advertising, seemingly increasing its salience in the minds of whisky-drinking consumers. Walker's had done a deal with Lyons' & Co., taking over their Throgmorton brand and whisky stocks. Having Walker's brands 'on sale in Messrs Lyons' establishments constituted a good advertising medium[,] having in mind the large number of visitors to these establishments from the country'. They also sold 4,000–5,000 cases of Walker's brand in a good year. Deals were negotiated with firms like Levy & Franks who owned a large estate of pubs in London (the originators of the Chef & Brewer chain), accounting for around 7,000 cases a year, and Carr's restaurants. At the same time, because 'of the importance from the point of view of advertisement for home and export trade', they granted maximum discounts to theatres, licensed

Cultural immersion: an independent cartoon of Johnnie Walker during the Great Depression, selling 'unemployed apples' by C.M. Meier, 1930

cinemas and music halls in order to ensure a highly visible brand presence.[85] Walker's also had a team of window-dressers who called on these key London accounts to ensure brands were displayed to their best possible advantage.

In addition to his responsibilities as managing director of John Walker & Sons, Sir Alexander Walker, and Francis Redfern, had become increasingly involved in the non-potable business of the Distillers Company, particularly the expansion of their chemicals business. When Sir Alexander relinquished his role at Walker's to Alfred Adams in 1936 to join the main board of DCL, he maintained his position as chairman, and his presence and authority over the company did not diminish. Nor did his workload, which was quite remarkable for a man of his age, as was his range of influential political contacts whom he could call on to help with business issues. In developing DCL's interests, as well as private business ventures he shared with his oldest son Jocelyn, he travelled widely on the Continent, especially in Germany.[86] He had become a personal member of the Anglo-German Fellowship, a group largely dominated by blue-chip British financial and industrial business interests, that existed to promote understanding and commercial relations between the two countries.[87] Walker later joined a host of establishment figures in MP Archibald Ramsay's Right Club, established in May 1939 to lobby for a peaceful reconciliation with Germany, although there is no indication to suggest that he had any sympathy with the more extreme views of the founder.[88] Indeed, his correspondence with Churchill suggests very clearly the opposite.

Sir Alexander Walker retired from his family's firm and the Distillers Company in April 1940, aged seventy-one. At a celebration of his career the following year he was remembered as an 'able man of

affairs with a balanced and scholarly mind, and the psychic qualities
of the idealist – a man of vision with the power to make his visions
take concrete shape'. He continued his chummy correspondence with
Churchill (and the dispatch every Christmas of two cases of Black
Label) to the end of his life, offering him praise in 1941 for invigorating
and uniting the spirit of the country, observing that 'while it seems
a hard thing to say, only war could regenerate and rouse the nation
out of its self-indulgent decadence'.[89] Churchill, always a courteous
correspondent, read his letters 'with interest'.[90] In 1946 Walker became
the first Freeman of the Royal Burgh of Troon, his adopted home to
whom his benefactions were abundant; he had served on the first town
council elected there as early as 1896 and had supported numerous
municipal, medical, educational and cultural good causes.[91] His utopian
vision was still in place, as he explained to Churchill in December 1945:
'In my retiral . . . I have been concentrating on local affairs, and in this
particular area have accomplished some of my ideals for the future.
Without undue vanity I think you might be interested to see what can
be done in a little area and I still hope that some day you may favour
us with a visit.'[92] Sir Alexander Walker and Churchill enjoyed one final
lunch together at Prestwick in May 1947; and after Walker's death in
May 1950 Churchill was among the first to send his condolences to the
family on the passing of 'my old friend'.[93]

Sir Alexander Walker was replaced as chairman by the
long-serving Alfred Adams, who continued in his role as managing
director. John Barr Cumming, who had joined the firm in 1926 after
the acquisition of Mortlach distillery, remained as the most senior
director. Export director Ronnie Cumming left in 1939 to take on the
role of managing director at James Buchanan & Co.; he was replaced
by Albert Green as export manager. A further departure from the

business was Edward Grahame Johnstone, who resigned to take on the role of advertising director at British American Tobacco.[94] At a senior level in the Walker business this was almost unheard of; managers were either transferred within the Distillers Company, or more commonly retired or died in post, longevity being the key to the survival of the 'family spirit' within the business once the Walker family had no presence. The veteran A. J. Hogarth, who had joined in Kilmarnock in 1898, retired as production director in the same year. Under the watchful eye of Alexander Walker blending at Kilmarnock had been the domain of Bernard Lewis, who had died prematurely in 1936 to be replaced by Harold Howie Laing, who in turn succeeded Hogarth as production director, with Thomas Boyd as his deputy.[95] George Thomson, originally a clerk at Cardow distillery before transferring to Kilmarnock as bond clerk, moved down to St George's Bond in London in 1936.[96]

Despite the decline in total sales caused by the Great Depression, production facilities both in London and Kilmarnock were at full stretch, and bottling in Birmingham had also been considered. The St George's Bond in Commercial Road, London, was gradually extended, not least to house the state-of-the-art transport fleet that was required to manage the movement of upwards of 100 hogsheads of full-strength blends that arrived from Kilmarnock early each day, and the distribution of cased stock to nearby bonds for onward shipment, and to customers in the home counties.[97] However, as sales increased in the years preceding the outbreak of war, and the Factories Act of 1937 made compliance at the Strand increasingly difficult, the company asked Howie Laing to find a new site in Kilmarnock 'capable of storing 1,500,000 gallons of blended whisky, housing a blending plant and bottling plant, with a capacity of output which could take care of the

present Kilmarnock output, the Birmingham output and a part of
the present London output', and give some contingency production
if required.[98] There were also to be plans for a new cooperage, offices
and joiner's shop. Laing identified a site owned by the London Midland
& Scottish Railway north of Kilmarnock Station at Hill Street, Sir
Alexander estimating the likely cost of the project as at least £250,000.
Whilst Laing reported in October 1939 that the new 'warehouse' was
almost complete, Walker added that the firm had offered the use of the
building to the government for the duration of the war.[99]

Grain-whisky distilleries started to close late in 1939 as
a result of scarcity of grain, and quotas were imposed on malt
distilleries in 1940, most of which had closed by October 1942.
Between the start of the war and 1943 the price of a bottle of Red
Label more than doubled, from 12s. 6d. to 25s. 9d. Supplies to the home
market were put on a quota system, set early in 1941 at 50 per cent
of pre-war levels, whilst attempts were made to encourage exports,
despite the difficulties encountered by shipping. With the increasing

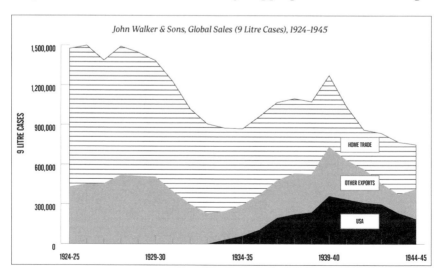

John Walker & Sons, Global Sales (9 Litre Cases), 1924–1945

scarcity of Scotch in the home market one of the most famous whisky victims of the war was the SS *Politician*, which foundered with her 22,000 cases of Scotch off Eriskay whilst trying to dodge enemy submarines in the Sea of the Hebrides in 1941. As the war went on, Walker's home-trade sales fell from 540,000 cases in 1939 to 324,000 cases in 1945, while exports fell from 734,000 to 430,000; in the USA shipments went from 363,000 to 147,000, although for most of the war the USA had taken the lion's share of the export total. As stocks were being drawn down and not replaced, one of the issues to be dealt with was the use of age statements, both for Red Label in the USA (which still had an 8-year-old declared age) and for Johnnie Walker Black Label. By 1944 the age statements had gone.[100]

At the start of the war most of the London staff were relocated to Kilmarnock, although John Barr Cumming and a skeleton staff remained at the Mincing Lane offices until they were 'rendered untenable ... through enemy action on the night of the 10th and 11th May 1941', after which they moved to the DCL offices in St James's. It was said that the bomb damage had destroyed the 'advertising suite' and the archive material it held.[101] During the First World War the brand had adopted a strongly jingoistic tone in its advertising. In the Second it was very different.[102] From 1940 through till early 1946, Johnnie Walker ran an inspired full-colour advertising campaign in the United Kingdom weeklies, illustrated by among others Clive Uptton and landscape artist Rowland Hilder ('the Turner of his generation'). The adverts placed the brand at the centre of the lives of everyone fighting on 'the home front', where everyday tasks and occupations such as 'digging for victory', bringing in the harvest, trawling for fish, or shipbuilding were all equally celebrated with the line 'Good work, good whisky'. In the final execution of the campaign published in early 1946 and brilliantly drawn by Uptton, the Johnnie Walker character (absent from most of the adverts) is pictured standing in an architect's drawing room admiring plans and designs for the reconstruction of blitzed London.[103] This was the same spirit of forward-looking optimism, mixed with defiance, that inhabited Bernard Partridge's 1921 'Goes Everywhere' poster. The real depth of character in a brand is displayed by how it behaves in adversity. Few could have done what Johnnie Walker did in this campaign so credibly: few brands were so deeply rooted in popular culture or held in such high esteem by the population as Johnnie Walker.

CHAPTER 10
TIME MARCHES ON

Casks of blended whisky being loaded onto a truck at the new Hill Street plant in Kilmarnock, 1955

'Scotch has never been an unfashionable drink
and if we do our job properly there is no reason
to think it ever will become one.'

JOHNNIE WALKER'S POSITION as the world's biggest selling and most successful Scotch whisky, the largest and most profitable brand within the Distillers Company portfolio, was cemented in the post-war years when an export drive delivered a remarkable rise in sales. Black Label, yet to regain its 12-year-old age statement, was a priority in markets like the USA, where sales would top 2 million cases in the 1970s. Markets around the world were cultivated by export directors and managers, who took advantage of the increasing availability of commercial flights to travel incessantly on behalf of the brand. Invaluable distributor partnerships, many going back to the early part of the century, were at the heart of much of the brand's overseas success, and these close relationships were assiduously developed both in-market and increasingly through visits to Scotland. These Walker senior managers and directors, many long-served with the business, were more often than not larger-than-life figures who brought the brand to life in themselves, and who lived to the full as part of the Johnnie Walker family. The brand's global footprint encompassed all the main regions of the world. One of its greatest assets, particularly in markets where little English was spoken, remained the square bottle, the distinctive slanting label, and the Johnnie Walker character. To keep up with the seemingly endless demand, primary production was vastly increased in the 1950s and 1960s, as were blending and bottling facilities in Kilmarnock and London. Changing tastes, changing economic conditions, and even changing political structures then contrived to slow this inexorable progress in the mid-1970s, and what had seemed an unassailable position in markets around the world was suddenly vulnerable to a variety of competitors, as was the Distillers Company to potential takeover.

When the now-retired Sir Alexander Walker celebrated his golden wedding in the spring of 1945 there was a deep symbolism in the choice of the three men who made a presentation to him on behalf of the company, a clearly written message that although this was now a family firm without a family, the family spirit of the business lived on in its employees. Chairman and managing director Alfred Adams, James Munn from the Kilmarnock offices, and James Macrae, foreman cooper at Kilmarnock, had between them '140 years of service' with a company 'which', said Adam, 'always had been and always would be a happy family'. Loyalty and longevity of service marked out the Walker workforce, from the board of directors to the bottling-hall floor. In return Walker's had always treated their employees with a generous, benevolent paternalism. You didn't leave John Walker & Sons, you either retired or died 'in service'.[1] This sense of continuity, a living connection with the past, was vital in helping Walker shape and retain its identity within the confines of DCL, particularly as the umbilical cord to the founding fathers was severed. At board level the men who would take the business into the second half of the century were all veterans who had spent their careers in the shadow of Sir Alexander. Alfred Adams (a protégé of Lord Stevenson), John Barr Cumming (whose roots were in Mortlach distillery), Harry M. Braid (son of the world-famous golfer James Braid, himself an intimate of Sir Alexander Walker) and Arthur Webb (London sales manager after the war, and a protégé of Alfred Adams) all had careers that went back to the early part of the twentieth century and had the old Walker ways of doing business in their blood; they also had a very rounded view of their business from primary production through to sales both at home and abroad. As we have seen, George Thomson, who became manager of the Kilmarnock Bond in 1949 and later production director, had started in the business at Cardow distillery. This sense of 'Walkerness' pervaded both the office and the factory floor: when Arthur Webb, by then managing director, remembered handing out long-service awards in Kilmarnock in 1966, he was pleased to recall that they had given 4 of 50 years, 37 of 40 years, and 122 of 25 years.[2]

Change did come, as with all things in the 1960s, both in the style and background of senior managers and directors, typified perhaps by the arrival of the 'cerebral' David Kerr. Born in the Argentine of Anglo-Scots parents and with an MA in economics from Edinburgh University, he had worked for Walker's in South Africa for five years in the early 1950s before returning to London as an export manager and then export director, becoming managing director in 1966.[3] In Kilmarnock, paternalism increasingly turned to polarisation in respect of industrial relations in the late 1960s and 1970s.

Scotch whisky was to play a pivotal role in the post-war reconstruction of Britain, in which Clive Uptton had rightly put Johnnie Walker at the heart. The need for hard currency to stimulate the war-ravaged economy was critical to successive governments' plans and exports of Scotch were at the heart of this strategy. 'On no account', Churchill had written as early as June 1945, 'reduce the barley for whisky. This takes years to mature and is an invaluable export and dollar producer. Having regard to all our other difficulties about export, it would be most improvident not to preserve this characteristic British element of ascendancy.'[4]

Between 1945 and 1955 total exports of Scotch increased by almost 170 per cent to nearly 12 million cases. Johnnie Walker's exports increased by 115 per cent to just over 1 million cases, with exports to the USA up by over 160 per cent to nearly 400,000 cases. However, after five years of almost negligible whisky production (there was no whisky made in Scotland in 1943–44), the government's demands on

the industry were stretching in the extreme. Self-imposed limits on
the sales of Johnnie Walker had been put in place during the war, over
and above government restrictions, in order to 'future-proof' supplies
to some extent. But the authorities didn't seem to be necessarily
mindful of the difficulties of the industry. A 'food before whisky' policy
curtailed the amount of grain being made available for new production
to back-fill an exposed inventory, and additional parcels of barley were
only made available on the basis of guarantees of more immediate
export sales. Shortages of both labour and materials compromised
initial attempts to increase output at distilleries.[5] One major concession
from the government which was to have profound consequences on
production was to relax long-standing excise regulations in 1946 that
prevented distillery operations like mashing, fermenting and distilling
from being carried out concurrently. They also permitted distilleries to
operate on a Sunday for the first time. The abolition of these Victorian
restrictions effectively allowed all distilleries to more than double their
production at a stroke, but at the same time fundamentally changed the
pace and cycle of the whisky-making process.[6] When senior members
of the DCL met with the Minister of Food, John Strachey, as late as
1950 the difficulty of the economic situation was being stressed, and it
became clear that it would be necessary to increase the sales of Scotch
whisky to 12,000,000 proof gallons (around 8 million 9-litre cases),
almost half of which would have to be exported to the United States,
with obvious consequences not only for stocks, but also for the home
trade and other 'soft currency' export markets. For Johnnie Walker
one particular difficulty was the expectation that much of what they
exported to the United States would be Black Label.[7]

In 1945 there were 57 distilleries operating in Scotland,
producing both single malt and single grain whiskies. By 1960 the

number was 106, and by 1978, at the peak of Scotch production, 123.
Malt whisky production doubled from nearly 6 million proof gallons in
1945, to 12 million in 1950. It was 26 million gallons in 1960, 55 million
in 1970, and peaked at 80 million in 1978. Grain whisky production
grew from 5 million proof gallons in 1945, to 50 million in 1960, to
100 million gallons in 1978. By 1950 the DCL had 37 malt distilleries in
operation, producing over 6 million gallons of spirit. This had almost
doubled by 1960, with stills being driven as hard as they could be,
but with strict processes in place to ensure that quality standards –
measured by the organoleptic assessment of individual whiskies by
the blenders at Walker's and the other companies – were maintained.[8]
By 1970 the combined DCL malt distilleries were producing over 24
million proof gallons; by 1978 it was 30 million.[9] The investment
that went into the Walker distillery at Cardow, much of it to replace
equipment that had been in place since the late 1890s, was typical of
what was required throughout Scotland to increase production levels
to satisfy the demands of government for increased exports, and to
ensure sustainable brand growth in the future. In 1951 the tun room
was rebuilt; the still house was partly rebuilt, and then extended in
1957 to accommodate a 'new' cast-iron low wines and feints receiver,
salvaged from Ardgowan distillery in Greenock. In 1960 it was reported
that 'a sudden deterioration in the condition of certain buildings at
Cardow Distillery now jeopardises production at this first quality
malt distillery', as a result of which a major redevelopment took
place, costing almost £500,000, which saw the remaining Victorian
plant stripped out, and production increased by 5,500 proof gallons
per week to 14,000. In 1966 the old floor maltings were taken out and
mechanical maltings installed to allow for a further increase in output,
and in 1971 the stills were converted from coal-fired to steam-heated.

Throughout these numerous changes the greatest care was taken not
to compromise the quality of the Cardow spirit, in order to ensure
that the Walker blenders got exactly what they needed. 'The quality of
Cardow, following conversion to steam distillation, had been considered
to be satisfactory', but it was crucial to 'pay particular attention to
samples from distilleries subsequent to conversion to steam distillation,
although so far, all companies considered that no reduction in quality
had been noted, rather the reverse'.[10] However, 1978 was to be the peak
year of malt whisky production; as the industry struggled to come to
terms with declining consumer demand both at home and in export
markets following the oil crisis and subsequent recession, output
fell to only 35 million proof gallons in 1983. DCL production of malt
whisky had fallen to a little over 10 million in the same year, and eleven
of its distilleries had been closed.[11] The 'whisky loch', the creation of
over thirty years of ever-increasing production, was well and truly
overflowing.[12]

Within the DCL, Walker had to compete with the other major
brands for shares of the overall inventory. There was at this point no
clearly stated strategy that Walker would be favoured as the biggest
brand; indeed if there was any strategy it appeared to be one of 'natural
selection', a battle between the rival brand-owning companies. In the
United States, Buchanan's held the ascendancy with Black & White,
which significantly outsold all the other DCL standard brands.[13] But
Johnnie Walker Black Label was the company's principal 'deluxe', or
premium, offering. No other brand, either within the Distillers Company
or without, had developed a premium offering with the same degree of
cachet or market penetration. This was, to a great extent, a mark of the
genius in introducing an age-defined range at the start of the century,
and the strategic forethought in having developed the whisky stocks to

Cardhu Distillery, substantially expanded, c.1971

do so. Black Label, it appeared, was unassailable in the United States, with only Haig's Pinch the other significant deluxe player, and as such it was imperative to release as much as possible onto the hard-currency export market. This presented the inventory managers at the DCL and the Johnnie Walker blending team, led by Christopher Vetters Smith following the retirement of Harold Howie Laing, with serious problems. The most intractable of these was the tension between meeting an overwhelming demand for both Black and Red Label while maintaining quality, and building up stocks to allow for the reintroduction of Black Label's cherished 12-year-old age statement.[14] Before the war the company had had an ambition of achieving an average 10-year-old age for Red Label and 15 (regardless of age statement) for Black, but the pressure from both government and equally aggressive distributors (particularly in the United States) to increase shipments meant that the thought of achieving targets of this nature by even the 1960s seemed impossible.[15] One concern, however, was the possibility of the American government reintroducing a minimum 8-year age for imported Scotch.[16] Another was the threat of competition, particularly from Sam Bronfman.

The Distillers Company had had a complex relationship with Bronfman's various businesses after the Prohibition era, and they clearly regarded him with some considerable respect as a formidable, if somewhat unpredictable, competitor to brands such as Johnnie Walker. Bronfman, always in awe of the Scotch establishment that brands such as Johnnie Walker represented, had sought to build a Scotch business in addition to his American whiskies such as Seagram's 7 Crown and 'VO'. In 1950 Bronfman publicly announced his intention to develop a 12-year-old Scotch whisky for the US market, which had long been in the planning.[17] In October 1951 Chivas Regal was launched at a price premium to Black Label, with an initial sales target of 60,000 cases a year, compared to Black Label's 150,000. It was supported by a promotional budget of $250,000; it was, said Bronfman's biographer, to be 'high priced and aristocratic', targeted at prosperous 'whisky connoisseurs', and making great play of its Scottish heritage and limited availability.[18] With Walker's in no position to reintroduce a 12-year-old label, a successful Chivas Regal threatened to undermine Black Label's formerly unassailable position in the market. It also opened up the danger of similar competition from the Hiram Walker brand Ballantine's. After the launch of Chivas, they put a 12-year-old age statement on their relatively small Grand Macnish brand, and began the process of building up stocks to support aged expressions of Ballantine's too. Ronnie Cumming worried that Walker's would 'undoubtedly experience difficulty in selling in the USA if two well-known and well-advertised outside brands decided to use an age label'. But the stock situation was still critical, regardless of a desire to reintroduce age statements, and it was clear that without significant investment in production capacity and purchasing, sales 'would be more or less static after the end of 1955'.[19]

A very different concern about increased deluxe sales was raised in November 1951 by Harry Braid, who reported that both distributors and representatives in 'certain' export markets were warning of 'the danger of Red Label being considered as a secondary brand' due to the unprecedented emphasis being given to Black Label. The Walker directors agreed that with the exception of the United States the emphasis of the business, as it had been since the early twentieth century, should be on the sale and promotion of Red Label.[20] The following year the Walker directors were even more alarmed that the continued heavy emphasis on Black Label was undermining consumer perceptions of Red, and 'that in view of the possibility of unfavourable repercussions in other markets, it would be unwise to increase sales of Black Label in the USA until the reputation of Red Label in relation to Black Label is on a sounder basis and is readily acceptable by the consumer as a leading brand and not as a secondary brand'.[21] In the year 1951–52 sales of Walker whiskies in the United States totalled 380,000 cases, of which 42 per cent, or around 160,300 cases, were Johnnie Walker Black. It was agreed that in future any additional allocation of whisky available to Walker for the United States would be dedicated to Red Label sales.[22] Another threat to the key Walker brand that became apparent as the 1950s progressed was the increasing favour being shown by American consumers towards 'lighter' blends of Scotch whisky, in both colour and flavour, at a time when vodka was beginning its inexorable rise to popularity there. Both Walker and the DCL more generally were becoming overdependent on the US market as a result of the earlier pressures from the British government; the rise of brands such as Cutty Sark and J&B, so different in flavour profile from Johnnie Walker Red Label, posed a clear and present danger.[23] Both were brands created by wine merchants in St James's in London; the whiskies were of a new light character, and traded heavily on the reputations of these long-established companies and their standing at the heart of London's clubland; 'It was significant that these blends' were being sold at a price premium to Red Label.[24] 'Scotch', wrote one commentator in the US, 'has become so light spirited its [sic] almost ghostly.'[25] Cutty Sark had established a significant business in the United States before the start of the Second World War, but 'J&B had made a phenomenal impact on the post-war market', its promotion being 'materially assisted by the presentation in London of gift bottles to visiting Americans'. The continued growth of both 'was a serious matter, and a solution was being sought. The longer they continued to make progress the more difficult it would be to dislodge them.'[26]

Such was the seriousness with which this threat was regarded that the DCL commissioned consultants Arthur D. Little to undertake a sweeping market review in the United States, including lengthy research with both consumers and retailers, as well as a thorough competitor review, which included an in-depth analysis of the language used to promote the two brands. The recommendations pointed to the need to take the competitors on directly with new brands, and to look closely at the relative merits of the different distributors used by the DCL brands. Canada Dry, which had distributed Walker since the end of Prohibition, had few distractions from its work on Scotch. But other distributors were more widely spread and lacked the focus that their brands required.[27] Fearing the cost involved in trying to establish completely new brands, in 1963 DCL launched two 'light' brand-variants in the United States, Vat 69 Gold and Black & White 'Extra Light', just as J&B was launched in the UK.[28] Ralph Cobbold of Justerini & Brooks, a thorn in the side of his St James's neighbours, provoked outrage and complaints with his advertising line, 'This is a Scotch with the rough edges off', and, following the US launches, wrote to DCL 'expressing his pleasure at the acknowledgement . . . of the merits of lightness'. It was noted that 'the tone of the letter was flippant, but the point was real'.[29] 'Extra Light' was little short of a disaster, and quite possibly the final nail in the coffin of Black & White's brand leadership in the United States, leaving the door open for Johnnie Walker to become the principal Distillers Company brand. This was reflected in the increasingly large amounts invested in Red and Black Label, both in the United States and other markets, compared to either Buchanan's, Dewar's or Haig. By 1971 Walker's global advertising budget, at just over £3 million, was almost twice as much as Buchanan's.[30] Walker's total exports were just over 6 million cases, over 12 per cent of the Scotch export market, of which almost 2 million were to the United States.

There had been some important developments in the Walker business in the US which had given even greater impetus to the brand's growth there. The relationship with Canada Dry had clearly been critical to post-Prohibition success, and in 1955 Walker's had welcomed Roy Moore and colleagues from Canada Dry to a board meeting to celebrate 'the happy relations which had existed between this Company and "Canada Dry" for more than 21 years'. Canada Dry expressed their great satisfaction at the perfect relationship and co-operation which existed between the two companies, and of course the significant profits that had accrued to both.[31] As trade-sales director Hugh Ripley recalled, lavish hospitality was extended to the American distributors when they were in London.[32] In 1964, Canada Dry had been acquired by Hunt Foods, subsequently Norton Simon Inc., and there had been concerns that all was not well with the management of the Walker business, now run there by Paul Burnside, a drinks-trade veteran since the repeal of Prohibition. Burnside had delivered twelve consecutive years of record-breaking growth for Walker since the early 1950s, and had just begun a record $4 million advertising campaign for Red Label ('Johnnie Walker Red, so smooth it's the world's best selling Scotch'). Personal relationships were absolutely key to the success of such ventures, and the Walker business was anxious that these changes in ownership didn't impede the renewal of their distribution deal. As contractual negotiations were coming to a head in 1968, Norton Simon went through a major reorganisation, as part of which Canada Dry announced that they had set up a new drinks division, Somerset Importers, with Burnside as president. The new deal was signed.[33] Burnside had been one of those pressing for the reintroduction of the 12-year-old age statement for Black Label, and inventory had finally been built up to allow for this in 1968. David Kerr, whilst acknowledging that 'Chivas would continue to stride ahead because of its age label and excellent presentation and advertising', feared that a US-only label would jeopardise sales elsewhere in the world, and demanded a global approach. Black Label sales there were 220,000 cases, around 20 per cent of the total Walker business, and highly profitable, giving huge prestige to the marque itself. But the carefully nurtured and expensively acquired stocks of aged whiskies could not extend beyond one market. Kerr conceded, and Black Label 12-year-old was quietly being shipped into the market by the middle of 1968.

In 1955 Johnnie Walker shipments to the United States had accounted for almost half of Walker's export sales; twenty years later they were only a quarter, despite having grown from around 400,000 cases to just over 2 million. During this time exports to other markets slowly increased as a variety of import restrictions around the world were eased or lifted entirely, and GDP began to rise sharply across Europe from the late 1950s. Between 1965 and 1975 non-US exports, principally for Johnnie Walker Red Label, more than tripled from just over 2 million cases to almost 7 million. Europe (not including the UK) accounted for 27 per cent of sales, Asia 14 per cent, and Africa 11 per cent (the largest market being the tourist destination of the Canary Islands). Central and South America, and Australasia each accounted for around only 6 per cent of sales. Although Walker's had originally opened up world markets at arm's length through trading houses in the late nineteenth and early twentieth

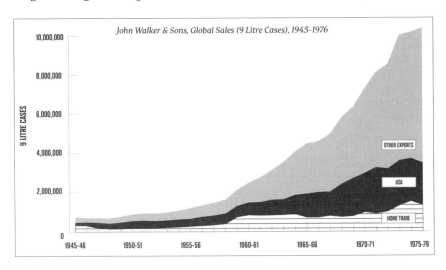

John Walker & Sons, Global Sales (9 Litre Cases), 1945–1976

centuries, with visits to markets being the exception rather than the rule, the model for delivering growth had changed as the market visit became the critical lever for delivering growth. It may well be that the typical Walker director or export sales manager was still something of a 'gifted amateur', public-school educated, a good regiment (preferably the Guards), increasingly with the gift of foreign languages, but the leg-work that was put into rebuilding the post-war export business was relentless. 'Our people', said David Kerr, who normally travelled for at least three months of the year, 'must acquire an intimate knowledge of local habits and trading conditions and feel thoroughly at home anywhere in the globe.'[34] In 1972, for example, Kerr personally visited at least eighteen markets, from the USA (twice) to Japan, Hong Kong and Singapore. Export director Neil Watt travelled to sixteen markets, including Ethiopia, the Territory of the Afars and Issas (present-day Djibouti), Malawi and Zambia. Anthony Westnedge, export sales manager, went to over fifteen markets, mostly in Latin America. And these were only three of a team of over a dozen executives who were constantly rotating between markets, building relationships with distributors and key stakeholders, gaining critical market intelligence, and laying the seeds for future long-term growth. As one later put it to the author, 'They exploited the post-war power of the British gentleman,' sharp-minded, slightly raffish, absolutely honest, with a stiff upper lip and the ability to withstand the most sustained and onerous hospitality.

Walker's two main continental European markets in the 1960s and 1970s were France and Italy – France consistently 20 per cent of the brand's business between 1965 and 1975, Italy growing from 8 to 18 per cent over the same period. In France, where Red Label was the leading brand through the sixties and seventies, the engine for Johnnie Walker growth, according to David Kerr, was 'what is generally described as the democratisation of Scotch. It is a well-known fact that the medical profession in France constantly recommend our product, and there is still a certain element of "snobisme" attached to drinking Scotch.' Advertising for alcoholic beverages was severely restricted in the 1960s and 1970s but relaxed somewhat in the early 1980s. Competitors included 'nightclub brands' such as Ballantine's and J&B, and the proliferation of cheap 'own label' whiskies often distributed through multiple retail channels; in addition the leading brands, particularly Red Label, suffered somewhat from 'irregular imports' from the grey market. By the early 1980s a particular concern was the appearance of locally bottled, aged, but low-priced malt brands, from stocks that had been put cheaply onto the open market as a result of the whisky loch. A Walker visitor to the market cautioned against complacency, warning that these new brands possessed 'a momentum which may be harming established brands more than we realise . . . both trade and consumers are developing loyalties which will not disappear overnight'.[35] Premium single malts like Glenfiddich were also beginning to gain a foothold in the market, buoyed by promotional work that questioned the quality and authenticity of blended Scotch whiskies.[36] But Johnnie Walker continued to grow in France, and by 1985 sales of over 600,000 cases made it the brand's largest European market.

In Italy, according to Kerr in 1963, 'In common with other European countries, Scotch Whisky is becoming more popular, and future increases will come about by a wider acceptance of our product by a broader section of the population'; this was the same process of 'democratisation' he had described in France.[37] However, there were instances of counterfeiting in the market at the time. In 1955 a Glasgow firm wrote to John Barr Cumming explaining they had received a letter asking them to supply 2,000 cases of whisky to a company in Italy.

'Their only essential requirement was that the colour should resemble that of Johnnie Walker as the Whisky was to be used for refilling Walker's bottles.' Their 'knowledge of Italian was limited', and thinking they had mistranslated the request they sent a query, 'but the Italian firm had now replied saying that they were quite right and this was what was proposed'.[38] The order was naturally rejected and swift action taken. In order to continue to grow Red Label, the Italian distributor Wax & Vitale asked in 1967 to use television advertising, which was relatively cheap and not being used by other brands. The DCL companies had an unwritten agreement not to advertise on television, partly to avoid the censure of the anti-drinks lobby in the United Kingdom, and feared 'if one brand used television the practice would spread'. The matter was dropped, but four years later, when Wax asked the question again, it was agreed that Italy could be an exception to the policy.

By 1974 Walker's were advertising on television in Italy, Austria, West Germany, Spain and Greece, although these markets were all still regarded as exceptions to an increasingly fractured rule. Advertising was certainly critical to growth in Italy, and as Red Label lost ground to competitors such as Ballantine's and J&B, new television advertising 'aimed at stressing the authenticity of the brand, is expected to generate renewed consumer demand'.[39] The brand's particular strength was in small bars and restaurants throughout the country. Due to an increased risk of adulteration at the time appropriate safeguarding measures were also introduced and supported by Kerr, who argued that 'the prestige of a brand was important', and that the use of effective deterrents would 'contribute to the image of his brands'.[40] Also challenging the Walker brands were the increasingly popular single malts, for which Italy was probably the largest market in the world, particularly 5-year-old Glen Grant, which experienced huge growth in the late 1970s and early 1980s, and Glenlivet 12-year-old, launched by Seagram in 1985, with the result that brands like Red Label 'have been squeezed both from above and below'.[41] Nonetheless, at almost 400,000 cases of Johnnie Walker, this was the brand's second-largest European market.

Despite the fact that Scotch and Johnnie Walker had been long present in countries with strong British expatriate communities such as Argentina, Latin America remained a difficult place to do business in the post-war world. Political and economic instability, currency problems, high duties and import restrictions, and the regional debt crisis of the early 1980s, all conspired against the sort of growth witnessed in North America or Europe. But as people like David Kerr knew, even though there was no immediate prospect of serious growth in Argentina, brands are built over the long term. Through the 1960s, annual Scotch imports fluctuated between zero to only around 80,000 cases. 'The Argentine', said a visitor in the early 1970s, 'is very brand conscious, but few can afford the luxury of imported Scotch.' By the late 1970s, total Scotch imports to Argentina had reached around 300,000 cases, with Red Label as the lead brand and with 'the potential to become a 400,000 case market over the next three years'.[42] One of the barriers to growing brands effectively in the region was cross-border trading which particularly impacted on Venezuela, the strongest market in the 1970s. It was estimated that 80 per cent of the Scotch imported to the Dutch Antilles was reshipped, principally from Aruba to Venezuela. Illicit trading threatened legitimate trade. Walker shipments to Paraguay, their second-largest market in the region, had grown to 85,000 cases by 1975, although much of this would have found its way to Brazil.[43] Shipments to Venezuela, hampered by high duties, grew only very slowly in the late 1960s, but then exploded in the short-lived period of post-oil-crisis prosperity in the seventies. Just as Johnnie Walker had followed gold in the nineteenth century, so it was to follow oil in the late twentieth. Case sales almost quadrupled in five years to nearly 400,000 cases, almost 70 per cent of Walker shipments to the region. Morris E. Curiel were Walker's long-standing distributors there (since at least 1928), and Black Label the principal Walker brand, growth being driven by the conspicuous consumption of luxury imported products by the newly wealthy. But by 1985 shipments were negligible and the two biggest Walker markets in the region became Colombia and Brazil, albeit total shipments less than they had been ten years before.

Walker's was keen to develop other geographies and wished to avoid over-dependence on a single market. Business had been done in Japan since the late nineteenth century, albeit in no great volumes. Nonetheless Johnnie Walker was the market leader in both standard and deluxe Scotch categories. Until 1971 the market for Scotch was driven by a strict licence system which controlled volumes. Locally produced brands had reappeared on the market in the early fifties and had benefited from the relative scarcity of Scotch and gained a foothold in the market. By the mid-1960s Suntory (whose leading brand was 'Red Label') were selling over 4 million cases in the domestic market, and Nikka over 1.5 million. Sales of single malt and vatted-malt Scotch to Japan, which were to increase rapidly following liberalisation in 1971, were used by some local blenders in their own whiskies. The domestic brands were being sold at much lower prices (for example Suntory Red Label sold at 15s. a bottle compared to over £3 for a bottle of Johnnie Walker).[44]

Walker's had been doing business in Asia since the early 1880s, and Caldbeck MacGregor had been their distributors for China since the early twentieth century; they got Walker's Japanese business at the end of the Second World War.[45] Caldbeck sales to Japan increased rapidly after 1971, from 190,000 cases to nearly 440,000 in 1976, some 34 per cent of Walker's Asia business (the next-biggest market was Hong Kong with 12 per cent). Red Label was still the leading standard brand, particularly strong in the off-trade, and a favoured brand for gift-giving, a very important growth driver for Scotch in the market. However, both Red and Black Label suffered from parallel imports from the United States and increasingly Europe; the same brands being sold at different prices confused consumers and damaged Walker's reputation and that of the category as a whole at the time.[46] By the early 1980s Scotch was also suffering from the 'premiumisation' of domestic blended whiskies, with beautifully packaged, super-deluxe products significantly out-pricing brands like Black Label. This, and massive investment in advertising (particularly on TV), had enhanced the reputation of local producers at the expense of brands like Walker. No surprise that as early as the 1970s Caldbeck MacGregor were discussing 'the need to introduce . . . in the future, a top price brand . . . highest quality, packaging and the supreme presentation of such a brand to be all important'. A mid-1980s economic slump, and an unanticipated boom in the consumption of domestically produced spirit *shochu*, was a brake on the growth of both Japanese and imported Scotch whiskies. Japan fell away badly in sales, leaving a rapidly growing Thailand as the largest Johnnie Walker market in Asia.[47]

In addition to counterfeiting, although dealt with effectively by increasingly efficient policing, being the biggest and most recognisable brand in the world exposed Johnnie Walker to some unusual trademark conflicts. Two long-standing disputes were over the use of the Johnnie Walker name in the United States for tobacco products. The American

Tobacco Company had started selling 'Johnnie Walker' cigarettes ('extremely mild . . . yet full flavoured') as early as 1924, and the Tampa Cigar Company registered a trademark for 'Johnnie Walker' cigars, advertised by an elegant man in top hat and monocle, in the same year.[48] It was to be a number of years before Walker's became concerned about these relatively minor brands, and then they felt a legal challenge would not be worth the 'risks and the expenses that would be incurred'. However, in the 1950s they moved aggressively against Tampa Cigar, eventually winning their case after a number of appeals.[49] Another more obvious use of the brand name was for shoes and boots both in the United States ('Johnnie Walker Shoes, the Young Man's choice') and markets as far afield as Burma and the Philippines, although litigation there was more difficult.[50] Motels were another favourite in the United States; Walker's had a long-running dispute with Boyle's of Yakima in Washington state, whose 'Johnnie Walker' motel, operating since at least 1958, featured a 'signboard bearing an imitation of the Johnnie Walker striding figure'. The company tried to find an amicable solution by offering to fund new signage for a new name, but the intransigent proprietors were finally issued with a restraining order in 1963.[51] Walker's 1969 action against John Walker Bethea and his 'Johnnie Walker' motel in South Carolina, advertised with the brand's red and black colours and 'old English type', was also successful, albeit a matter of some local controversy. In order to prove their case Walker's carried out surveys with the local and travelling populace to demonstrate awareness of their brand, and thus possible confusion over the use of the name; Bethea countered, unsuccessfully, that there could be no confusion as his guests were 'influenced by Protestant denominations which prohibit drinking; South Carolina is a poor state and Scotch is expensive – this is bourbon country.'[52] More prosaic attempts to trade on the brand's good will around the world included the manufacture of sports goods, men and women's clothing, underwear, playing cards and even branding for taxi companies. The company failed in an action against a Burmese patent medicine because of 'the lack of a likelihood of confusion as the mark was used on different goods, namely whisky and blood tonic', and the outcome of a case against the Myawaddy Pharmacy, Rangoon, who were selling 'Johnnie Walker Wind Medicine' remains unknown.[53]

The victim of the post-war largesse that the British government gave to export markets such as the United States was the home market. The quota system that had been put in place at the start of the war was continued, but decreased to as low as 20 per cent of pre-war sales in 1948; Walker sales fell to an all-time low the following year of a mere 145,000 cases; to add insult to injury the price of a bottle of Red Label was increased to 33s. 4d., compared to the pre-war price of 12s. 6d. The quotas were increased to 25 per cent in 1950, and then 30 per cent in 1954, before being gradually increased to 50 per cent by 1958, when they were abolished, with Red Label by then at over 37s. a bottle. It is hardly surprising that Compton Mackenzie's 1947 novel, *Whisky Galore*, made into a film in 1949, was so popular, as the plight of the whisky-starved residents of Hebridean islands Great and Little Todday perfectly reflected the everyday experience of the man on the Clapham omnibus – assuming he didn't have access to black-market supplies, which it was estimated accounted for a third of all the whisky sold in the country.[54] As quotas were lifted Walker sales in the home market rose to around 400,000 cases, over 95 per cent of which was Red Label. They then doubled within two years, and by 1972 home-trade sales director Sir Hugh Ripley reported to the board that sales had easily surpassed a million cases, only marginally behind market leader, Haig. He confidently predicted continued growth.[55]

Ripley had drifted into the Scotch whisky business after the war, having worked as a tea-plantation manager in British Ceylon before returning to enlist in 1939. On the basis of an off-chance letter of application he had been interviewed by John Barr Cumming ('steeped in the tradition of Scotch whisky and . . . an acknowledged expert in his field') in Walker's London offices in 1947 ('the whole place seemed to me to have style written all over it'), a gruelling conversation that 'ranged over the beauty of Scotland, salmon fishing, stalking and shooting'. Ripley clearly charmed Cumming and soon found himself dispatched to Scotland for a year to learn the fundamentals of the business, including distilling at Glen Elgin and Linkwood, and of blending and flavour in Kilmarnock with C. V. Smith. He also spent time in the bond at Kilmarnock learning how blends were put together and bottled, before completing something of a dissertation for Cumming on his return to London. He soon learned there was a certain mystique about Scotch, and an audience always eager to learn more: 'I was flattered by the attention and was already beginning to consider myself an expert after barely two years in the business.' Even though Scotch was still on quota, Ripley found himself working in a reformed home-trade sales force, visiting customers (mostly local brewers) who hadn't seen a sales representative from Walker's for over ten years. Travelling the Midlands, Wales and the West Country, rather like Lindsay Anderson's 'Oh lucky man', with golf clubs and fishing rod carefully packed, Ripley soon fell into the heavy cycle of socialising that was characteristic of the Scotch business at the time. Client meetings were followed by lengthy lunches, dinners and nightcaps. Having got bored of that routine he appealed to Harry Braid for a promotion, and found himself working for Arthur Webb, looking after Greater London and rebuilding relationships with high-end Soho and Mayfair accounts 'with unlimited expenses'. Lunch at Bentley's, an afternoon nap at Boodle's, evenings in the Embassy Club, golf tournaments, Licensed Victuallers' dinners, race meetings (until 1973 Walker's had for many years sponsored the Ebor Handicap), and fishing trips to Scotland; all this clearly qualified the now 'Sir' Hugh Ripley for the post of home-trade director in 1963 (having first been appointed to the board with George Thomson in 1957). 'I settled myself into a fine room in St James Street. A new drinks cabinet was installed, together with a television set (for the racing) ... I always kept my putter and a few balls in the corner of the room.'[56]

Walker's may have disbanded their sales force, but the brand was kept alive in the minds of consumers by advertising throughout the quota period, and of course beyond. In the immediate post-war years the 'Good work' campaign had developed to 'Time Marches On', where the Johnnie Walker character's stride bridged the old world and the new, introducing consumers to the brave new post-war world, again strikingly illustrated by Clive Uptton. This was followed by the mostly sporting-themed 'The smooth round whisky in the square bottle', and then 'Thank you Johnnie Walker' (1955), again first illustrated by Uptton with a drawing of a sophisticated couple heading out for a party (men and women enjoying Scotch together would be an increasingly common leitmotif of these UK adverts). This campaign marked a more conscious move towards 'lifestyle' advertising, and the slow relegation of the Johnnie Walker character to a sign-off for the advertisements, rather than being a key actor. Illustrations became less important, photographic treatments more common. As sales, and competition, increased, there was also a return to explicit, liquid-focused 'reason why' campaigns, mixing product truths with brand heritage. What makes Johnnie Walker Red Label different? 'It's the subtle and superbly smooth result of 42 whiskies being blended together with 142 years of skill . . .' Semi-advertorial executions introduced individuals from various parts of the production process, from barley to bottle, explaining the care and the quality that lay behind every bottle, with the assurance that this was the drink 'strictly for whisky drinkers'. There was also an attempt to educate consumers, with Jonathan Miller commissioned to make a film about the production process from barley to bottle; *Scotch*, described as an 'art-house' treatment, certainly mystified some of the directors, who felt 'the film did not sufficiently advertise our product'. It rewarded Miller handsomely, and he bought a holiday home in Archiestown, near Cardow, with the proceeds.[57] Progressively there was a move to the unashamedly aspirational (albeit humorous), with adverts like 'When the head waiter starts knowing your name', followed by the 'Johnnie Walker Guide to Success'. This coincided with the arrival of advertising manager Charles Euman from Rothman's, who had also worked on the agency side. A protégé of Kerr's (to whom he reported directly) he became, after some argument, a Walker board member in 1971.[58] Ripley disliked the slant of the new advertising, claiming it 'introduced some issues involving the field of class distinction to some extent on the theme of running down the little man'; it was agreed that 'a softer and less jagged' approach would be taken in future.[59] Walker's budget for advertising in the home market increased from around £250,000 as quotas were removed, to £450,000 in 1966, and over £1 million ten years later. In 1970 the global budget was £2.3 million; by 1980 it was £12 million, and by 1986 £24 million.[60]

A number of important changes had taken place to the get-up of both Red and Black Label since the war began. 'Old Highland', the original brand name used by Walker's, was changed to 'Old Scotch' in 1941, and in 1959 the Kilmarnock crest that had been used by the company since at least the first registered label of 1877 (for which they stated a first-use date of before 1867) was also removed from the label, cork and capsule at the request of the Lord Lyon, with effect from the following year.[61] In 1956, following the grant of a royal warrant from Queen Elizabeth, the royal arms were added to the foot label of both Red and Black Label.[62] During and immediately after the war the availability of materials, particularly cork, had led to a degree of pragmatism in terms of closures used for sealing bottles, and shortages of lead for the manufacture of capsules led to strip stamps being used in their place. Following a lengthy review in the sixties, Walker's decided to introduce a moulded 'ROPP' closure for both Red and Black Label in 1967, at the same time phasing out the wrapping of individual bottles in tissue paper.[63] Swing had also had a label change as the use of the Kilmarnock crest ended, and in Europe was renamed 'Celebrity' for certain markets. David Kerr had seen an opportunity to develop sales of Swing in the United States and Asia as a super-deluxe brand, priced above Black Label and with a 15-year-old age statement ('If there were a market for super deluxe it was worth providing a brand,' said Kerr), but the highly conservative DCL Management Committee refused to countenance it and would only support a 12-year-old brand, which would clearly have cannibalised Black Label.[64] In 1983 the company did launch Johnnie Walker Old Harmony in Japan, a 'semi-premium' brand aimed at combatting the erosion of Red Label's position by domestic whiskies.[65]

In the early 1960s, Walker launched an 8-year-old Cardhu in small quantities, apparently at the insistence of Sir Ronnie Cumming; 'It seemed that the Cardhu exercise might commit the Company to provide age labels for all single malts,' grumbled Alex MacDonald, then DCL chairman. It was packaged in individually numbered bottles with a carton and a booklet, and received a relatively large advertising

The opening of the new Hill Street plant in Kilmarnock, 1956, with Harry M. Braid (far left) and chairman of John Walker & Sons, Leonard Elgood (second from left), with representatives from Canada Dry

Cask-filling in the newly opened Hill Street plant in Kilmarnock, 1956

allowance in 1966 and 1967 of £15,000 for the UK, with full-page adverts in the *Illustrated London News* and the *Tatler*. It was also launched in Italy, where Cumming reported it was doing 'quite well'.[66] Later in the year MacDonald complained that it had only sold 462 cases, and that 'Mr Kerr should examine the situation and decide whether the promotion of Cardhu was worthwhile.' Concerned that 'advertising a single malt as something special was not perhaps knocking standard brands', the promotional budget was withdrawn, and sales restricted to the home market. Even then in 1968 MacDonald, commenting on the worldwide success of Walker, couldn't refrain from wondering 'if the promotion of Cardhu Highland malt whisky was still worthwhile'.[67] In 1970 the tenacious Kerr tried again with Cardhu, at the same time as trying to move Swing into the super-deluxe segment, but his attempts to covertly fund a promotional campaign were met with fury by MacDonald, who 'felt that this disregard for Management Committee directives should not be tolerated and that Walker should be required to abandon their plans for the promotion of Cardhu'. Instead it was quietly relaunched as a 12-year-old, the standard age for premium malts, with a lighter colour spirit, as was preferred in Italy, by then the lead market for malts in the world.[68] The brand languished until the early 1980s, when in very different circumstances, with the Distillers Company desperate to shed its 'stodgy image' with investors, Cardhu (now both brand and distillery name) was relaunched with a new pack and significant investment in home and export markets in both advertising and public relations, with journalists being fêted on trips to the distillery, a published history written by DCL executive Brian Spiller, and even newly installed distillery manager Evan Cattanach (who was to be a redoubtable ambassador for both his distillery and Johnnie Walker) releasing an 'LP and cassette in the form of a Cardhu Ceilidh'.[69]

Tourists were actively encouraged to visit the distillery, a licence was obtained to allow sales of whisky to them, and in 1987 a major programme was announced to build a new visitor centre. As licensees of Talisker distillery, Walker had already substantially upgraded visitor facilities (including the provision of a shop) there in 1982.[70]

The two decades of continued growth that the Walker brand had experienced around the world since the end of the war imposed huge strains not only on the inventory of whisky available to their blenders, but also the bonding, blending and bottling facilities available to the company. The St George's Bond in London had suffered damage as a result of multiple bombing raids, and the Strand premises were increasingly unfit for purpose. The developments planned for Hill Street in Kilmarnock (to provide bottling capacity of 2 million dozens per annum) had been put on hold as the site had been given over to the armed forces, and when the plans were revisited costs had escalated to over £700,000 compared to some £214,000 before the war. Eventually they would rise to over £1 million.[71]

With the new facility still not ready by early 1955, capacity was 'not sufficient to present requirements, although both Kilmarnock and London Bottling establishments are working late'. Slater Rodger, the long-standing Walker subsidiary in Glasgow, took the deficiency of 6,000 dozen bottles per week. The seven-acre site at Hill Street was fully operational later in 1955, and was officially opened in September 1956 with Scotch-thirsty distributors from all over the world (not least Ray Moore and his colleagues from Canada Dry) in attendance to admire the massive barrel-vaulted ceiling of the new bottling hall, and to witness this guarantee of sustained, growing and regular supply to their businesses.[72] However, by 1964 the company was suffering bottlenecks in production and missed orders, and already looking at plans to expand the site with a new bottling hall and six new lines, capable of adding over 2.5 million cases to output a year. While all the possible spare capacity within the DCL was put at their disposal, plans were eventually agreed in 1965 for an expansion, costing in excess of £1.5 million, with the new bottling hall at Hill Street and a disgorging, blending and bottling plant at Hurlford on the outskirts of the town. This additional capacity led to the closure of St George's Bond in 1967, and the end of blending in the Strand, which had continued through the 1960s.[73] For all of this the apparent insatiable thirst for Scotch whisky around the world led to further expansion plans in 1970, which included doubling the capacity of the new bottling hall, and taking advantage of three of the new bottling lines at a new Distillers Company plant at Leven in Fife.[74] It was acknowledged that by 1974 yet more capacity would be required, and with no further opportunities for expansion at Hill Street, plans were agreed to develop the Shieldhall plant, on the banks of the Clyde on the outskirts of Glasgow.[75]

In 1970 John Walker & Sons celebrated their 150th anniversary with 135 representatives from distributors around the world joining guests in London and then Gleneagles, for banquets and a conference, to celebrate the achievements of the world's largest-selling Scotch whisky. Even with a newly buoyant home trade, the story was all about the global success of the brand; with sales of over 7 million cases and growing, and numerous Queen's Awards for Export to their credit, Walker's stood at the pinnacle of the country's most valuable industry. To celebrate the occasion the company created a special blend which was gifted to all the guests, and anniversary decanters were sold all over the world.[76] From Gleneagles parties toured distilleries and Kilmarnock for an immersion in the whisky-making process, an increasingly important and undoubtedly powerful tool in building relationships with distributors and their customers.[77] Welbeck PR had been employed to develop and manage visits for both trade and the press, and placed a five-page advertorial on the company and its celebrations in the *Illustrated London News* in May.[78]

Yet, despite volumes growing till the mid-1970s, storm clouds were gathering; Red Label had been starting to lose share in the UK to brands like Bell's and Famous Grouse, there was a looming recession, and increasing EEC legislation was challenging some long-established practices in the Scotch whisky industry. Walker's had operated a dual pricing system in Europe for many years, with appreciably lower prices for Red and Black Label in the domestic market. This had led to a growth in the parallel trade from the UK to Europe, particularly to large retail chains and traders, which damaged local distributors' sales and profits. The dual pricing system was open to challenge under European trading laws, and although the issue affected all Scotch whisky companies, a test case was brought by the European Commission against Walker and the Distillers Company in the summer of 1977, and a judgement against them was issued in December.[79] Various options were considered by way of response, but finally the unprecedented decision was taken to withdraw Red Label from the home market entirely. As home-trade director Hugh Ripley observed with an uncharacteristic touch of understatement, 'The upshot of this tricky situation was unfortunate for me.'[80]

Taking a 1.25 million-case brand out of a market overnight obviously not only threatened business performance, but also had the potential to massively disrupt whisky production schedules and long-laid inventory plans. Stocks had been built up for Johnnie Walker

over decades on the basis of eventually returning Black Label to a
12-year-old age statement around the world, and sustaining growth of a
7- to 8-year-old blend of something like 15 per cent a year. Now that was
turned on its head by taking more than 10 per cent of Walker's total
volume out of the system. The Walker board and the DCL Management
Committee believed this risk could be mitigated by the introduction of
a new brand to replace Red Label in the home market. 'John Barr' (the
name had apparently been suggested by Ripley as a tribute to his old
mentor John Barr Cumming) was a brand not from Johnnie Walker – in
order to comply with the EEC ruling – but from subsidiary George
Cowie & Sons of Mortlach distillery. This new blend ('which is quite
different from Red Label'), in a square bottle but with a large, straight
body label, and a male silhouette on the shoulder, was the subject of
some considerable debate among directors, and was likely originally
designed as much by lawyers as it was by creatives. David Kerr (now
on the DCL Management Committee) feared that there was too much
optimism about the potential sales of the brand, while John Connell
(soon to be DCL chairman) observed 'that attempts by other members
of the industry to thrust a new brand into public acceptance by massive
promotion had failed'. Nonetheless, moved by the argument from
Walker's managing director Peter Whitely that 'a brand could only be
launched once', an initial launch budget of £310,000 was increased to
over £500,000 as John Barr went on shelf and optic in the summer of
1978. Provincial newspapers declared it was 'The whisky man's whisky',
created with 160 years of whisky heritage behind it. Testimonials from
consumers vouched for its exceptional smoothness and mellow flavour.
Ripley's Johnnie Walker racing sponsorships were overnight transferred
to John Barr. Drinks writers extolled the brand's virtues in the press.
Free tastings, free bottles, free glasses and even competitions for free

weekends in a castle in Scotland ('Live like a laird for a long weekend') were used to try persuade drinkers to try the new brand.[81] However, only a few months later Kerr was handing budget back, reporting 'difficulty' in persuading larger customers to take on the new brand.[82] The launch was not a success, although as Ripley recalled, 'At least it was fun bashing around the countryside with the sales team promoting the new stuff – even if sometimes a bit exhausting.'[83]

'Smaller distillers', said *The Times*, were 'scrambling to mop up the sales gap left by the departure of Johnnie Walker.'[84] Red Label's departure, and the failure of John Barr to make the hoped-for impact, opened the door for brands like Bell's and Famous Grouse to achieve leading positions in England and Scotland. In addition, it spelled opportunity for the 'new' single malt brands such as Glenfiddich, Glenmorangie and Macallan, which had already been gaining a foothold in some continental European markets. Black Label, albeit with an increased price to prevent parallels to Europe, had not been allowed to thrive in the home market and an underdeveloped 'deluxe' market was particularly vulnerable to these ambitious and novel newcomers. Hence Walker's launch of the repacked Cardhu in 1983. With a new managing director, David Connell, in charge the company pushed hard to get Red Label back onto the home market, which they achieved in the same year. But after six years' absence, and in a highly competitive yet declining market, it would not regain its former pre-eminence. In order to grow 'significantly and rapidly', Walker's were proposing to invest millions into television advertising, a first in the UK, but the ultra-cautious DCL Management Committee refused, still concerned about 'the political and social implications of seeking to advertise a brand of spirits on television'.[85] Exports were also suffering, and in the United States Scotch simply seemed to have lost its cachet with drinkers, who had turned instead to white spirits. Distributors were concerned about the 'frequent references which commentators in the USA had made in recent months to a levelling off in demand for Scotch Whisky', arguing that more effort should be directed at journalists and influencers. In 1981 Somerset were renegotiating their credit terms for Walker shipments. In 1984 the DCL bought Johnnie Walker's American importers outright.[86] This perfect storm of circumstance saw the Distillers Company's substantial whisky loch ready to burst its banks. Production schedules were revised downwards, and eventually in 1983 eleven malt-whisky distilleries were closed by the company, including now legendary names such as Brora and Port Ellen.[87] Similarly, short-time working was introduced at Kilmarnock in April 1981, followed by redundancies in 1984 as the Distillers Company closed plants in Edinburgh and Glasgow.[88]

By this time the Distillers Company had become an easy target for critics in the City of London, its leadership characterised as old and out of touch. In many respects the company's reputation likely still suffered from the damage caused by its venture into the distribution of foreign-made pharmaceuticals and its connection to the Thalidomide tragedy of the 1960s. Its critics carped at a lack of diversification, of mismanagement of brands like Haig in the home market, and of the virtual surrender of its domestic position to hungrier and more aggressive upstarts with the withdrawal of Johnnie Walker Red Label in 1978. The relaunch of Red Label was seen by some commentators as the last roll of the dice; 'Scotch has never been an unfashionable drink and if we do our job properly there is no reason to think it ever will become one,' said David Connell on the eve of the relaunch.[89] Some continued to doubt the directors' ability to do their job properly. In the autumn of 1985, James Gulliver, chairman of the Argyll group of food retailers, made his first move to acquire the Distillers Company, which provoked an acrimonious takeover battle, seen by some as a David and Goliath confrontation. Others thought it a 'Gentlemen vs Players' affair, with Gulliver characterised (unfairly) as a minor retailer trying to take on the whisky aristocracy. The drawn-out and complex dealings which saw the Irish brewers Guinness (who had recently acquired the Bell's Scotch whisky brand) emerge as a 'white knight' to aid the Distillers Company, finally ended with Guinness acquiring DCL in April 1986.[90] As Walker's had in many respects operated as an independent fiefdom within the Distillers Company, it could be argued that over 170 years of history had come to an end with this change, and with it possibly the future of the brand. But Johnnie Walker was a brand of great resilience. If its history showed anything it was that this was a company with *esprit de corps*, and most of all a brand that was adept at managing changed circumstances, and which thrived most when facing potential adversity. It was hardly conceivable that it would do anything other than keep walking.

EPILOGUE
'KEEP WALKING'

*The reimagined Striding Man
introduced in 2015*

'Analyse the proposition this way: We take the idea "walking" – there is nothing ambitious about it when spelled out in plain English. But substitute for the printed words a picture of a man walking; then what is our subject? One person says, "a man". Others say "a suit of clothes". "A hat". "A street". The expression of the idea has become indefinite.'[1]

THE JOHNNIE WALKER brand was owned by United Distillers and Guinness for ten years, during which time the brand grew from 7.3 million cases to 10.8 million, more or less equivalent to the growth it had experienced between 1970 and 1975, when global sales were at 10.3 million. During the decade 1987–1997 global Scotch sales remained at around 71 million cases, and although a general decline had set in to sales of blended Scotch compared to single malts, Johnnie Walker's share had increased from 10 to 15 per cent. There were also significant shifts in the geography of the business, reflecting some success for the new regional structure that United Distillers had put in place.

In 1997 Europe was the largest region (30 per cent of all sales), but the home market, where the new company also had the (ailing) market-leader Bell's, had fallen to only 215,000 cases, a fall of more than 1 million since the withdrawal and then unsuccessful relaunch of Red Label in the seventies and early eighties. France, the single biggest European market, was in decline, whilst sales of Red Label in particular were growing at breakneck speed in Greece, and to a lesser extent Spain. The United States' share of the global business had fallen from 19 to 11 per cent, although more than half of these 1.5 million cases were of the highly profitable Black Label. Latin America had grown from 9 to 16 per cent, the fastest-growing market being Brazil (almost 500,000 cases), which had more than doubled sales. In Asia Pacific, which had grown from 12 to 17 per cent of global Johnnie Walker sales, Thailand was the largest market – although already in the grip of a fierce recession in which sales fell from almost 1 million cases to around 700,000 in a year – followed by Japan and Australia. Globally, duty-free sales accounted for almost 16 per cent of the Walker business. In the regions, in order to enhance profitability, a significant margin was clawed back through the ending of many long-standing distributor arrangements, and the establishment of local offices or joint ventures.

Johnnie Walker Black Label remained at around 30 per cent of all global sales, but the percentage in different regions and markets varied enormously, from around 10 per cent of all sales in Europe to 55 per cent in Asia, and 6 per cent in Greece to over 95 per cent in Venezuela. The mantras of the new business were 'trading up', 'drink less but drink better', and 'premiumisation'. This new outlook opened up the super-premium category for Walker, which the Distillers Company had been reluctant to develop. Tom Jago had been brought in to United Distillers to lead innovation, and under his tutelage Johnnie Walker 'Oldest', soon after to be known as 'Blue Label', was launched in 1987, a non-aged blend of old and rare whiskies.[2] Proudly bearing the words attributed to Alexander Walker, 'Our blend cannot be beat', and with a bottle that harked back to the late nineteenth century, this new brand represented a step change in whisky packaging and marketing.[3] Shortly afterwards 'Premier', a heavily sherried blend aimed at Asian premium-spirits market, was launched, at what the *Aberdeen Evening Express* considered the eye-watering wholesale price of £100 a bottle.[4] By 1997 Blue Label was selling almost 50,000 highly profitable cases, Premier 30,000. Other innovations aimed at the duty-free channel were less successful, but by 1997 Walker's had also launched Gold Label (originally in Japan as a 15-year-old) and Green Label, a 15-year-old 'pure malt' created by Mike Collings, who also substantially repackaged Cardhu single malt.[5]

Investors and analysts cautiously welcomed this return to growth. But further acceleration faced a fundamental challenge which key decision-makers were slow to recognise. Advertising was increasingly the preserve of the key regions and lead markets within them, resulting in a considerable degree of inconsistency around the world. If there was a thread of an idea that held the brand together it was the notion that it represented 'masculine success' (a somewhat generic 'category truth'), although more often than not expressed in ways that made both the brand, and the category, look stale, clichéd and out of touch with a new demographic for whom Scotch was no longer the first choice of spirits.[6] The brand had also made a headlong dive into massive expenditure on golf sponsorship. It clearly had an authentic connection to the brand's past (as did, it was to turn out later, motor racing); Alexander and his children (sons and daughters) were all enthusiastic golfers, and it seemed that few at the senior end of the business were ever far away from a golf course, or in Hugh Ripley's case, his putters. And from the hole-in-one competition of the 1920s to the sponsorship of the various Johnnie Walker championships in the early 1980s, it seemed like a fixture in the brand's promotional budget. But from the late 1980s, working in close association with Mark McCormack's International Management Group (IMG), Johnnie Walker sponsored the Ryder Cup (from 1987) for five tournaments, and then from 1991 to 1995 promoted the not-entirely-successful Johnnie Walker World Championship, and the Johnnie Walker Asian Classic.[7] All, of course, were intended to reach global audiences through the McCormack media network. The business also increasingly looked to, and invested in, Scotland as a global resource of both knowledge and brand support, enlisting distillery managers to travel to markets to espouse the liquid credentials of the Walker brands, and welcoming ever more frequent visits to Cardhu and other distilleries from marketing teams, customers and consumers.

Meanwhile, in 1997 it was announced that Guinness and its spirits subsidiary, United Distillers, would merge with rivals Grand Metropolitan, which included brands such as J&B Scotch, Smirnoff and

Bailey's, to form a new company called Diageo.[8] This new company possessed an unrivalled portfolio of spirits brands and an unlikely collection of 'diversifications', from burgers to ice-cream (the majority of which were relatively quickly disposed of), and initially seemed not to recognise the importance that Scotch would have to its overall performance and future growth.[9] Moreover, Johnnie Walker now found itself fighting for share of mind and resources alongside J&B Scotch, in which many executives in the new business had a lot of emotional investment.

Over and above delivering significant cost savings, there was an expectation that this new drinks marketing giant would supercharge the performance of its most potent brands, none more so than Red and Black Label.[10] However, Johnnie Walker sales were stuttering and its market share falling, and Diageo, particularly the Johnnie Walker global brand director Alice Avis, was under huge pressure to demonstrate that the merger could deliver something very special from this extra-special brand. In sharp contrast to the usual development process of regional advertising, and the out-dated clichés often used, Avis determined to develop a global positioning for the brand working with a small group of regional marketeers and members of her own team. An extensive global masculinity study revealed that there was a universal and profound idea connected to 'masculine success' which related to the idea of progress – 'A man was judged a success not by where he was, but where he was going.'[11] This insight was the basis of a brief – that 'in every corner of the world Johnnie Walker would be a symbol of personal progress' – delivered to advertising company Leo Burnett and industry outsiders Bartle Bogle Hegarty (in whom Burnett had just acquired a majority stake). At the same time, championed by its senior marketing men Jack Keenan and Ivan Menezes, Diageo had agreed to a five-year plan for Walker's that included critical investment in mature and developed markets to recruit a new generation of drinkers, partly through the global roll-out of the 'Johnnie Walker Mentoring Program', an educational programme with the art of blending at its heart which had been developed by a senior brand marketeer, Michael Stoner, in the United States. Critically this new strategy, which took into account the issue of geographical inconsistencies in marketing plans and executions, was destined to embody and articulate the idea of Johnnie Walker as a global icon-brand.

Ultimately it was to be a trip to consult the Johnnie Walker Archives, including years of forgotten advertising from Tom Browne's very earliest pieces, that would unlock the idea that BBH presented back to Walker's of 'Keep Walking'. What the BBH team saw in the work of Browne, Basil Partridge, Leo Cheney and Clive Uptton was that 'the Striding Man represented the pioneering and entrepreneurial zeal of the Walker family'; it had the 'strength of heritage' but was also progressive, and 'inherently dynamic'. In appreciating this they had unlocked the idea of the brand's inherent vitality and progressiveness that underpinned the original brief that James Stevenson and Paul E. Derrick had developed, and which led to the creation of the icon in 1908. As BBH later wrote:

> *The Striding Man forged a deep connection between the universal human desire to progress and the Johnnie Walker brand. It was essential to be pro-active, to inspire progress in our consumers not merely celebrate it in the brand. From this the campaign idea was born, encapsulated in the powerful exhortation, 'Keep Walking'.*

They also, controversially, turned the figure round to walk from left to right (although in truth over the years he had wandered the world quite freely at will). Brought to life first in a series of powerful short films (which like the original poster advertising in 1908 made no mention of whisky) and then in a variety of poster and print executions, and designed to allow markets to adapt the core idea to local circumstance, the campaign launched in 2000, by which time Stephen Morley was running the Global Brand team. In eight years the Keep Walking campaign ran in over 120 markets, with over 50 television executions and more than 150 print executions, with a degree of global consistency that the brand had not witnessed for generations. And when the sales needle started moving, it moved dramatically, taking the brand from 10 million cases to 15 million by 2008. Latin America had increased to over 3 million cases, a third of which were in Brazil, and almost a third of which were Johnnie Walker Black Label. Asia was also selling over 3 million cases, about a third of which was from a reinvigorated Thailand, and across the region half of which were Johnnie Walker Black Label. The United States had increased sales to 1.5 million cases, more than half of which were Black Label. In addition, high-margin super-premium variants, from Green Label upwards, added almost 500,000 additional cases. At the same time Walker's volume, and more significantly value, share of the total Scotch market increased. Moreover, the campaign not only galvanised the brand, but also the new business; indeed it's possible that if Diageo hadn't been under quite such pressure to demonstrate it could build brands, the ideas created by the Johnnie Walker team and brought to life by BBH might never have been approved.[12]

In July 2009 Diageo announced that it would be closing the Hill Street bottling plant in Kilmarnock as part of a major restructuring programme, and despite a vociferous campaign fronted by the First Minister of Scotland to retain the Johnnie Walker link with its founder's home, the closure was confirmed a few months later; the last bottle of Red Label was filled there on Friday 23 March 2012, with production transferred to the company's modern plants in Glasgow and Fife. Part of the Hill Street site was gifted to Kilmarnock College and has now been redeveloped as a new campus for Ayrshire College. The remainder of the site was then also gifted to the community along with a £2 million investment in the Halo Urban Regeneration project, a community-focused initiative that will see the site redeveloped for business, leisure and residential use.[13] John Walker's home in India Street had long been engulfed by the expansion of his son's and grandson's business at Hill Street in the 1950s, but the building that housed his original shop in King Street still survives. Alexander Walker's large house in London Road has been subdivided into apartments, and his much-prized garden is no more, although his other house, Crosbie Tower in Troon, has recently been dramatically restored; the very large garden there has long since been developed for housing. A large part of his monument to the growth and success of Walker's whisky in the Strand at Kilmarnock still stands, much of it occupied by the offices of East Ayrshire Council. The modest but elegant house built by his son Sir Alexander Walker, also at Troon, is now Piersland House Hotel, much frequented by golfers; Sir Alexander's grave and that of his brother Thomas are close by in the Troon cemetery. John Walker's grave is in the St Andrew's churchyard in Kilmarnock, his son Alexander's, as already mentioned, a small Celtic cross in the 'new' Kilmarnock Cemetery, a most articulate memorial to the modesty and character (if not the often fiery temperament) of the man who laid the foundations for the world's largest Scotch whisky brand.

The dramatic sales lift that was demonstrably attributable to the Keep Walking campaign continued. By 2018 the brand's total sales were just shy of 19 million cases, almost double the figure at the start of the Keep Walking campaign. Ten million cases were Red Label, that recruitment engine for the Scotch whisky category around the world, and 6 million Black Label. Asia and Latin America each accounted for around 20 per cent of total sales, Europe 17 per cent, Africa 12 per cent. The United States, at almost 2 million cases, remained the single largest and most profitable market for the brand, followed by Mexico, Brazil and Thailand. A new global sponsorship of a Formula 1 racing team, announced in 2005 and running until 2014, had brought the brand to millions of Grand Prix followers around the world, many in markets where spirits advertising was severely restricted. It acknowledged the achievements of Jack Walker's grandson Rob Walker, who managed one of the last great privateer racing teams in the 1950s and 1960s. And initially at least it was blessed with outstanding success on the circuit. Between 2014 and 2019 Johnnie Walker strengthened its involvement in Grand Prix and became 'the official whisky of Formula 1'.

Continued innovation delivered some notable successes, particularly Johnnie Walker Double Black, introduced in 2009 as a smokier version of Black Label, which was selling almost 1 million cases a year. Most recently, between 2018 and 2020, the astonishingly successful tie-in with the HBO series *Game of Thrones* for a limited edition variant, White Walker by Johnnie Walker, introduced a new demographic to Scotch. Super-premium innovations had included 'The John Walker', a tribute to the founder, and 'King George V', a celebration of the award of the company's first royal warrant in 1934. In 2012, Johnnie Walker master-blender Jim Beveridge blended by hand rare malt and grain whiskies that had been distilled in, and maturing since, 1952 to make a special-edition Scotch whisky to celebrate Her Majesty the Queen's Diamond Jubilee, supported by more than sixty craftspeople involved in the making of the elaborate packaging. Just sixty editions of Diamond Jubilee by John Walker & Sons were created for sale and, as a result, £1 million was donated to the Queen Elizabeth Scholarship Trust (QEST) to support its mission to preserve excellence in British craftsmanship, as symbolised by the Royal Warrant of Appointment.

'Two hundred years later and Johnnie's still walking,' said the actor in the film *The Man Who Walked Around the World*, commissioned by then Walker brand director David Gates in 2009, and intended to build passion, commitment and pride for the brand within Diageo. It ended up being a hit, described as 'one of Johnnie Walker's best ever ads'. By then of course John Walker & Sons strode the world not just of Scotch, but of whisky and spirits in general, like a Colossus. A brand of size and scale unimaginable to John Walker the founder, and inconceivable to his son Alexander, in so many respects the intuitive genius behind the success of the firm, and to his handful of carefully picked and long-serving (and in some respects long-suffering) staff. Sir Alexander Walker, the longest-lived of John's grandsons to work in the business, only saw sales reach around 1.5 million cases. Even that was a remarkable achievement, given the capital and logistical organisation required to deliver that many bottles of Scotch, all 'guaranteed the same quality throughout the world'. But would he, or his elder brother George, or James Stevenson, or the men they recruited who were still running the business into the 1950s and 1960s, have imagined 5 or 10, let alone 15 or almost 20 million cases of Johnnie Walker whisky a year? Would they have understood, all of them, the remarkable role they played in this remarkable achievement, particularly in overcoming successive threats of adversity – floods, hostile fiscal regimes, wars, Prohibition, economic depression – and each time emerging stronger?

If Scotch was Scotland's gift to the world, then these were the men, and latterly women, who parcelled it up and made sure it was delivered safely to every corner of the globe. In so doing they built the engine for growth of the whole category, and importantly a brand which firmly remains the world's No. 1 Scotch whisky.

Keep walking: the Striding Man through the ages

ACKNOWLEDGEMENTS

I would like to thank Christine McCafferty and her team in the Diageo Archive for all their help and patience, and for generally putting up with me for such long periods of time whilst I was working through the records of John Walker & Sons and other material in the collection. The staff in the Newspaper Room at the British Library were unfailingly helpful, as were the staff at the National Archives of Scotland, the National Library of Scotland, the Mitchell Library in Glasgow, the London Library, the Ayrshire Archives in Ayr and Kilmarnock, the East Sussex Record Office in Brighton, and the History of Advertising Trust. I am also immensely grateful to Laura Chilton, a tenacious research assistant who spent months searching, often in vain, for the elusive John Walker & Sons in newspapers from all around the world.

Simon Thorogood and his colleagues at Canongate have been a pleasure to work with since my first meeting with them in Edinburgh.

Among my colleagues at Diageo I would like to thank for their assistance Jim Beveridge, Gillian Cook, Duncan Elliot, Philip Garden, James Higgins, Lieke Hompes, Marie Kennedy, Jeremy Lindley, Stephen MacDonald, Graham Penter, Ian Smith, and last, but by no means least, Jerome Stewart.

The following friends and former colleagues all wittingly (or sometimes unwittingly) made contributions large (you know who you are) and small (but important) for which I am very grateful: Alice Avis, Mark Bastable, Karen Bennett, Ben Bond, Chantal Bristow, Dave Broom, Michael Burkham, Alex Conway, Ronnie Cox, Jonathan Driver, Andrew Ford, David Gates, Peter Gordon, Isabel Graham-Yooll, Ailana Kamelmacher, Nick Kendall, Michael Laird, Keith Law, Lana Lindsley,

Charlie Maclean, Chris Middleton, Tarita Mullins, Alessandro Palazzi, Tom Patrick, Lucy Pritchard, Patrick Roberts, Ian Ross, Noah Rothbaum, Sam Simmons, Peter Smith, Cat Spencer, Martin Spurrier, Chris Stokes, Anthony Westnedge.

     If you also helped and I have failed to mention you then I can only profusely apologise.

Nicholas Morgan

IMAGE PERMISSION CREDITS

In addition to any acknowledgement or credit that has been given in captions and text, specific credit is given for the following images.

Chapter 1

p. 4 Map of Kilmarnock, reproduced with the permission of the National Library of Scotland

Chapter 5

p. 107 London Street Scene © The Francis Frith Collection/Almay Stock Photo

Chapter 8

p. 178 Bootlegged whisky bottles © Siiddeutsche Zeitung Photo/Alamy Stock Photo

p. 190 Lord Stevenson, by permission of East Ayrshire Council / East Ayrshire Leisure

PLATE SECTION IMAGES

Section 1

p. 1 Kilmarnock Cross – Octavius Hill c. 1840, by permission of East Ayrshire Council/East Ayrshire Leisure

p. 2 Aquatint Print of Men Drinking, Historical Picture Archive/Corbis Historical via Getty Images

p. 4 Showcard for John Walker & Sons, whisky merchants, c. 1882, Science and Society Picture Library/SSPL via Getty Images

Section 2

p. 8 'Keep Walking' campaign in New York by permission of New Tradition, c/o Lucas Klappas

NOTES

AA: Ayrshire Archives, Ayr and Kilmarnock
DA: Diageo Archives, Menstrie
NLS: National Library of Scotland, Edinburgh
NRS: National Records of Scotland, Edinburgh

'The Story of the World's No. 1 Scotch Whisky': Johnnie Walker is the no. 1 Scotch Whisky in the world (The IWSR 2020, volume and value data 2019)

Prologue

1   DA, JW&S Letter Book A11/2, p. 137, John Blaikie to AW, 30.7.1886
2   Aeneas MacDonald, *Whisky* (Edinburgh, 1930), p. 23. Aeneas MacDonald was a pseudonym adopted by Leith-born George Malcolm Thomas: see George McKechnie, *The Best Hated Man* (Glendaruel, 2013), pp. 29–30
3   DA, JW&S Letter Book A11/1, p. 50, AW to Daniel Wilson, Sydney, 8.11.1882
4   Ian Wisniewski, *The Whisky Dictionary: An A–Z of Whisky, From History and Heritage to Distilling and Drinking* (London, 2019). On reflection, the title is not very A–Z.

Chapter 1: Tea and Whisky: A Grocery Shop in Kilmarnock

1   *The Kilmarnock and Riccarton Post Office Directory 1846–1847* (Kilmarnock, 1846), p. v
2   DA, JW 1819 'Inventory'
3   William Scott Douglas, *In Ayrshire: a descriptive picture of the County of Ayr* (Kilmarnock, 1872), p. 42
4   Scott Douglas, *In Ayrshire*, p. 42
5   Alexander Mackay, *History of Kilmarnock* (Kilmarnock, 1858), pp. 161–9
6   Mackay, *History of Kilmarnock*, p. 172
7   *The New Statistical Account of Scotland* (Edinburgh, 1834–45), pp. 537–8, p. 554
8   'I am sending you a small Kilmarnock prize cheese this afternoon as a Christmas present,' wrote Alexander Walker to Robert Hendry at Christmas 1886. DA, JW&S Letter Book A11/3, p. 172, AW to Robert Hendry, 15.12.86. See also *Brief Historical Reminiscences of . . . Ayr* (Scottish Post Office Directories, Ayr, 1830), p. 53; Douglas, *In Ayrshire*, pp. 40–41
9   Mackay, *History of Kilmarnock*, pp. 91–3

10 AA, Kilmarnock Burgh Town Council Minutes 1792–1824, bk 1/1/2/2, 28.7.1819
11 Mackay, *History of Kilmarnock*, pp. 185–93; AA, Kilmarnock Burgh Town Council Minutes 1792–1824, bk 1/1/2/2, 31.1.1820; 1825–43, bk 1/1/2/3, 18.8.1826; *Glasgow Herald*, 14.4.1820, 17.4.1820, 21.8.1826: 'The fear of the scarcity of meal has produced some mobbing and rioting in Kilmarnock, and five men . . . have been in consequence committed to prison.'
12 James Walker, *Old Kilmarnock* (Kilmarnock, 1895), pp. 69–70; AA, Kilmarnock Burgh Town Council Minutes 1792–1824, bk 1/1/2/2, 1.2.1820
13 *The Old Statistical Account of Scotland* (Edinburgh 1792), pp. 94–5; *New Statistical Account* (Edinburgh, 1845), p. 564; See also AA, Kilmarnock Burgh Town Council Minutes 1825–43, bk 1/1/2/3, 23.4.1832
14 T. C. Smout, *A Century of the Scottish People 1830–1950* (London, 1986), p. 133
15 David Daiches, *A Wee Dram* (London, 1990), pp. 23–5; *Scotsman*, 14.6.1823
16 Alexander Peddie, *The Hotel Inn Keeper Vintner and Spirit Dealer's Assistant* (Glasgow, 1825), p. 276
17 Peter Mackenzie, *Reminiscences of Glasgow* (Glasgow, 1866), vol. 2, pp. 429–30
18 Peddie, *The Hotel Inn Keeper*, p. 23
19 John Dunlop, *The Philosophy of Artificial and Compulsory Drinking Usage in Great Britain and Ireland* (London, 1836), p. 6, quoted in Smout, *A Century of the Scottish People*, p. 134
20 Nancy Cox, *The Complete Tradesman: A Study of Retailing 1550–1820* (Abingdon, 2016), pp. 170–76. A successful apprenticeship was also a way of developing enduring business contacts in the local community.
21 Robert Kemp Philip, *The Shopkeeper's Guide* (London, 1853), p. 33
22 Philip, *The Shopkeeper's Guide*, pp. 80–4
23 For details see, for example, William Clarke, *The Publican and Inn Keeper's Practical Guide*; and *Wine and Spirit Dealer's Director and Assistant* (London, 1830)
24 W. H. Simmonds, *The Practical Grocer* (London, 1911), vol. 1, p. 13; see Jon Stobart, *Sugar and Spice: Grocers and Groceries in Provincial England 1650–1830* (Oxford, 2013), pp. 140–64
25 Stobart, *Sugar and Spice*, p. 110–11; Hoh-Cheung Mui and Lorna H. Mui, *Shops and Shopkeeping in Eighteenth Century England* (London, 1989), p. 287
26 Mui and Mui, *Shops and Shopkeeping*, pp. 254–5
27 For a detailed description of Chinese teas, see *Tea and Tea Blending* (2nd ed., London, 1887), pp. 53–80
28 *The Tea Purchaser's Guide* (London, 1785), pp. 29–30
29 *The Tea Purchaser's Guide*, pp. 43–8, 'The Art of Mixing one quality of Tea with Another'

30 *Deadly Adulteration and Slow Poisoning Unmasked, or Disease and Death in the Pot and Bottle* (London 1839; reprinted Fairford 2016), p. 54. For tea merchants in China, see Hoh-Cheung Mui and Lorna H. Mui, *William Melrose in China: 1845–1855* (Edinburgh, 1973)

31 *The Tea Purchaser's Guide*, pp. 30–38; *Deadly Adulteration and Slow Poisoning Unmasked*, pp. 54–6

32 Mui and Mui, *Shops and Shopkeeping*, pp. 272–7; *Glasgow Herald*, 28.6.1820 and 10.12.1821, advertisements for the London Genuine Tea Company

33 DA, JW Shop Inventory 1825, p. 1; for Scottish tea trade see Mui and Mui, *Shops and Shopkeeping*, pp. 263–6

34 Mui and Mui, *William Melrose*, pp. lx–lxi

35 DA, JW Shop Inventory 1825, p. 1

36 *Caledonian Mercury*, 21.3.1805, 24.12.1808, 10.2.1820, 22.9.1821

37 *Caledonian Mercury*, 27.11.1824

38 *Scotsman*, 14.6.1823

39 *Caledonian Mercury*, 8.2.1823; *Scotsman*, 25.1.1823

40 See, for example, John M'Donald, *The Maltster, Distiller, and Spirit Dealer's Companion* (Elgin, 1828), passim.

41 Evidence of James Mackinlay, *Royal Commission on Whisky and Other Potable Spirits, Minutes of Evidence* (London, 1908), p. 237

42 Peddie, *The Hotel Inn Keeper*, pp. 280–93

43 *Tea and Tea Blending*, p. 119

44 Simmonds, *The Practical Grocer*, vol. 11, pp. 52–3

45 Scotland's Places *Shop Tax, 1785–1789*, vol. 3

46 J. F. T. Thomson, 'John Walker 1805–1857', typescript notes, East Ayrshire Central Library, the Dick Institute, Kilmarnock

47 NRS VR004600001/60, 1855, Kilmarnock Burgh, p. 60

48 James Walker, *Old Kilmarnock* (Kilmarnock, 1895), pp. 38–42; Grocers were 'firmly tied into polite lifestyles and consumption practices, their shops as well as their wares being set alongside other makers of domestic sociability: the china dealer, toy shop, draper and upholsterer.' Stobart, *Sugar and Spice*, p. 111

49 Walker, *Old Kilmarnock*, pp. 10, 13; AA, bk 1/1/2A/1/2, 1828–1849, Kilmarnock Police Commissioner Minute Book, 6.5.1835

50 DA, JW Shop Inventory 1825, p. 3; George B. Wilson, *Alcohol and the Nation: A Contribution to the Study of the Liquor Problem in the United Kingdom from 1800–1935* (London, 1940), pp. 118–19. The act 'clearly separated retail liquor licences into two main classes – "on" and "off" – and provided that publicans should not sell groceries and that grocers should not sell liquor for on-consumption'.

51 See, for example, NLS, handbill of Montgomery, Confectioner and Grocer, 30 Princes Street, Edinburgh (William Aitken, 1820)

52 *Kilmarnock Directory for 1833*, compiled by William Brown (Kilmarnock, 1833), photocopy in the Burns Monument Centre, Kilmarnock

53 Walker, *Old Kilmarnock*, pp. 36–7

54 *Kilmarnock and Riccarton Post Office Directory, 1846–1847*, Advertisements pp. 3–4; *Ayrshire Directory 1851–1852*, p. 30, p. 67

55 Walker, *Old Kilmarnock*, pp. 32–6; *Glasgow Herald*, 10.10.1873; *Ardrossan & Saltcoats Herald*, 11.10.1873

56 I. G. C. Hutchison, *A Political History of Scotland 1832–1924* (Edinburgh, 1986), pp. 3–4

57 AA, bk 9/1, 1833–1875, 'List of Burgh Voters in Kilmarnock'

58 Walker, *Old Kilmarnock*, p. 10

59 *Scotland's Places: Ayrshire OS Name Books 1855–1857*, vol. 34, OS1/3/34/11

60 NRS VR004600001/102, Kilmarnock Burgh, 1855, p. 102; NRS Census 597/2/30, 1851, p. 30

61 Before setting out on his fateful Mediterranean cruise in the spring of 1889 Alexander Walker wrote: 'You might also ask him what clothes he thinks I should take. My opinion is that a tweed suit and a blue serge one would be sufficient as I would not care to take a dress suit.' DA, JW&S Letter Book A11/5, p. 169, AW to Blaikie, 4.2.1889

62 *New Statistical Account*, pp. 546–7, 551–2

63 *North British Daily Mail*, 10.3.1848, 5.5.1848; Kilmarnock Burgh Town Council Minutes, 1843–1865, bk 1/1/2/4, 7.4.1848

64 Mackay, *History of Kilmarnock*, pp. 256–7

65 *Kilmarnock and Riccarton Post Office Directory, 1846–1847*, pp. 10–11; *Ayrshire Directory 1851–1852*, pp. 14

66 DA, JW&S Annual Balances 1857–86, p. 3

67 Mackay, *History of Kilmarnock*, pp. 241–55

68 *Kilmarnock Standard*, 16.5.1903

69 DA, JW&S Annual Balances 1857–86, pp. 1–2

70 NRS SC6/44/24, Ayr Sheriff Court, pp. 949–54

71 That is, stored in a government certified warehouse free of duty charges, which were only imposed when the goods were taken 'out of bond' for sale or blending.

72 DA, JW&S Annual Balances 1857–86, pp. 1–15

73 NRS SC6/44/24, Ayr Sheriff Court, pp. 945–9

Chapter 2: A 'Great Gulf Stream of Toddy'

1 *Ayrshire Express*, 13.11.1863

2   DA, JW&S Letter Book A11/3, p. 71, AW to Blaikie, 20.7.86

3   DA, JW&S Letter Book A11/5, p. 166, AW to Blaikie, 1.2.1889: 'I have been a little seedy for two days and was not at business yesterday. I got a bit of a tooth extracted last week and rarely got any sleep for two or three nights … the weather here at present is very disgusting more especially [for] mercurial temperaments like mine.'

4   DA, JW&S Letter Book A11/3, p. 27, AW to Blaikie, 6.11.1888

5   NRS SC6/44/24, Ayr Sheriff Court, Will and Inventory of John Walker, 28.11.1857

6   John was fourteen years old. NRS, Census 597/2/5, 1861, p. 5; 644/64/13, 1861, p. 18

7   DA, JW&S, A12/1, Annual Balances 1857–1886; *Edinburgh Gazette*, 25.8.1865; NRS Valuation Rolls VR004600011/78, Kilmarnock Burgh. It has not been possible to establish exactly when Robert Walker travelled to Australia.

8   DA, JW&S, A12/1, Annual Balances 1857–1886, between balances for 1864 and 1865

9   George B. Wilson, *Alcohol and the Nation* (London 1940), Tables 1, 3, 4, 9, 11 and 14, pp. 331–70. John Hume and Michael Moss, *The Making of Scotch Whisky* (Edinburgh, 2000), Table 5, p. 220; Smout, *A Century of the Scottish People*, pp. 139–44

10 Wilson, *Alcohol and the Nation*, pp. 38–40

11 Charles Tovey, *British and Foreign Spirits: their history, manufacture, properties etc.* (London, 1864), pp. 150–51

12 Tovey, *British and Foreign Spirits*, pp. 130–33; George Saintsbury, *Notes on a Cellar-Book* (London, 1978), pp. 78–9

13 *Morning Chronicle*, 10.8.1846

14 *Inverness Courier*, 22.2.1848; *Glasgow Sentinel*, 21.12.1850; *Greenock Advertiser*, 30.3.1852

15 For M'Lachlan, see *North British Daily Mail*, 16.2.1859 and 2.8.1860; *Glasgow Morning Journal*, 3.1.1862, 7.12.1865; *Glasgow Herald*, 16.12.1862; *Glasgow Evening Citizen*, 16.3.1866; *Morning Advertiser*, 8.10.1866

16 *Victualling Trades Review*, 13.7.1891

17 *Ridley and Co.'s Monthly Wine and Spirit Trade Circular*, 12.3.1921

18 DA, W. & J. Gilbey Minute Book No. 1, 26.4.1889

19 Ridley's, 12.3.1921

20 *Saturday Review*, 'Sherry Poison', 29.11.1873; see also 'Counting House Alcoholism', 15.4.1871, 'Drawing Room Alcoholism', 21.1.1871

21 Ridley's, 12.1.1886

22 Ridley's, 12.3.1887, commented on the preference trade buyers had for whiskies 'bonded in sherry-wood, the prices of which … have ruled higher than those bonded in plain casks. Despite the enormous price to which sherry casks have been driven by the demand upon a continually diminishing supply, they

still seem to be indispensable to blenders, and to do for the whisky what no substitute of added wine or colour can effect.'

23 DA, JW&S Annual Balances 1857–86, balance for 1866
24 DA, Letter Book A11/1, p. 133, AW to J. W. Teage, Oporto, 17.9.1883; p. 338, AW to Captain Lipscombe, Southsea, 2.5.1885
25 DA, JW&S Annual Balances 1857–86, balance for 1866
26 Joseph Pacey, *Reminiscences of a Gauger* (Pitlochry, 2007), p. 66
27 *Kilmarnock and Riccarton Post Office Directory 1868* and *1872* (Kilmarnock, 1867 and 1871)
28 DA, JW&S Annual Balances 1857–86
29 Douglas, *In Ayrshire*, p. 44; *Kilmarnock Standard*, 8.2.1879; *Ardrossan & Saltcoats Herald*, 23.8.1873
30 Gordon Jackson and Charles Munn, 'Trade, Commerce and Finance', in Hamish Fraser and Irene Maver (eds), *Glasgow 1820–1912* (Manchester, 1996), pp. 80–83
31 John Hume, *The Industrial Archaeology of Scotland, 1: The Lowlands and Borders* (London, 1976), pp. 61–2; 'The Architects have taken much trouble to make basically dull buildings visually attractive.', John Butt, *The Industrial Archaeology of Scotland* (Newton Abbot, 1967), p. 225
32 *Kilmarnock Standard*, 8.2.1879; *Ayr Advertiser*, 13.2.1879; DA, JW&S 257/106, 'Fire Insurance Policy Croft Street and Strand Street', 1873
33 *Ayr Advertiser*, 20.1.1881; in 1885 Alexander Walker, along with Thomas Kennedy, was lobbying for an increase in telephone provision in the town and county: DA, JW&S Letter Book A11/1, p. 356, AW to William Pollock, Ayr, 23.6.1885. The following year he installed a telephone in London Road to allow him to talk with the office, complaining that delays and 'difficulties arise in a matter of this kind where one possibly sees nine months before his neighbours', Letter Book A11/3, p. 19, AW to Blaikie, 7.4.1886. He subsequently wrote to Blaikie in London: 'Don't bother anything about the telephone for its advantages are its disadvantages': Letter Book A11/3, p. 26, AW to Blaikie, 12.4.1886
34 *Caledonian Mercury*, 26.4.1794
35 *Newcastle Courant*, 16.11.1855
36 The National Archives, 'Drawing of John Walker and Son's trademark, two squirrels supporting shield', Copy 1/26/266
37 *Trademark Journal*, 8.8.1877, p. 1344. First use was indicated as 'above 10 years before 20 June 1877'.
38 NRS, CS248–6764, closed record in suspension and interdict, John Walker & Sons against James Haddow & Company, 7.11.1882
39 DA, 259/1, JW&S London Accounts 1874–1886, 4.11.1874, John Blaikie to AW with attached stock sheet

40 *Glasgow Herald*, 15.9.1862

41 *Rothesay Chronicle*, 6.1.1875

42 DA, JW&S Letter Book A11/3, p. 10, AW to GPW, 2.4.1886

43 DA, JW&S 257/9, John Walker & Sons' London Accounts 1874–1886, 4.11.1874, Blaikie to AW; 13.2.1875, Blaikie to AW; 19.2.1876, Blaikie to AW; 14.2.1877, Blaikie to AW; 6.3.1878

44 DA, JW&S Letter Book A11/1, p. 27, AW to Blaikie, 2.5.1882

45 DA, JW&S Letter Book A11/1, p. 25, John Kilgour to Blaikie, 19.4.1882; p. 27, AW to Blaikie, 2.5.1882; p. 100, AW to Blaikie, 24.8.1883; p. 108, AW to Kilgour, 30.8.1883; p. 108, AW to Kilgour, 30.8.1883; p. 116, AW to John Piper, 4.9.1883; p. 128, AW to JW&S London, 14.9.1883; p. 136, AW to McCosh, 21.9.1883; p. 156, AW to Kilgour, 12.11.1883; p. 166, AW to Ed Upton, London, 4.12.1883; DA, JW&S 257/9, John Walker & Sons London Accounts 1874–1886, 4.11.1874; Blaikie to AW, 13.2.1875; Blaikie to AW, 23.2.1881; list of Mr Piper's customers, JW&S 257/9, 19.2.1884 London Balance

46 NRS, CS248–6764, closed record in suspension and interdict, John Walker & Sons, 7.11.1882

47 DA, JW&S Letter Book A11/2, p. 427, Blaikie to Davenport, 15.12.1887. Robert Walker, 'Merchant, Sydney', gave evidence on behalf of John Walker & Sons in the proceedings.

48 *Sydney Morning Herald*, 16.1.1832; Samuel Morewood, *A Philosophical and Statistical History of the Inventions and Customs of Ancient and Modern Nations in the Manufacture and use of Inebriating Liquors* (Dublin, 1828), pp. 258–9

49 *Sydney Morning Herald*, 3.5.1847; *The Age*, 18.7.1857

50 *Sydney Morning Herald*, 15.8.1856, 4.12.1869 and 8.8.1874

51 *Sydney Morning Herald*, 5.11.1879; *Sydney Evening News*, 28.5.1881

52 *Sydney Mail*, 24.1.1896

53 *Sydney Morning Herald*, 1.12.1879

54 Robert Walker's ill-health and semi-destitute condition, and the upbringing of his children, were a cause of constant concern for Alexander Walker, and worry for his mother. He was paid a regular allowance via Mason Brothers and may still have been working for them when able. These payments continued, as a charge against Alexander Walker's estate, until at least 1895: DA, JW&S Letter Book A11/2, p. 935, Kilgour to trustees of late A. Walker, 15.2.1895, 'payments to Robt Walker for year, £33.8/–'

55 *Bulletin*, vol. 3, 29, 14.8.1880

56 DA, JW&S Letter Book A11/1, p. 223, AW to Daniel Wilson, Sydney, 8.7.1884

57 *Sydney Morning Herald*, 6.11.1880

58 *Sydney Morning Herald*, 1.4.1881, 16.9.1881; *The Age*, 9.4.1881; *Australian Sketcher*,

9.4.1881; *Illustrated Sydney*, 9.9.1881. See also Stephen Grad and Michael Rush, *A Tyrone Lad on the Clarence* (Thirlmere, 2011), pp. 171–3

59 DA, JW&S Letter Book A11/1, p. 160, AW to Blaikie, 14.11.1883

60 *Sydney Morning Herald*, 12.12.1881

61 DA, JW&S Letter Book A11/1, p. 223, AW to Daniel Wilson, Sydney, 8.7.1884

62 DA, JW&S Letter Book A11/1, p. 160, AW to Blaikie, 14.11.1883

63 DA, JW&S Letter Book A11/1, p. 19, AW to Blaikie, 16.3.1882; p. 50, AW to Daniel Wilson, Sydney, 8.11.1882; NRS, CS248–6764, closed record in suspension and interdict, John Walker & Sons against James Haddow & Company, 7.11.1882; *Sydney Morning Herald*, 9.1.1883; *Sydney Morning Herald*, 6.5.1883

64 DA, JW&S Letter Book A11/1, p. 4, AW to James Cullen, Sydney, 4.11.1881

65 *Sydney Morning Herald*, 1.12.1879

66 DA, JW&S Letter Book A11/5, p. 94, AW to Mrs Reid, London, 25.12.1888

67 *Ardrossan & Saltcoats Herald*, 17.9.1881

68 DA, JW&S Letter Book A11/3, p. 178, AW to H. H. Norrie, Union Bank, Edinburgh, 20.12.1886

69 DA, JW&S Letter Book A11/2, p. 309, AW to James MacMurtree, Ayr, 21.4.1887; A11/1, p. 414, AW to Simpson, 1.9.1885

70 DA, JW&S Letter Book, A11/3, p. 472, AW to Mr Comrie, 30.9.1887

71 DA, JW&S Letter Book A11/1, p. 434, AW to W. A. Robertson, Glasgow, 28.9.1885; DA, A11/3, p. 438, AW to W. A. Robertson (R&B, Glasgow), 15.9.1887

72 For Alexander Walker at his misanthropic best, see DA, JW&S Letter Book A11/3, p. 19, AW to Blaikie, 7.4.1886: 'Mr Blair has gone to Glasgow today instead of me and in place of being able to attend to business in the afternoon I have a lot of friends to meet, and I presume afterwards give them dinner, which I abominably hate.'

73 DA, JW&S Letter Book A11/2, p. 603, Blaikie to AW, 25.9.1888; A11/1, p. 456, AW to Mrs McMichael, 17.11.1885

74 DA, JW&S Letter Book A11/1, p. 100, AW to Blaikie, 24.8.1883; A11/1, p. 483, AW to James Calder, 6.1.1886; A11/1, p. 94, AW to Mrs Reid, London, 25.12.1888

Chapter 3: 'Our Blend Cannot Be Beat'

1 Evidence of James Mackinlay, *Royal Commission on Whisky*, p. 238

2 DA, JW&S Letter Book A11/1, p. 317, JW&S to Messrs A. Wool [?] & Sons, Glasgow, 20.3.1885

3 DA, JW&S Letter Book A11/1, p. 147, AW to James Cullen, Sydney, 27.10.1883; p. 446, AW to Kirkland, 28.10.1885; p. 473, AW to Kirkland, 22.12.1885

4 AW wrote thus of Lipscombe: 'I need not tell you how sad I feel and don't know

what to do as I have all along been looking forward to the assistance of one in whom I had the greatest possible confidence, and during his 12 years with me I don't think I ever once had to say an angry word to him, neither did I ever hear his name mentioned in public as having done anything stupid or wrong.' DA, JW&S Letter Book A11/1, p. 417, AW to Blaikie, 1.9.1885

5   DA, JW&S Letter Book A11/2, p. 844, Blaikie to Lipscombe, 30.7.1889
6   'Mr Walker wired twice today requesting Mr John the first if he could be spared to send him down at once and intimating that they leave Troon on Friday, the second twenty minutes later, to the effect that Mr John now to come down tonight Pullman car and Mr Walker would see him at Troon tomorrow. Mr Walker left for his shootings immediately after and asked me to repeat your reply to him at Dalry but up to this hour I have no wire from you. Mr Walker wished John down here at once and he will have a long talk with him before he goes up to London. Mr Walker intends sending Mr George up to take Mr John's place until such time as Mr John recovers from his present indisposition.' DA, JW&S Letter Book A11/1, p. 47, Kilgour to Blaikie, 30.9.1882
7   DA, JW&S Letter Book A11/1, p. 122, AW to Andrew Stewart, Glasgow, 6.9.1883; p. 113, AW to James Cullen, Sydney, 4.9.1883
8   DA, JW&S Letter Book A11/1, p. 66, AW to Blaikie, 12.4.1883
9   DA, JW&S Letter Book A11/1, p. 191, AW to Daniel Wilson, Sydney, 12.5.1884; *Edinburgh Evening News*, 22.4.1884
10   *Table Talk*, 29.10.1886; *The Herald*, 3.9.1887; DA, JW&S Letter Book A11/3, p. 323, AW to Kilgour, 2.5.1887; p. 326, AW to Kilgour, 4.5.1887
11   For these proposed investments see DA, JW&S Letter Book A11/3, p. 449, AW to Jack Walker, 20.9.1887; p. 466, AW to Jack Walker, 26.9.1887
12   DA, JW&S Letter Book A11/3, p. 464, AW to Blaikie, 26.9.1887
13   DA, JW&S Letter Book A11/1, p. 47, Kilgour to Blaikie, 30.9.1882; p. 445, AW to Mrs Arnot, 28.10.1885; p. 446, AW to Kirkland, 28.10.1885; p. 426, AW to Blaikie, 22.9.1885: 'I yesterday made arrangements that Mr James Blair of Rankin & Co come into this firm. He is simply in Mr Lipscombe's place and I have an idea that his being here will give me a great deal less to do. No doubt when it comes out it will be a sad blow to Rankin & Co but it is no part of my seeking, as Mr Blair gave notice two months ago that at the end of six months he would no longer remain in the Firm. I understand he is a good buyer and a very steady fellow, and we must just hope for the best.'
14   DA, JW&S Letter Book A11/3, p. 434, AW to Davenport, 14.9.1887
15   *Kilmarnock and Riccarton Post Office Directory 1868*, advertisements, p. 11; NRS, Census 1871, 597/2/2, p. 2; DA, JW&S Letter Book A11/1, p. 108, AW to Kilgour, 30.8.1883

16 DA, JW&S Minute Book No. 1, 15.12.1886 and 4.7.1890

17 DA, JW&S Letter Book A11/2, p. 569, Blaikie to GPW, 15.8.1888; A11/1, p. 509, AW to Blaikie, 16.3.1886; p. 520, AW to Blaikie, 22.3.1886. For all this, few doubted his contribution to the firm. 'Hodge is very much interested in the success of the business and has shown ability and energy in the prosecution of it,' wrote Blair (A11/2, p. 8, Blair to Jack Walker, 1.4.1886). Alexander Walker wrote to Blaikie in November 1886 when Hodge was again unwell: 'You will now understand the necessity of having some one else besides Mr Hodge as I could not help being impressed with the fact that he was working too hard.' A11/3, p. 156, AW to Blaikie, 12.11.1886

18 DA, JW&S Letter Book A11/3, p. 29, AW to Blaikie, 19.4.1886; p. 235, AW to Kilgour, 18.1.1887

19 DA, JW&S Letter Book A11/1, p. 100, AW to Blaikie, 24.8.1883; p. 293, AW to Mr K. D. Dunlop, America, 2.2.1885

20 *Kilmarnock and Riccarton Directory 1872*; NRS, SC6/44/38, Ayr Sheriff Court, Samuel Dunlop Inventory, 24.3.1875; SC6/46/10, Ayr Sheriff Court, Samuel Dunlop Will, 24.3.1875

21 DA, JW&S Letter Book A11/3, p. 320, AW to JW&S London, 29.4.1887; A11/3, p. 336, AW to Blaikie, 16.5.1887; p. 337, AW to John Dunlop, 16.5.1887; A11/2, p. 272, Blaikie to AW, 2.7.1887; A11/3, p. 389, AW to Blaikie, 4.7.1887; A11/3, p. 398, AW to Kirkland, 20.7.1887. Alexander Walker had learned his lesson and determined to be more firm with other personal debtors: 'I have made up my mind to put the whole of my private a/cs into the hands of Mr McCosh, Dalry. I merely warn you of this as you must make some arrangement as to what you owe me. I am determined to know the best or worst of my private affairs, and I think you cannot blame me.' A11/3, p. 393, AW to W. G. Walker, Ayr, 19.7.1887

22 'I have never yet been connected with any concern which could not bear the strictest investigation and I should not like this paltry thing to be a stain on my name as a Director in a Company where I feel I am so far from close connection with the man at the wheel.' DA, A11/5, p. 76, AW to Blaikie, 19.12.1888

23 DA, JW&S Letter Book A11/1, p. 50, AW to Daniel Wilson, Sydney, 8.11.1882

24 DA, JW&S Letter Book A11/5, p. 213, AW to Blaikie, 16.4.1889; A11/2, p. 308, Blaikie to AW, 3.9.1887; A11/2, p. 219, AW to David Wilson, Sydney, 2.2.1887

25 DA, JW&S Letter Book A11/5, p. 76, AW to Blaikie, 19.12.1888

26 DA, JW&S Letter Book A11/1, p. 222, Blaikie to Wilson, 9.2.1887; p. 835, Blaikie to Jack Walker, 7.6.1889. Mason Brothers were desperately trying to sell the Camdenville Foundry as a going concern (*Sydney Morning Herald*, 17.8.1888).

27 DA, JW&S Letter Book A11/3, p. 53, AW to Blaikie, 11.6.1886; A11/2, p. 595, Blaikie to AW, 13.9.1888

28 DA, JW&S Letter Book A11/3, p. 222, AW to Kirkland, 13.1.1887; p. 410, AW to Blaikie, 29.4.1887

29 DA, JW&S Letter Book A11/5, p. 14, 'Copy of letter sent by Mr A. Walker to Mr D. Wilson, dated 25/10/1888 but not sent till 2/11/1888'

30 DA, JW&S Letter Book A11/2, p. 578, Blaikie to AW, 25.8.1888; p. 603, Blaikie to AW, 25.9.1888

31 DA, JW&S Letter Book A11/5, p. 14, 'Copy of letter sent by Mr A. Walker to Mr D. Wilson, dated 25/10/1888 but not sent till 2/11/1888'; A11/2, p. 835, Blaikie to Jack Walker, 7.6.1889; A11/5, p. 223, AW to Mrs Shearlaw, Linlithgow, 14.5.1889. Shareholders included not just the great and good of Kilmarnock, but even the likes of Homewood, 'one of the conductors of the Pullman Cars . . . [who] is anxious to get rid of his shares in Mason Brothers as he is obliged to assist his father in getting a farm'. A11/3, p. 100, AW to James Smith, Mason Brothers, London, 11.9.1886

32 DA, JW&S Letter Book A11/1, p. 219, AW to Jack Walker, London, 4.7.1884; JW&S Minute Book No. 1, 15.12.1886

33 *Mercantile Gazette*, 6.1.1870. Mackie, Dunn & Co reported 'that diamonds continue to arrive by every post from the frontier'.

34 DA, JW&S Letter Book A11/2, p. 347, AW to JW&S London, 28.5.1887; *Ardrossan & Saltcoats Herald*, 1.6.1910, obituary of David Sneddon; A11/2, p. 280, Blaikie to AW, 21.7.1887: 'We have had Mr Sneddon with us today and had the Cape business pretty well discussed.'

35 DA, JW&S Letter Book A11/2, p. 533, Blaikie to Rolfes Nobel & Co., 12.6.1888; p. 847, Blaikie to Blair, 24.10.1889

36 DA, JW&S Letter Book A11/2, p. 27, Blaikie to AW, 27.11.1884; p. 646, Blaikie to Jack Walker, 2.11.1888; p. 455, Blaikie to Wilson, 13.1.1888; p. 866, Advertising Expenditure May 1890

37 DA, JW&S Letter Book A11/2, p. 751, Blaikie to Gibbs, Bright & Co., Melbourne, 25.1.1889; p. 764, Blaikie to Jack Walker, 1.2.1889

38 DA, JW&S Letter Book A11/2, p. 72, Blaikie to AW, 17.3.1886; p. 131, Kilgour to AW, 12.7.1886

39 DA, JW&S Letter Book A11/1, p. 82, AW to Blaikie, 13.7.1883; A11/3, p. 302, AW to Blaikie, 20.4.1887

40 DA, JW&S Letter Book A11/1, p. 185, AW to J. Wilson Reid, London, 'Confidential', 22.3.1884

41 DA, JW&S Letter Book A11/3, p. 78, AW to Blaikie, 29.7.1886; p. 93, AW to Dr J. H. Stoddart, Glasgow, 30.8.1886; p. 95, AW to Thomas Inglis, 2.9.1886; A11/2, p. 144, Blaikie to AW, 4.8.1886; p. 146, Blaikie to AW, 5.8.1886; p. 153, Blaikie to Wilson, 10.9.1886

42 *Saturday Review*, 12.4.1874; Peter H. Hoffenberg, *An Empire on Display* (London, 2001), pp. 279–80

43 *Saturday Review*, 20.7.1872; 'Far from the world being enamoured of exhibitions, it is dead sick of them. There have been too many Exhibitions. And while it is possible to have too much of a good thing Exhibitions are among the good things that those who have had too much of them absolutely detest.' *Saturday Review*, 2.12.1876. See also Ridley's *Monthly Wine and Spirit Trade Circular*, 8.6.1911: 'How to obtain a gold medal'

44 *Sydney Morning Herald*, 21.4.1880 and 29.7.1880; *The Age*, 14.5.1881

45 DA, JW&S Letter Book A11/1, p. 453, AW to John Dunlop, Paris, 16.11.1885

46 DA, JW&S Letter Book A11/2, p. 335, Blaikie to AW, 23.9.1887; A11/3, p. 464, AW to Blaikie, 26.9.1887; p. 473, AW to Blaikie, 30.9.1887; p. 458, AW to Sanderson, 23.9.1887

47 DA, JW&S Letter Book A11/1, p. 4, AW to James Cullen, Sydney, 4.11.1881

48 DA, JW&S Letter Book A11/1, p. 147, AW to James Cullen, Sydney, 27.10.1883

49 DA, JW&S Letter Book A11/3, p. 473, AW to Blaikie, 28.9.1887 and 30.9.1887

50 DA, JW&S Letter Book A11/3, p. 402, AW to Cullen, 20.7.1887

51 DA, JW&S Letter Book A11/1, p. 223, AW to Daniel Wilson, Sydney, 8.7.1884; p. 414, AW to Simpson, 1.9.1885

52 DA, JW&S Letter Book A11/3, p. 131, AW to Blaikie, 26.10.1886

53 DA, JW&S Letter Book A11/2, p. 455, Blaikie to Wilson, 13.1.1888

54 DA, JW&S Letter Book A11/2, p. 648, Blaikie to AW, 3.11.1888; A11/5, p. 23, AW to Blaikie, 5.11.1888

55 DA, JW&S Letter Book A11/5, p. 141, AW to Blaikie, 22.1.1889; A11/2, p. 753, Blaikie to AW, 25.1.1889; p. 751, Blaikie to Gibbs, Bright & Co., Melbourne, 25.1.1889

56 DA, JW&S Letter Book A11/2, p. 166, Blaikie to GPW, 8.10.1886

57 DA, JW&S Letter Book A11/3, p. 123, AW to Blaikie, 15.10.1886

58 DA, JW&S Letter Book A11/3, p. 201, AW to the Midland Hotel, 31.12.1886; p. 208, AW to Blaikie, 7.1.1887

59 DA, JW&S Letter Book A11/3, p. 115, AW to Blaikie, 11.10.1886, 'Confidential'; James Walker, *Old Kilmarnock* (Kilmarnock, 1895), p. 32. Alexander Walker wrote to Mrs Rankin: 'I hope you will have no reason to regret the association of the respectable old firm of William Rankin & Son with that of John Walker & Sons. I may say that there is no desire on my part for the amalgamation, the idea originated with Mr Blair who I assure you wishes you to obtain all the benefits he can arrange for, and I trust that these may be such as to make the change in every way satisfactory to you.' A11/3, p. 335, AW to Mrs Rankin, 16.5.1887

60 DA, JW&S Minute Book No. 1, 23.11.1886; A11/3, p. 197, AW to Blaikie, 29.12.1886

61 DA, JW&S Letter Book A11/3, p. 121, AW to William Calder, 12.10.1886. Alexander's son George was to marry Calder's daughter, Helen, in 1891.

62 DA, JW&S Letter Book A11/3, p. 341, AW to Kirkland, 19.5.1887; p. 384, AW to George Lipscombe, 27.6.1887. The Letter Books record ever more frequent visits to hydropathic hotels and spa resorts in both England and Scotland.

63 DA, JW&S Letter Book A11/3, p. 394, AW to Blaikie, 19.7.1887

64 DA, JW&S Letter Book A11/1, p. 459, AW to Blaikie, 25.11.1885; 'Yours to hand with plan of the Ceylon [a boat]. I cannot possibly make up my mind what to do. I am of opinion that I shall feel so much better for being at Matlock that I think I shall abandon the Ceylon trip. However I think I shall be in London next week and shall then decide; and if spared it is a cruise I could possibly take at some other time.' A11/1, p. 486, AW to Blaikie, 9.1.1886. In September 1887 AW wrote to his friend Turner: 'I have been away in Ireland for ten days wanting to get rid of everything and really forget whether I replied to yours of 19th . . . my wife and I have had a fine trip on the lakes of Killarney and elsewhere in Ireland.' A11/3, p. 417, AW to F. J. Turner, Mansfield, 1.9.1887

65 DA, JW&S Letter Book A11/3, p. 87, AW to Blaikie, 11.8.1886

66 DA, JW&S Letter Book A11/3, p. 15, AW to Mr Campbell, 6.4.1886

67 'I have made up my mind that the Bay of Biscay shall never see me again.' DA, JW&S Letter Book A11/5, p. 66, AW to Andrew Stewart, Glasgow, 11.12.1888; p. 98, AW to Blaikie, 2.1.1889; p. 196, AW to Andrew Stewart, 3.4.1889; p. 211, AW to Dr Turner, Gibraltar, 8.4.1889; p. 239, AW to Dr Turner, Gibraltar, 27.5.1889; A11/2, p. 774, Blaikie to Jack Walker, 1.3.1889

68 DA, JW&S Letter Book A11/5, p. 198, AW to GPW, 4.4.1889

69 DA, JW&S Letter Book A11/5, p. 258, AW to Jack Walker, 14.6.1889; p. 160, AW to John Erskine Esq., Glasgow, 26.1.1889; p. 183, AW to J. D. Thomson Esq., Kingencleuch, Mauchline, 15.2.1889; p. 184, AW to John Erskine Esq., Glasgow, 15.2.1889. The scheme was abandoned soon after Alexander's death.

70 DA, JW&S Letter Book A11/5, p. 271, AW to GPW, 9.7.1889

71 DA, JW&S Letter Book A11/2, p. 774, Blaikie to Jack Walker, 1.3.1889

72 *Kilmarnock Standard*, 20.7.1889

Chapter 4: Modern Times

1 Evidence of James Greenlees, *Royal Commission on Whisky and other Potable Spirits, Minutes of Evidence* (London, 1908), p. 205

2 Evidence of John Ross, *Report from the Select Committee on British and Foreign Spirits with Minutes of Evidence* (London, 1891), p. 18; *Brewer's Gazette*, 16.2.1911

3 'In 1873, the halcyon days of the sherry trade, the quantity cleared for home consumption amounted to 6,034,494 gallons, and this has now fallen to 2,964,494

– yet this altered state of things is due more to fashion and medical nostrums than to any real cause.' Ridley's *Monthly Wine and Spirit Trade Circular*, 12.1.1885

4   *Sporting Life*, 13.8.1890; *Sportsman*, 8.11.1890; evidence of James Greenlees, *Royal Commission on Whisky*, p. 203–204; Ridley's, 9.4.1907

5   Ridley's, 12.12.1890

6   *British Medical Journal*, quoted in an advert for W. & A. Gilbey's Castle Grand whisky in the *Eastbourne Gazette*, 5.7.1882. Although always urging moderate consumption, the medical profession was nonetheless critical in shaping popular tastes for alcoholic beverages in the nineteenth century.

7   Evidence of Andrew Drysdale, *Select Committee on British and Foreign Spirits*, p. 29

8   Evidence of James Greenlees, *Select Committee on British and Foreign Spirits*, p. 63

9   Ridley's, 12.9.1890

10 Evidence of James Greenlees, *Royal Commission on Whisky*, p. 213

11 'High ball' starts appearing in newspaper advertisements and columns in the United States around 1894 (e.g., *Minneapolis Star Tribune*, 10.12.1893). In 1898 the *North British Daily Mail* wrote that 'a Scotch high ball is the latest popular mixed drink in St Louis', *North British Daily Mail*, 19.4.1898

12 *Times of India*, 30.5.1885; *Kendal Mercury*, 27.8.1880

13 *Illustrated London News*, 27.7.1889; *Leeds Mercury*, 21.5.1890

14 *Illustrated London News*, 14.10.1893, 'What is Rosbach and Whisky?'

15 *Sportsman*, 10.12.1890

16 *Standard*, 5.6.1890

17 *The Times*, 8.3.1861; *Wine & Spirit Trade Record*, 1.10.1898

18 For visits to Mr and Mrs Begg, see *Illustrated London News*, 4.10.1873, 23.10.1880 and 12.11.1881; *Lady's Own Paper*, 11.4.1848; *Aris's Birmingham Gazette*, 11.12.1848; *The Era*, 24.12.1848

19 *Wine & Spirit Trade Record*, 1.10.1898; 'I wished [Gladstone] to reduce the duty on whisky,' wrote Begg in his diary, 'saying it would be a great boon to the trade, but he would not as he wished to encourage the sale of French cheap wine.'

20 NRS, SC6/44/50, 'Inventory of Alexander Walker', 17.7.1889; SC6/46/20, 'Will of Alexander Walker', 10.9.1889

21 For Jack Walker's debts to his father, see NRS, SC6/44/50, 'Inventory of Alexander Walker', 17.7.1889; DA, JW&S Letter Book A11/2, p. 771, Blaikie to Jack Walker, 15.2.1889; p. 786, Blaikie to Jack Walker, 29.3.1889

22 DA, JW&S Letter Book A11/1, p. 223, AW to Daniel Wilson, Sydney, 8.7.1884; p. 255, AW to Blaikie, 27.10.1884; p. 255, AW to Blaikie, 29.10.1884; Letter Book A11/2, p. 969, Kilgour to Blaikie, 17.4.1896

23 DA, JW&S Letter Book A11/2, p. 870, Blaikie to Blair, 6.6.1890; p. 847, Blaikie to Blair, 24.10.1889

24 DA, JW&S Letter Book A11/5, p. 283, Thomas Kennedy to Messrs J. Copeland & Co., Engineers, Glasgow, 24.3.1890. In addition to Kennedy the trustees were: banker David Gairdner, accountant John Easton, William Robertson of Robertson & Baxter, and Jack and George Walker.

25 Alexander Mackay, *History of Kilmarnock* (Kilmarnock, 1858), p. 333; AA, Kilmarnock Dean of Guild Court Minute Book, 3/1/1, 1879–1893, 13.5.1889; DA, Letter Book A11/2, p. 847, Blaikie to Blair, 24.10.1889

26 DA, JW&S Letter Book A11/2, p. 859, Blaikie to Blair, 2.12.1889 and 5.12.1889

27 AA, Kilmarnock Dean of Guild Court Minute Book, 3/1/1, 1879–1893, 25.11.1890 and 20.4.1891

28 DA, JW&S Minute Book No. 1, 24.6.1891 and 18.6.1892

29 Alfred Barnard, *John Walker & Sons, Brokers, Wholesale Blenders and Exporters* (London, 1893), passim; *Victualling Trades Review*, April 1896, p. 79, 'Walker & Sons Distillery Kilmarnock: a gigantic concern'; *The Bulletin*, 15.9.1894, wrote: 'The famous whisky-distilling firm of John Walker and Sons, Limited, have issued a beautifully bound illustrated pamphlet, describing their distilleries and offices at Kilmarnock, Cardow, Arran and London. The author of the little work is Mr Alfred Barnard, writer of "The Whisky Distilleries of the United Kingdom", and apart from the mere advertisement, the brochure tells an interesting narrative of the rise and progress of the great business concern, and of distilleries which are not only themselves historical, but which have been immortalised by Robert Burns.'

30 *Report from the Select Committee on British and Foreign Spirits with Minutes of Evidence* (London, 1891), p. 65

31 Ridley's, 12.12.1883

32 DA, JW&S, A1/19, Bills Payable 1881–1896

33 *DCL Gazette*, April 1930, p. 61. He also received a 'technical grounding' from Robertson & Baxter.

34 Evidence of Alex Walker, *Royal Commission on Whisky*, p. 225

35 DA, JW&S Minute Book No. 1, 24.6.1891, 2.12.1892 and 23.6.1893

36 Brian Spiller, *Cardhu: The World of Malt Whisky* (London, 1985), pp. 9–20; see also Alfred Barnard, *John Walker & Sons, Brokers, Wholesale Blenders and Exporters* (London, 1893), pp. 57–67; information supplied to the author by Ronnie Cox

37 Spiller, *Cardhu*, pp. 21–6; Alfred Barnard, *Whisky Distilleries of the United Kingdom* (Newton Abbott, 1969 reprint), pp. 211–12

38 Spiller, *Cardhu*, pp. 27–34; DA, JW&S Minute Book No. 1, 19.9.1893

39   DA, JW&S Minute Book No. 1, 9.12.1893. Alex Walker also acquired shares in Ardgowan distillery on behalf of the company: DA, JW&S Minute Book, 11.9.1896

40   Ridley's, 12.8.1887, 12.9.1887, 12.10.1887 and 12.1.1888; DA, JW&S Letter Book A11/1, p. 147, AW to James Cullen, Sydney, 27.10.1883

41   DA, JW&S Minute Book No. 1, 3.12.1888; Ridley's, 12.1.1888

42   'The Pattison "Smash": a number of wholesale traders in Glasgow who were interviewed all agree in believing that the troubles of the firm were caused by too lavish expenditure in the pushing of their business. This expenditure was absorbed chiefly in unusual methods of advertising. Not only did the firm advertise extensively in all kinds of newspapers and magazines; Pattison placards were familiar on street hoardings and at railway stations all over the kingdom. It was, indeed, carried to extraordinary lengths; an advertisement even floats on top of the Himalayan mountains.' *Wine & Spirit Trade Record*, 2.1.1899; Hume and Moss, *The Making of Scotch Whisky*, pp. 125–7

43   *Victualling Trade Review*, 15.11.1899

44   DA, JW&S 257/9, 'London Stock', 1.2.1876

45   DA, JW&S Letter Book A11/1, p. 223, AW to Daniel Wilson, Sydney, 8.7.1884; *Sydney Morning Herald*, 4.1.1879; DA, JW&S 257/9, 'London Stock', 12.2.1880, 23.2.1881

46   DA, JW&S 257/9, 'London Stock', 1.2.1876, 12.2.1880, 23.2.1881

47   DA, JW&S Letter Book A11/3, p. 197, AW to Blaikie, 29.12.86; p. 205, GPW to Blaikie, 4.1.1887; p. 267, AW to JW&S London, 14.3.1887. 'It is most unfortunate that my ideas about bottling in squares should have come so true. A larger and more profitable trade could have been done if my wishes had been carried out at first. This leads me on to reflect on the management of the London business which I will not allude to further in the meantime, but I'm sorry to say it causes me considerable anxiety.' p. 234, AW to Blaikie, 18.1.1887

48   DA, JW&S Letter Book A11/2, p. 648, Blaikie to AW, 3.11.1888; A11/3, p. 23, AW to Blaikie, 5.11.1888; A11/2, p. 654A, Blaikie to AW, 6.11.1888

49   *Sydney Morning Herald*, 21.4.1894, 11.10.1894; *The Bulletin*, 1.12.1894

50   DA, JW&S Sample Book Price Lists 1906–1933

51   'Rankin's Kilmarnock Whisky – this is the celebrated Square Whisky', *Rockhampton Morning Bulletin*, 24.10.1881; *Pacific Commercial Advertiser*, 22.7.1882; *Rockhampton Morning Bulletin*, 22.3.1902

52   DA, JW&S Letter Book A11/2, p. 557, Kilgour to Johnstone Sadler & Co., London, 9.7.1888; p. 878, GPW to Johnstone Sadler & Co., 1890; DA, JW&S Minute Book No. 1 1886–1920, 8.1.1912

53   DA, JW&S Minute Book No. 1 1886–1920, 30.6.1898

54   On London whisky: Ridley's, 12.7.1887; *Sporting Life*, 29.11.1889; *Sportsman*, 14.5.1890; *Illustrated London News*, 5.10.1895. 'For us to supply these large

holders of "pubs" would just be ruinous.' DA, JW&S Letter Book A11/3, p. 309, GPW to Blaikie, 19.4.1887. On loans to licensees, see DA, JW&S Minute Book No. 1 1886–1920, 24.4.1909

55 Evidence of Alex Walker, *Royal Commission on Whisky*, p. 227

56 DA, JW&S, AW's blending notebook; *Royal Commission on Whisky*, p. 204; Ridley's of 9.4.1907 reported: 'Blenders are not dumping together their blends just prior to sale or bottling as of yore. They are blending Whiskies in classes, Highlands, Islays, Lowlands, Campbeltown, Grains, and from these vatted categories making up the final vat which reached the public lips. This mode is greatly to the advantage of quality, both as to homogeneity of style and uniformity. Indeed the more we look into the inwardness of the Scotch Whisky Trade, the more one is struck with the advances in all means which provide satisfactory quality and maturity for the public.'

57 Evidence of Alexander Walker, *Royal Commission on Whisky*, pp. 224–5

58 Barnard, *John Walker & Sons*, pp. 53, 85; Evidence of James Greenlees, *Royal Commission on Whisky*, p. 213

Chapter 5: The Triumph of Blended Scotch Whisky

1 *Wine & Spirit Trade Record*, 8.6.1907, 'The Sign of the Time'

2 *Advertising World*, March 1911, p. 300

3 'I attribute it [the growth of blended Scotch Whisky] to advertisements, to a large extent. It has been advertised to a perfectly extraordinary extent, and everybody knows how it has been advertised, through London even, with those electric lighted things which go up and down. You see them in the Strand, and everywhere. People do not know what Scotch whisky to get, and these are largely advertised, under highly respectable and well known names, and I think they are sold on the strength of those names.' Evidence of Arthur Brammall, *Royal Commission on Whisky and other Potable Spirits, Minutes of Evidence* (London, 1908), p. 29

4 *Printers' Ink*, 18.8.1909, 'The Diffident Distiller. Keeping the word whisky off the billboards'

5 *Wine and Spirit Trade Gazette*, 1.8.1899

6 *Singapore Free Press and Mercantile Advertiser*, 13.7.1899

7 *Wine and Spirit Trade Gazette*, 8.1.1905

8 *Graphic*, 3.3.1900; Ridley's, 12.2.1904

9 *The Sportsman*, 14.2.1900; see also *Wine and Spirit Trade Record*, 2.9.1901: 'Tell a woman that it will improve her complexion, beautify her figure, and reduce

her weight to drink water, and she will meekly become a water drinker. Tell her that whisky will make her fat and bring out spots, and she will never touch another drop.'

10   *Reporter*, 16.12.1899

11   *Globe*, 30.1.1899; *Daily Telegraph*, 22.1.1900, 4.5.1900

12   *Illustrated Police Budget*, 30/12/1899

13   *Morning Post*, 25.12.1899; *Daily Telegraph*, 5.1.1900

14   *Graphic*, 6.10.1900

15   *The Era*, 30.12.1899

16   *Norfolk News Sheet*, 23.12.1899

17   'I attribute the necessity for blending, in the first instance, to the fact that it is impossible to make whisky in a pot still without getting too much flavour . . . the grain whisky . . . may be admixed in order to bring down the flavour to a certain extent and keep it within popular taste. That, of course, has gone on increasing as the popular taste has gone to lighter articles.' Evidence of Alexander Walker, *Royal Commission on Whisky*, p. 225

18   Ridley's, 12.5.1886. 'Glenlivet' was used throughout the industry at the time as a generic description for Highland, and more particularly Speyside, whiskies.

19   Ridley's, 8.5.1908

20   Ridley's, 12.8.1887

21   *Harper's Wine & Spirits Trade Gazette*, 29.6.1889

22   *Wine & Spirit Trade Record*, 8.3.1910

23   'Proprietary brands and the wine merchant', *Victualling Trades Review*, March 1932, pp. 182–6. See also 'Whiskies bulk and proprietary', *Wine & Spirit Trade Record*, 8.5.1905

24   For an account of the Gilbey business, see Jane Kidd, *Gilbeys, Wine and Horses* (Cambridge, 1997)

25   DA, W. & J. Gilbey Minute Book No. 4, 10.6.1901, 8.7.1901

26   For the Pattison Brothers, see R. B. Weir, *The History of the Distillers Company 1877–1939* (Oxford, 1995), pp. 106–20. Both brothers were found guilty and imprisoned.

27   See, for example, *The Lancet*, 21.2.1903, pp. 542–3; 21.3.1903, pp. 820–21; 2.5.1903, pp. 1254–5

28   *Victualling Trades Review*, July 1896, p. 137

29   *Printers' Ink*, 22.12.1909

30   *Evening Standard*'s series 'A Nation's Drink' by 'The Expert' first appeared on 18.2.1905. Gilbey's interest in the outcome of the affair was so great that Arthur Gold maintained a series of scrapbooks of relevant cuttings, and the company

special files, not all of which appear to have survived. DA, W. & J. Gilbey, 'A. S. Gold Scrapbook'

31 *Standard*, 1.1.1903, 19.5.1903

32 Thomas Harding, *Legacy: One Family, a Cup of Tea and the Company that Took on the World* (London, 2019), pp. 154–7

33 DA, W. & J. Gilbey Minute Book No. 5, 7.12.1903, 18.1.1904. Sir Herbert Maxwell, 'a good literary man', was shortly afterwards commissioned to write a history of Gilbey's celebrating their first fifty years in business, see Herbert Maxwell, *Half-a-century of Successful Trade: Being a Sketch of the Rise and Development of the Business of W. & A. Gilbey, 1857–1907* (London, 1907). It was common practice at the time for lobbying groups to draft bills and find sympathetic MPs to promote them in Parliament.

34 'It may be assumed therefore, that the consumer is in the main satisfied with what he gets so why seek to perplex him with differences which after all, are so in name only? The individual palate of the consumer may be safely allowed to regulate his taste in whisky. It is true, of course, that there are "cranks" who profess to know about whisky who can even undertake to instruct the most proficient member of our trade as to how he should conduct his business. Yet these so-called authorities will swallow with a very wise look, a blend of malt and grain whiskies and be ready to pronounce it "pure malt" if they are told it is so! Fortunately, these individuals are a minority but that they can and do make themselves troublesome at times almost all of our trade knows by practical experience.' *Wine & Spirit Trade Record*, 8.4.1905

35 Ridley's, 9.1.1906

36 *Wine & Spirit Trade Record*, 8.6.1907

37 DA, W. & J. Gilbey Minute Book No. 4, 3.11.1902, Minute Book No. 5, 11.12.1905, 7.5.1906

38 DA, W. & J. Gilbey Minute Book No 5, 3.7.1905, 29.1.1906. Alfred Gilbey also 'recommended that Mr Vasey of "The Lancet" be asked to rewrite his pamphlet on whisky making it applicable to blended spirit'.

39 See Weir, *History of the Distillers Company*, pp. 122–33 for a blow-by-blow account

40 Ridley's, 8.11.1905

41 DA, DCL Minute Book No. 10, 21.12.1906

42 DA, DCL Minute Book No. 10, 25.10.1906

43 Ridley's, 10.7.1906

44 *Era*, 2.12.1905, 9.12.1905, 23.12.1905; see also Harvey Macnair & Co., *The Truth About Whisky* (London, 1907), John Johnson Collection of Printed Ephemera, Bodleian Library, Oxford

45 *The Times*, 8.10.1909

46 Ridley's, 10.4.1906; *Wine & Spirit Trade Record*, 8.9.1908

Chapter 6: The Birth of 'Johnnie Walker'

1 Paul E. Derrick, *How to Reduce Selling Costs* (New York, 1920), p. 101

2 These developments are all dealt with at greater length in the following chapters.

3 DA, JW&S Sample Book, Price Lists 1906–1933, pp. 7–8

4 Evidence of Alexander Walker, *Royal Commission on Whisky and other Potable Spirits, Minutes of Evidence* (London, 1908), p. 224

5 See Allen Andrews, *The Whisky Barons* (London, 1977), p. 59; Thomas R. Dewar, *A Ramble Around the Globe* (London, 1894), passim. For James Buchanan and the turf, see Brian Spiller, *The Chameleon's Eye: James Buchanan and Co. Ltd, 1884–1984* (London, 1984), p. 46–8. Dewar and Buchanan made regular appearances in the society columns of magazines such as the *Illustrated London News, Vanity Fair* and the *Tatler*.

6 *Victualling Trades Review*, 15.11.1899

7 *Manchester Courier and Lancashire General Advertiser*, 14.12.1907, 'Johnnie Walker's Popularity'. The language used in this article reads very much as if it was taken from a press release issued by the company.

8 *Dundee Evening Post*, 1.12.1903

9 'This is to be sung for the first time on Monday and will vie with the cake walks and the Lambeth Walks and the like in popularity. You have heard of the "gin crawl", this is the "Johnny Walker Walk" and will I fancy turn out to be a staggerer.' *Islington Gazette*, 20.6.1902; *The Era*, 14.6.1902, 11.10.1902

10 *Hampshire Advertiser*, 21.1.1893; *Barnet Press*, 9.4.1892; *South London Chronicle*, 19.12.1896

11 *Yorkshire Evening Post*, 27.2.1901

12 *Printers' Ink*, 22.12.1909

13 In 1886 Alexander Walker, then aged fifty-two, complained to a friend of the strong influence his mother had over him. DA, JW&S Letter Book A11/3, AW to Mr Campbell, 6.4.1886

14 See for example *Bristol Times*, 4.12.1905, 14.12.1905

15 See for example *Country Life*, 4.4.1906; *The Globe*, 22.4.1906. The firm had also run a campaign of small notices in a variety of titles dealing specifically with the 'What is Whisky' question, 'which continues to agitate the public. It is no doubt gratifying to the large number of consumers of the "Walker's Kilmarnock Whisky" to be authoritatively informed that Messrs John Walker & Sons Ltd, of Kilmarnock, guarantee all the whiskies sold under their labels. Of the firm's

position as holders of malt whisky in Scotland there is no need to speak': *The Referee*, 15.3.1906; *Leeds Mercury*, 29.3.1906; *Sporting Times*, 7.4.1906

16   *Bradford Daily Telegraph*, 18.10.1907

17   *Advertising World*, October 1907, p. 524; 'I recommend Johnnie Walker', John Johnson Collection of Printed Ephemera, Bodleian Library, Oxford; *Sheffield Daily Telegraph*, 4.10.1907

18   Derrick, *How to Reduce Selling Costs*, pp. 96–7, p. 132

19   Derrick, *How to Reduce Selling Costs*, p. 133

20   Derrick, *How to Reduce Selling Costs*, p. 194

21   Somerville 'did some strenuous work for Mr Derrick among the non-advertising manufacturers of this country and landed some sizeable fish.' *Advertising World*, July 1922, p. 52. Horace Barnes' 'mind leapt to the complete advertising scheme almost before the details of a proposition were unfolded. He could "get it down" in verse with almost the same facility, as the more ordinary form of copy, and, as to prose, I still treasure some advertisements written by him as very pearls of indescribable simplicity and charm.' *Advertising World*, September 1922, p. 280

22   *Printers' Ink*, 18.8.1909, 12.12.1909

23   A. E. Johnson, *Brush, Pen and Pencil: The Book of Tom Browne* (London, 1909), p. 1, pp. 20–22: 'The circulation went up with a bound to 600,000 copies weekly'; Robert Machray, *The Night Side of London* (London, 1902): 'The artist and the author worked together, visiting the places described, and seeing the scenes herein set forth; the volume is therefore the result of what may be called their common observation'; A. St John Adcock, *The World that Never Was* (London, 1908)

24   *Printers' Ink*, July 1915, pp. xii–xiii

25   'Sunny Jim has not lived. Why did he not live? Because he lacked one important characteristic in a mascot; he didn't carry the name of the goods about with him. Johnnie Walker was the nickname of Walker's whisky before the late Tom Browne first drew his admirable figure for my friend Mr Paul E. Derrick.' Thomas Russell, *Commercial Advertising* (London, 1923), pp. 162–4. For Waukenphast ('Walking Fast') see, for example, the *Naval and Military Gazette*, 2.5.1883. The Waukenphast figure was radically redrawn in 1912 – see the *Bystander*, 17.7.1912. It's possible that Browne was working from an image of John Walker supplied to him by the Walker family.

26   *Advertising World*, December 1908, p. 104 and February 1911, pp. 178–84

27   *Tatler*, 2.12.1908, 14.12.1910

28   *Sporting Times*, 18.11.1909

29   *Advertising World*, February 1911, pp. 178–84

30   *Printers' Ink*, 22.12.1909

31   *DCL Gazette*, July 1928, p. 10, July 1930, p. 119; *Daily Herald*, 19.11.1932. The provenance of the Savoy lunch story is as yet unclear.

32   *Advertising World*, December 1913, pp. 922–24

33   *Printers' Ink*, 22.12.1909

34   *Advertising World*, November 1924, pp. 108–14

Chapter 7: The Scotch Whisky Triumvirate

1   *Bristol Times*, 14.12.1905

2   For Hodge Brothers, see DA, Letter Book A11/2, p. 947, GPW to Hodge Bros, 127 Fenchurch Street, 29.8.1895; p. 950, 'Accounts of James Hodge', trading as 'Hodge Bros', 19.12.1895; p. 952, GPW to Goldberg & Langdon, 19.12.1895; p. 954, GPW to George and William Hodge, 19.12.1895

3   DA, Letter Book A11/2, p. 964, GPW to George Hunter Esq, New York, 21.2.1896; DA, JW&S Minute Book No. 1, 8.4.1896, 27.6.1898

4   *DCL Gazette*, April 1930, p. 62; *Victualling Trades Review*, 15.7.1902: 'This important agency [Birmingham] is under the management of Mr James Stevenson, who received his training in Kilmarnock, and who, since his appointment as the Messrs. Walker's representative in the Midlands, has done excellent work'; DA, JW&S Minute Book No. 1, 7.10.1907

5   DA, JW&S Minute Book No. 1, 24.6.1895

6   DA, JW&S Minute Book No. 1, 29.6.1902, 6.1.1908; *Kilmarnock Herald*, 18.3.1910; *Ardrossan & Saltcoats Herald*, 18.3.1910; *Kilmarnock Standard*, 19.3.1910. In December 1895 Leander Jameson, encouraged by Cecil Rhodes, led an abortive uprising against the South African republic to seize control of Johannesburg and its goldfields.

7   DA, JW&S Minute Book No. 1, 9.12.1893, 4.5.1894; DA, Letter Book A11/2, p. 903, GPW to Mr Rolfe, 10.1.1893

8   DA, Letter Book A11/2, p. 906, Jarvis Soutter & Co. to JW&S London, 17.7.1893; p. 912, Kilgour to B. Lewis, 7.11.1893

9   DA, JW&S Minute Book No. 1, 4.7.1890

10   *Photographic Review*, 12.1.1894; *The Bulletin*, 12.1.1894, 6.6.1896; *Sydney Daily Telegraph*, 21.8.1896, 16.12.1896; *Sydney Evening News*, 16.12.1896; *Daily Commercial News and Shipping List*, 23.10.1896

11   DA, JW&S Minute Book No. 1, 11.9.1896, 30.6.1898; *New Zealand Times*, 3.7.1897; *Sportsman*, 7.7.1896

12   The shipment data is taken from the annual summaries of 'the year in the United States' published in Ridley's *Wine and Spirit Trade Circular* in February of each year. Ridley's 11.2.1882; *Wine & Spirit Trade Record*, 1.2.1900

13 *Wine & Spirit Trade Record*, 1.1.1900

14 Ridley's, 12.2.1904

15 Ridley's, 8.2.1905

16 *Wine & Spirit Trade Record*, 8.2.1912

17 Ridley's, 8.2.1905, 8.2.1906, 8.2.1911; *Wine & Spirit Trade Record*, 8.12.1912

18 DA, Letter Book A11/1, p. 55, Kilgour to Blaikie, 1.2.1883

19 DA, Letter Book A11/1, p. 255, AW to Blaikie, 27.10.1884; A11/2, p. 387, JW to William Page Ponsford Esq., Cold Harbour, Willesden Green, 18.11.1887; 'One brand and one quality, always kept to the highest standard, have made "Kilmarnock" a most popular brand in Canada, and it is reported that sales are showing a large increase in every part of the dominion.' *Wine & Spirit Trade Record*, 1.6.1900

20 *Courier Journal*, 7.11.1894; *Pittsburgh Daily Post*, 12.10.1894; *Baltimore Sun*, 29.9.1902; *New York Tribune*, 26.3.1906

21 DA, JW&S Minute Book No. 1, 30.6.1909, 10.10.1909, 11.4.1910, 29.12.1910, 23.4.1912, 1.4.1913, 15.8.1914; JW&S AC 257/3, 'Advertising Year Ended 1910'

22 'Of course, as Scotch increased in popularity [in the United States] the imitations of it also increased. This evil will have to be combatted.' *Wine & Spirit Trade Record*, 1.2.1902; 'In the raid on the establishment of Witteman Bros [Chicago], which was made on 20th October, the following articles were seized. About 1,000,000 labels of numerous different well-known brands of foreign wines and spirits, 25,000 counterfeit capsules, 10,000 to 20,000 corks with the brands of leading foreign shippers, 500 cuts, stencils and plates for the printing of labels, 500 empty branded cases, 500 filled cases, sawed lumber cut and stamped and ready to be made into counterfeit cases (an amount sufficient to make 10,000 cases or more), wire netting sufficient to cover 2,000 bottles, 5,000 lead seals for fastening the bottles, and a great amount of other stuff used in the manufacture of counterfeit cases and labels. The attorneys also carried away 20 cases of Gilka Kummel, 25 Hennessy brandy, 20 Martell brandy, 20 Boonekamp bitters, 25 bottles of Old Tom gin, 40 of De Kuyper's gin, and a number of others.' *Victualling Trades Review*, January 1898

23 *Wine & Spirit Trade Record*, 1.6.1900

24 *Harper's Weekly*, 25.7.1891

25 *Wine & Spirit Trade Record*, 1.6.1900, 1.1.1901

26 Ridley's, 8.3.1910

27 DA, Letter Book A11/2, p. 5, JW&S London to JW&S Kilmarnock, 29.3.1884; A11/1, p. 4, AW to James Cullen, Sydney, 4.11.1881

28 Ridley's, 8.3.1907, for a case involving Dewar's packaging components being shipped to South Africa; *Victualling Trades Review*, March 1896, on the skills of forgers

29 *Windsor Star*, 6.3.1897, 16.1.1907

30 *The Times*, 13.9.1908; *Wine & Spirit Trade Record*, 8.7.1908, 8.8.1908, 8.11.1909; *The Globe*, 13.3.1909

31 DA, JW&S Minute Book No. 1, 11.4.1910, 4.7.1910, 27.3.1910; *Wine & Spirit Trade Record*, 8.7.1910, 8.7.1911; *Brewer's Gazette*, 6.1.1910

32 DA, JW&S Minute Book No. 1, 26.2.1912

33 DA, JW&S Minute Book No. 1, 23.4.1912, 1.4.1913; DA, JW&S Sample Book, 'The NR Fitment' brochure; *Observer*, 5.5.1912

34 *Wine & Spirit Trade Record*, 8.7.1912; Ridley's, 9.7.1912

35 For Robert Brown, proprietors of the Four Crown's brand, see the *National Guardian*, 17.1.1908; Charles Craig, *The Scotch Whisky Industry Record* (Dumbarton, 1994), p. 497

36 'The Old Wilson in the New Bottle', *Washington Evening Star*, 16.12.1910

37 *Sydney Morning Herald*, 1.4.1914, 7.4.1914; *Ottawa Citizen*, 31.10.1914; *New York Tribune*, 8.12.1914; DA, JW&S Minute Book No. 1, 24.1.1916

38 Edward Meigh, *The History of the Glass Bottle* (Hanley, 1972), pp. 25–30; DA, Letter Book A11/2, p. 207, Blaikie to GPW, 15.11.1886; DA, JW&S Minute Book No. 1, 26.9.1910

39 'Are we threatened by a bottle famine in Scotland? This is evidence by the busy state of the home and foreign trade in bottled whisky. There has been tremendous pressure of late on the bottle makers, and many wholesale houses are quite unable to get their orders executed. Some of them are face to face with a rather serious state of things, being unable to execute their orders for whisky for want of the wherewithal to put it into. Some of the very large wholesale houses have contracts with the bottle makers for the delivery of so many bottles per annum; many houses, however, give their orders as they require them, and according to the state of trade, it is the latter class that will suffer . . . the bottle manufacturers in the North of England, and at Portobello, near Edinburgh, have more than they can do, and even the voracious Germany cannot take on hand to execute large orders before the end of the year.' *Victualling Trades Review*, 15.8.1900; DA, JW&S Minute Book No. 1, 2.12.1913

40 Jack K. Paquette, *The Glassmakers, Revisited* (Bloomington, IN, 2011), pp. 23–5; Meigh, *The History of the Glass Bottle*, pp. 44–8

41 DA, JW&S Minute Book No. 1, 29.12.1910, 9.10.1911, 2.12.1913, 2.3.1914, 15.6.1914, 15.11.1915

42 DA, JW&S Net Sales 1886–1922, ex. 'Goods a/c' in Kilmarnock Private Ledger Series A9/1, 9/2, 9/3

43 George B. Wilson, *Alcohol and the Nation: A Contribution to the Study of the Liquor Problem in the United Kingdom from 1800–1935* (London, 1940), p. 335

44 DA, JW&S Minute Book No. 1, 6.10.1908, 11.1.1909, 24.4.1909, 11.4.1910, 26.9.1910, 29.12.1910, 16.6.1911, 9.10.1911

45 Ridley's, 8.5.1909; DA, JW&S Sample Book, Budget Price Increase, pro forma letters re. cash payments. For the 'People's Budget', see Weir, *History of the Distillers Company*, pp. 133–7

46 Ridley's feared the consequences of the use of cheap German sherry, with a lower duty rate, to reduce whisky: 'Other expedients are sure to be resorted to by the unscrupulous first, and then by those who are more scrupulous, but must live. A good deal of talk is now current about the increased use of the cheapest sherry for reducing whisky. These sherries can be had from Hamburg and indeed from Spain, of a strength a little under thirty degrees, and therefore paying the 1s 3d duty. The matter can be put thus: every gallon of this "wine" which a spirit dealer can use in his spirit stock will provide him with say twenty-nine degrees of proof spirit at a duty cost equal to about 4s 4d per proof gallon, as against 14s 9d if that proof gallon alcohol were used in the form of spirits.' 8.2.1910

47 For a highly detailed listing of the private Walker meetings to prepare proposals for these discussions, see DA, JW&S 2066, Redfern Hunt & Co., detailed billing re. proposed amalgamation, 1908–1912; DA, JW&S Minute Book No. 1, 26.9.1910, 19.12.1910, 9.10.1911, 23.4.1912, 17.6.1912

48 DA, DCL AC301, Files Relating to Combine, 1908–1915

49 DA, DCL AC301, Files Relating to Combine, 1908–1915

50 DA, DCL AC301, Files Relating to Combine, 1908–1915

51 DA, DCL AC301, Files Relating to Combine, 1908–1915

52 DA, DCL AC301, Files Relating to Combine, 1908–1915

53 DA, DCL AC301, Files Relating to Combine, 1908–1915

54 DA, DCL AC301, Files Relating to Combine, 1908–1915

55 DA, DCL AC301, Files Relating to Combine, 1908–1915

56 DA, DCL AC301, Files Relating to Combine, 1908–1915

57 DA, DCL AC301, Files Relating to Combine, 1908–1915

58 See graph Chapter 6, p. 138, JW&S Advertising Expenditure 1887–1922

59 Evidence of Arthur Bramall, *Royal Commission on Whisky and other Potable Spirits, Minutes of Evidence* (London, 1908), p. 29

60 *Wine & Spirit Trade Record*, 8.10.1909

61 Derrick, *How to Reduce Selling Costs*, p. 110

62 See for example *Illustrated London News*, 30.1.1897

63 See for example *Illustrated London News*, 21.3.1904, 5.3.1905, 10.12.1905

64 Raghunath Singh Rao, Rajesh K. Chandy and Jaideep C. Prabhu, 'The Fruits of Legitimacy: Why Some New Ventures Gain More from Innovation Than Others', *Journal of Marketing*, July 2008

65 *Advertising World*, December 1913, p. 922–4

66 In 1915 William Heath Robinson was also commissioned to produce a series of humorous drawings showing 'The Making of Johnnie Walker Whisky', in a style for which he would later become world famous. Geoffrey Beare, *Heath Robinson's Commercial Art* (London, 2017), pp. 17, 70–74

67 *Advertising World*, July 1914, p. 33; *Printers' Ink*, 20 October 1909, pp. 39–40

68 *Advertising World*, September 1912, p. 259

69 *Printers' Ink*, April 1912, p. 15

70 DA, JW&S Minute Book No. 1, 12.8.1914, 25.1.1915

71 DA, JW&S Minute Book No. 1, 15.11.1915, 5.4.1916

72 DA, JW&S Minute Book No. 1, 24.1.1915, 15.11.1915

73 DA, JW&S Minute Book No. 1, 24.1.1916, 3.4.1916, 15.6.1916, 23.10.1916

74 Sales graph and US imports graph, Ridley's, February 1917

75 'The new offices of James Buchanan & Co. Ltd at 29 Broadway are among the finest in the wine and spirit trade in New York.' *Wine and Spirit Trade Record*, 8.7.1906; 'Rumours are proverbially unreliable, but one which has recently reached us is well worthy of the attention of those interested in the Scotch Whisky Trade in the United States. This is to the effect that Messrs James Buchanan & Co., Ltd, are seriously considering the advisability of giving up their own offices and staff in New York.' Ridley's, 8.4.1913; DA, DCL AC 301, Files Relating to Combine, 1908–1915

76 DA, JW&S Minute Book No. 1, 15.8.1914, 5.4.1916, 3.7.1916

77 DA, JW&S Minute Book No. 1, 2.3.1914, 15.6.1914, 28.6.1915, 15.11.1915, 24.1.1916

78 DA, JW&S Minute Book No. 1, 25.6.1915

79 DA, JW&S Minute Book No. 1, 5.4.1916

80 Ridley's, 8.5.1909

81 *Sports Special* ('the Green 'un'), 26.6.1915

82 *Kilmarnock Herald*, 18.5.1915; M. J. Lewis and Roger Lloyd Jones, *Arming the Western Front: War, Business and the State in Britain* (London, 2016), pp. 174–5

83 *Kilmarnock Herald*, 16.12.1917; *Liverpool Daily Post*, 16.2.1917; for Churchill's speech see *The Times*, 9.11.1923; DA, JW&S Minute Book No. 1, 9.12.1918; draft letter to George Paterson Walker from the Ministry of Munitions, University of Sussex Special Collections SxMs 42/2/1, 19.12.1918

84 DA, JW&S Minute Book No. 1, 18.3.1910, 14.6.1911, 3.7.1911, 29.9.1913, 10.6.1915, 24.6.1918

85 *Scotsman*, 8.1.1919

86 Ridley's, 9.5.1916

87 Ridley's, 10.5.1918

88 Ridley's, 14.12.1920; *The Times*, 30.10.1925. See also University of Sussex Special Collections SxMs 42/1/4, Laurence Guillemard to James Stevenson, 26.10.1921
89 Ridley's, 14.6.1926

Chapter 8: Carry On

1   Ridley's, 14.8.1925
2   Ridley's, 10.9.1918
3   DA, JW&S Sample Book, pro-forma letters, post-WW1 allocations and shortages
4   DA, JW&S Minute Book No. 1, 9.12.1918
5   'This is the centenary year of the firm, and it is satisfactory that the results constitute a record. It is necessary, however, to point out that the profits this year have been increased by abnormal conditions that are not likely to recur, and that higher costs all round, in addition to increased taxation, are likely to prove adverse factors in the near future.' DA, JW&S Minute Book No. 1, 5.7.1920; see graph p. 139, Annual Sales 1881–1924; see graph p. 156, Annual Profits 1882–1924
6   *Illustrated London News*, 24.1.1920; John Walker & Sons Ltd, *Around the World: 'We sailed wherever ship could sail'* (London, 1923), passim
7   See *Bystander*, 31.3.1920
8   *Advertising World*, April 1920, pp. 373–4
9   *Advertising World*, May 1921, p. 494
10 DA, JW&S Minute Book No. 1, 2.2.1920
11 DA, JW&S Minute Book No. 1, 5.7.1920; Minute Book No. 2, 27.6.1921
12 *Kilmarnock Herald*, 31.12.1920. The Kilmarnock war memorial, opposite the Dick Institute, was not opened until May 1927: *Kilmarnock Herald*, 12.5.1927
13 See James Watson, 'The Scotch Whisky Export Trade', *Journal of the Leith Chamber of Commerce*, January 1920; Ridley's, 10.8.1918
14 DA, JW&S Minute Book No. 1, 15.8.1914, 16.19.1914, 25.1.1915; 15.6.1916; 25.3.1917; 24.6.1918; Minute Book No. 3, 7.11.1927
15 Ridley's, 14.1.1926
16 Ridley's, 14.4.1924
17 *Kilmarnock Herald*, 10.6.1921; see also the *Southern Reporter*, 16.6.1921, 'Wrestling Influenza'
18 *The Times*, 7.10.1920; Ridley's, 12.2.1921
19 Ridley's, 12.3.1920, 12.2.1921, 14.9.1922. This did, however, allow Scottish distillers to experiment with the use of American whisky casks for maturing Scotch: 'The result has been very unsatisfactory, as from the amount of charring in the inside of the casks, the spirit has become discoloured, and in some cases nearly black.' Ridley's, 12.5.1920

20 DA, JW&S Minute Book No. 1, 12.1.1920

21 Ridley's, 12.2.1920; Weir, *History of the Distillers Company*, p. 205

22 Ridley's, 11.6.1918; DA, JW&S Minute Book No. 3, 22.12.1925

23 DA, JW&S Minute Book No. 1, 12.1.1920

24 DA, DCL AC 301, 30.7.1923, draft agreement Buchanan, JD&S, Lowrie's and JW&S to acquire business of James Watson & Co.; Ridley's, 12.4.1921, 14.10.1922, 14.6.1923

25 DA, JW&S Minute Book No. 3, 20.7.1923

26 DA, JW&S Minute Book No. 2, 11.1.1923; Minute Book No. 3, 16.9.1923

27 DA, JW&S Minute Book No. 1, 2.3.1914, 15.6.1914, 26.10.1914, 25.1.1915, 7.7.1919, 23.2.1920

28 DA, JW&S Minute Book No. 1, 4.10.1921, 11.1.1923

29 Ridley's, 14.3.1923

30 Sir Peter Mackie to Lord Dewar, 30.5.1923, quoted in Weir, *History of the Distillers Company*, p. 203

31 Weir, *History of the Distillers Company*, pp. 203–206. The four firms were particularly exercised about the fate of the 'Haig & Haig' brand, whose residual popularity in the United States made it ripe for exploitation.

32 Ridley's, 14.9.1923

33 DA, JW&S Minute Book No. 2, 22.1.1925, 29.1.1925, 26.2.1925, 18.3.1925; Weir, *History of the Distillers Company*, pp. 207–13, 218–21

34 Ridley's, 14.2.1925

35 Ridley's, 14.8.1925

36 DA, JW&S B1/1, H&E Joint Meeting, 8.7.1926

37 DA, JW&S B1/2, H&E Joint Meeting, 2.11.1926

38 *Advertising World*, June 1911, pp. 675–6; Ridley's, 9.5.1911, 8.11.1911, 10.12.1912

39 Lord Stevenson had made the suggestion to purchase Derrick's agency: DA, JW&S B1/1, H&E Joint Meeting, 8.7.1926

40 DA, JW&S B1/3, Propaganda Committee, 3.1.1927; *Western Morning News*, 8.12.1926; *Nottingham Evening Post*, 23.12.1926; *The Times*, 18.2.1927; *Nottingham Journal*, 8.3.1927; *Illustrated Sporting and Dramatic News*, 18.12.1926; *Sphere*, 18.12.1926. Herd was former Managing Director of James Watson & Co. in Dundee, and a future chairman of the DCL.

41 DA, JW&S B1/2, Malt Distilling & Blended Whisky Sales Committee (MDBWSC), 7.12.1926

42 DA, JW&S B1/2, MDBWSC, 24.1.1928

43 DA, JW&S B1/2, MDBWSC (Joint), 7.2.1928

44 Letter from Winston Churchill 'in the train' to David Lloyd George, 30.1.1921, the Churchill Archive, CHAR 2/114/29-31; Letter from Winston Churchill [War Office] to David Lloyd George, 8.1.1920, CHAR 2/114/6

45 Handwritten note, undated and unsigned, on 'The Wembley Garden Club'

headed notepaper. University of Sussex Special Collections, SxMs 42/1/1. See also the Churchill Archive, CHAR 1/188/38, citation letter from Stella, Lady Stevenson, to Winston Churchill, 11.6.1926

46 Letter from Sir James Stevenson to Winston Churchill, 14.3.1923, the Churchill Archive, CHAR 2/126/18-19

47 Following Scotland's victory against England in a Home International football match at Wembley in 1977, fans invaded the pitch in order to carry trophies of war home: 'I then started digging up the Wembley turf. I handed out hundreds of bits of the turf and kept some for myself.' See the *Guardian*, 12.11.1999

48 *Kilmarnock Standard*, 12.6.1926

49 *The Times*, 3.8.1923

50 *The Times*, 25.6.1924

51 University of Sussex Special Collections, SxMs 42/1/7, 8 December 1924, Stevenson to D. N. Dunlop, British Electrical & Allied Manufacturers Association

52 DA, JW&S B1/2, H&E Joint Meeting, 18.3.1926, 23.3.1926, 13.4.1926

53 'Lord Stevenson as I knew him' by Barrington Hooper CBE, *Advertising World*, July 1926, p. 248

54 *Kilmarnock Standard*, 12.6.1926

55 *The Times*, 19.6.1928; circular letter from Brendan Bracken, Eyre and Spottiswoode Ltd, 6 Middle New Street, London, announcing the recommendation for Lord Stevenson memorial scholarships, 29.6.1927, the Churchill Archive, CHAR 2/152/123–124

56 *Kilmarnock Standard*, 12.6.1926

57 Letter from Brendan Bracken to Edward Marsh, 4.7.1927, the Churchill Archive, CHAR 2/152/146–147

58 *The Times*, 13.7.1928

Chapter 9: 'Good Work, Good Whisky'

1 *Kilmarnock Herald*, 16.7.1920; *Kilmarnock Standard*, 10.7.1920, 5.4.1941

2 *Kilmarnock Herald*, 16.7.1920

3 DA, DCL AC 301/2. The comment was attributed to both his brother George, and James Stevenson.

4 *National Guardian* (supplement), 16.2.1929

5 *Kilmarnock Herald*, 23.2.1923

6 *Leading Men of London: A Collection of Biographical Sketches* (London, 1895), p. 448; *DCL Gazette*, January 1927, p. 7

7 *Bystander*, 1.2.1922; *Graphic*, 18.2.1922; *Illustrated London News*, 18.2.1922; *Tatler*, 22.2.1922; *Sphere*, 11.3.1922

8   *Derbyshire Advertiser*, 8.7.1927; DA, JW&S Minute Book No. 3, 28.1.1927

9   *Kilmarnock Herald*, 8.8.1902

10 *London Gazette*, 6.6.1913; James Borland Walker Medical Card, National Archives, WO 372/20/182850

11 *Tatler*, 21.9.1943, 6.6.1945, 5.9.1945; *The Times*, 6.5.1958

12 *Sketch*, 31.8.1927; *DCL Gazette*, January 1928

13 *Sketch*, 8.5.1929, 15.5.1929, 19.2.1930; *Bystander*, 17.5.1933, 9.11.1938, 21.6.1939; *Illustrated London News*, 11.5.1929; *Tatler*, 17.11.1937; *Sphere*, 18.2.1950

14 *Advertising World*, April 1927, pp. 804–806

15 *Advertising World*, June 1927, p. 179

16 *Advertising World*, December 1926, p. 178; November 1930, p. 410; April 1932, p. 240; November 1934, p. 91; *Publicity World*, 21.12.1929

17 DA, JW&S Minute Book No. 3, 26.7.1935

18 For Crawford's, see G. H. Saxon Mills, *There is a Tide . . . The Life and Work of Sir William Crawford* (London, 1954), especially pp. 54–67. There is no mention of Paul E. Derrick, or his agency, in the book. DA, JW&S Minute Book No. 4, 23.1.1936, 31.1.1936, 15.10.1936

19 See for example DA, JW&S B1/7, Blending Committee, 11.2.1930

20 DA, JW&S B1/7, Blending Committee, 29.4.1930, 22.7.1930, although Redfern did also wonder 'how the gin companies within the Group would view our action in trying to push whisky cocktails'.

21 DA, JW&S B1/7, Blending Committee, 24.6.1931

22 *Advertising World*, 25.10.1934

23 Ridley's, 8.5.1913, 14.4.1927; *Wine and Spirit Trade Record*, 8.6.1913

24 DA, JW&S B1/4, Malt Distilling and Blended Whisky Sales Committee, 7.2.1928, 22.5.1928

25 *Illustrated London News*, 19.5.1928, 23.6.1928, 11.8.1928, 18.8.1928, 8.9.1928

26 *The Times*, 18.10.1928, 26.10.1928, 9.11.1928, 30.11.1928; *Daily Mail*, 5.12.1928

27 DA, JW&S B1/5, Blending Committee, 16.10.1928

28 *Aberdeen Press and Journal*, 5.12.1928

29 *Illustrated London News*, 17.4.1920

30 *Sketch*, 12.1.1910

31 *Printer's Ink*, 22.12.1909; DA, JW&S Sample Book, Costumes, 1920s

32 *Hendon and Finchley Times and Guardian*, 22.4.1932

33 Postcard in possession of the author, franked 1928; *Berwickshire News and General Advertiser*, 21.4.1925

34 *West London Observer*, 30.11.1928; *Belfast Newsletter*, 31.1.1931; *Kent & Sussex Courier*, 15.7.1932; *Fife Free Press*, 29.12.1934

35 *Era*, 5.10.1932; *Loughborough Echo*, 22.1.1915; *Manchester Evening News*, 16.11.1915

36 *Illustrated London News*, 10.3.1928

37 DA, JW&S Sample Book, 'Hole in One', 1926–1933; *Birmingham Daily Gazette*, 11.6.1932

38 *Printers' Ink*, 22.12.1909

39 Christopher Martin Jenkins, *Ball by Ball: The Story of Cricket Broadcasting* (London, 1990), pp. 6–44

40 *Wine & Spirit Trade Record*, 14.7.1930

41 *Nottingham Journal*, 11.6.1930, 17.6.1930

42 *Bucks Examiner*, 5.9.1930

43 *South of England Advertiser*, 21.8.1930; *Illustrated London News*, 23.8.1930

44 See for example the *Cricketer*, 17.3.1930, 14.6.1930, 9.8.1930; *Wisden's Cricketers' Almanack* (London, 1931), p. 16, 'Johnnie Walker Makes 1930 Cricket History'; *Graphic*, 16.8.1930

45 *Cricketer*, 30.6.1934

46 Redfern advised only a few months later that 'it would be necessary to spend at least £50,000 in bringing the plant of this company up to date'.

47 'Visit to the works of Messrs John Lumb', *Journal of the Society of Glass Technology*, 1924, pp. 57–8. See also Michael Cable, 'Mechanization of Glass Making', *Journal of the American Ceramic Society* (82), 1999, p. 1097

48 *Popular Science*, April 1928, p. 54; DA, JW&S Minute Book No. 3, 19.6.1926

49 DA, JW&S Minute Book No. 3, 10.1.1929, 1.2.1933, 12.5.1933, 11.5.1934

50 *DCL Gazette*, April 1929, pp. 68–73

51 James Barbican (Eric Sherbrooke Walker), *The Confessions of a Rum Runner* (New York, 2016), passim

52 DA, JW&S B1/3, Malt Distilling and Blended Whisky Sales Committee, 12.7.1927

53 *The Times*, 15.10.1925, 27.1.1935; *Liverpool Echo*, 2.7.1926. For the record, the files in the National Archives relating to Attfield's gun-running activities in 1924 are still deemed too sensitive to be made available to the public.

54 DA, JW&S B1/1, Home & Export Committee, 23.6.1925

55 DA, JW&S B1/7, Blending Committee, 9.4.1930; *Winnipeg Tribune*, 3.12.1923, 26.1.1929

56 *DCL Gazette*, April 1929, p. 72

57 Barbican, *Confessions of a Rum Runner*, pp. 282–3

58 DA, JW&S B1/10, Blending Committee, 22.6.1932, 14.7.1932, 17.1.1933

59 Ridley's, 14.10.1932, 14.12.1932, 14.9.1933

60 DA, JW&S B1/11, Blending Committee, 25.4.1933, 30.5.1933, 7.2.1933; the other potential candidate was K. & A. Taylor, also of New York, DA, JW&S Minute Book No. 3, 8.9.1933

61 DA, B1/11 Blending Committee, 15.8.1933, 26.9.1933

62 DA, JW&S Minute Book No. 3, 6.10.1933; *DCL Gazette*, January 1934, pp. 6–8; *Hartford Courant*, 1.12.1933

63 See for example the *Democrat and Chronicle*, 25.5.1924; *Brooklyn Daily Eagle*, 8.6.1924, 22.5.1927

64 *Evening World*, 2.2.1920; *New York Times*, 1.7.1919, 20.11.1921

65 *Daily News*, 13.1.1923: 'Ginger ale is the most popular drink in the country according to 555 soft drinks manufacturers gathered in annual convention.'

66 *New York Tribune*, 10.7.1919

67 *New York Tribune*, 5.7.1919, 3.10.1920, 9.5.1921; *New York Herald*, 18.10.1919; *Daily News*, 2.5.1921, 6.1.1929

68 *Daily News*, 18.5.1929, 30.10.1929

69 *Daily News*, 24.3.1933

70 *Brooklyn Daily Eagle*, 12.2.1928; *Time*, 4.7.1927

71 *Daily News*, 19.3.1929

72 *Brooklyn Daily Eagle*, 10.12.1933; *Detroit Free Press*, 27.12.1934

73 *Brooklyn Daily Eagle*, 23.9.1936

74 DA, JW&S B1/13, Blending Committee, 10.9.1935

75 DA, JW&S AC 257/6, 1915–1916, J. G. MacQueen to Alex Walker, 29.5.1916, London, Export Department

76 DA, JW&S AC 2061/10, G. A. Bode to Wm Dunlop, 24.3.1923; DA, JW&S B1/6, Blending Committee, 29.5.1925

77 DA, JW&S B1/2, Home and Export Committee, 26.4.1926; for Corio see Weir, *History of the Distillers Company*, pp. 257–9

78 DA, JW&S Minute Book No. 3, 24.10.1932

79 DA, JW&S B1/8, Blending Committee, 21.4.1931, 28.4.1931

80 DA, JW&S B1/8, Blending Committee, 24.6.1931, 14.7.1931

81 DA, JW&S B1/7, Blending Committee, 14.5.1930, 9.9.1930

82 DA, JW&S B1/12, Blending Committee, 18.7.1934; *Ridley's*, 14.6.1933, 14.7.1933

83 DA, DCL Management Committee Minutes, 21.4.1936, 23.9.1937, 4.10.1937, 8.3.1938, 18.4.1929

84 *Scotsman*, 13.12.1938. For the trial and judgement, see *The Times*, 13–17.12.1938, 20–21.12.1938, 31.1.1939

85 DA, JW&S B1/10, Blending Committee, 13.12.1932

86 Sir Alexander Walker to Winston Churchill, 23.12.1938, the Churchill Archive, CHAR 8/596

87 The Anglo-German fellowship was supported by German Foreign Minister Joachim von Ribbentrop, who owned a business importing luxury wines and spirits which had distributed Johnnie Walker in Germany from 1924. Tim Bouverie, *Appeasing Hitler: Chamberlain, Churchill and the Road to War*

(London, 2019), p. 113; Richard Griffiths, *Patriotism Perverted: Captain Ramsay, the Right Club, and British Anti-Semitism, 1939–1940* (London, 1998), pp. 35–9. DA, JW&S Minute Book No. 3, 8.7.1924; JW&S B1/1, Home and Export Committee, 18.8.1925; JW&S B1/7, 22.7.1930. Paul Schwarz, *This Man Ribbentrop* (New York, 1943), pp. 56–9; Michael Bloch, *Ribbentrop* (London, 2003), pp. 14–16, 47, 61

88 Bouverie, *Appeasing Hitler*, p. 387; Griffiths, *Patriotism Perverted*, p. 155; Robin Saikia, *The Red Book: The Membership List of the Right Club – 1939* (London, 2010), pp. 60–61, 82–3, 130. See also Gavin Bowd, *Fascist Scotland* (Edinburgh, 2013), p. 106

89 *Kilmarnock Standard*, 5.4.1941; Sir Alexander Walker to Winston Churchill, 16.12.1935, the Churchill Archive, CHUR 1/272/106; Sir Alexander Walker to Churchill, 21.2.1941, CHUR 2/142

90 Sir Alexander Walker to Winston Churchill, 29.1.1945, the Churchill Archive, CHUR 2/157 A-B

91 *Kilmarnock Standard*, 23.11.1946, 13.12.1947

92 Sir Alexander Walker to Winston Churchill, 31.12.1945, the Churchill Archive, CHUR 2/142

93 Like his father one of the last things Sir Alexander did before his death was play a round of golf at Troon. Sir Alexander Walker to Miss E. Elliott, 9.5.1947, the Churchill Archive CHUR 2/251; Jocelyn Walker to Winston Churchill, 17.5.1950; Churchill to Jocelyn Walker, 10.12.1950, both CHUR 2/178

94 DA, JW&S Minute Book No. 4, 6.3.1939, 3.6.1940

95 DA, JW&S Minute Book No. 4, 6.3.1939, 7.3.1939, 23.1.1936; *Kilmarnock Herald*, 6.12.1935; *DCL Gazette*, January 1936, p. 61, *DCL Gazette*, Summer 1939, pp. 202–03

96 *DCL Gazette*, June 1972, pp. 14–15

97 DA, JW&S Minute Book No. 3, 19.6.1923, 7.11.1927; *Commercial Motor*, 25.2.1930. Similar fleets were maintained in both Kilmarnock and Birmingham.

98 DA, JW&S Minute Book No. 4, 18.10.1937, 14.1.1938

99 DA, JW&S Minute Book No. 4, 19.5.1938, 6.10.1938, 26.10.1938

100 DA, DCL Production Committee Minutes, 30.11.1943, 12.4.1944, 5.10.1944; DCL Management Committee, 8.9.1943

101 DA, JW&S Minute Book No. 4, 26.10.1939, 20.6.1942; *DCL Gazette*, Winter 1946, p. 102

102 Having said that, the broad principle behind the Great War advertising, as explained by Paul E. Derrick, informed the approach to that for the Second World War: 'Since the beginning of the war they have courageously gone forward with their advertising with practically no change in their previous policy; nor is any change contemplated for the future. I would point out that this policy is not merely to "carry on", but recognises the extraordinary power

of their advertising in developing the goodwill of their business, and the realisation of the importance of keeping their brand prominently before the public in order to secure the greatest possible benefit from the return to normal trade conditions.' *Advertising World*, September 1915, p. 256

103 *Illustrated London News*, 8.6.1940, 11.9.1940, 14.10.1944, 1.1.1944, 19.1.1946

Chapter 10: Time Marches On

1   *DCL Gazette*, Spring 1845, p. 5
2   *DCL Gazette*, Autumn 1966, p. 168
3   *DCL Gazette*, Winter 1966, p. 257; July 1976, p. 11
4   Quoted in Hume and Moss, *The Making of Scotch Whisky*, p. 186
5   Hume and Moss, *The Making of Scotch Whisky*, pp. 188–93
6   Charles Craig, *The Scotch Whisky Industry Record* (Dumbarton, 1994), pp. 257–8
7   DA, DCL Management Committee, 22.2.1949
8   DA, DCL Production Committee, 29.8.1960; in April of that year the committee recorded: 'Arising from a complaint by one member regarding the quality of Glenlochy, it was reported that a detailed investigation at this distillery had disclosed a build up of accumulated fatty acids in the cooling worms of both Wash and Spirit Stills: the worms had been thoroughly cleaned out, and this action, it was contended, had effected a marked improvement in the quality of the spirit. Two other members confirmed that, in their view, this was so.' DA, DCL Production Committee, 29.4.1960
9   DA, DCL Production Committee, 5.1.1971, 4.12.1978
10   DA, DCL Production Committee, 3.9.1951, 4.7.1958, 1.4.1960, 29.4.1960, 29.5.1961, 12.4.1966, 6.9.1971. See also Spiller, *Cardhu: The World of Malt Whisky*, pp. 64–72
11   DA, DCL Production Committee, 9.1.1984 and 4.12.1982
12   'The Costly Result of Whisky Galore', *The Times*, 13.10.1983
13   DA, DCL Management Committee, 22.9.1948
14   See for example DA, DCL Management Committee, 14.9.1949, 13.12.1949, 26.11.1950
15   DA, DCL Management Committee, 30.5.1935, 25.1.1938, 12.2.1941
16   DA, DCL Management Committee, 5.5.1954
17   DA, DCL Management Committee, 27.6.1950, 3.7.1951, 12.9.1951
18   Michael R. Marrus, *Samuel Bronfman: The Life and Times of Seagram's Mr Sam* (Hanover, New England, 1992), pp. 372–6; Nicholas Faith, *The Bronfmans: The Rise and Fall of the House of Seagram* (New York, 2006), pp. 133–7

19 DA, DCL Management Committee, 5.5.1954, 8.6.1954, 13.7.1954

20 DA, JW&S Minute Book No. 5, 30.11.1951; DCL Management Committee, 4.2.1953

21 DA, JW&S Minute Book No. 5, 21.8.1952

22 DA, JW&S Minute Book No. 5, 21.8.1952

23 DA, DCL Management Committee, 11.12.1957, 29.10.1957

24 DA, DCL Management Committee, 29.10.1957

25 *Emporia Gazette*, 8.3.1968

26 DA, DCL Management Committee, 13.9.1961

27 DA, DCL Management Committee, 16.10.1962, 31.10.1962, 8.4.1963

28 DA, DCL Management Committee, 10.11.1964

29 DA, DCL Management Committee, 16.10.1962, 8.4.1963, 14.5.1963, 28.5.1963

30 DA, DCL Management Committee, 12.1.1971

31 DA, JW&S Minute Book No. 5, 21.9.1955

32 Hugh Ripley, *Whisky for Tea* (Lewes, 1991), pp. 138–9

33 DA, DCL Management Committee, 1.7.1964, 15.9.1964, 12.9.1967, 12.12.1967, 28.3.1968; *Miami News*, 10.5.1966; *Chicago Tribune*, 29.3.1968; *Los Angeles Times*, 17.5.1968; *Daily News*, 15.12.1974

34 *Illustrated London News*, 30.5.1970, p. 19

35 DA, Market Reports France, JW 1.2.1983

36 DA, DCL Management Committee, 18.9.1973

37 DA, Market Reports Italy, JW 1.5.1963

38 DA, DCL Management Committee, 19.7.1955

39 DA, DCL Management Committee, 14.11.1967, 16.2.1971, 19.3.1974; DA, Market Reports Italy, JW 20.11.1985

40 DA, DCL Management Committee, 25.5.1971, 13.7.1971

41 DA, Market Reports Italy, JW 20.11.1985

42 DA, Market Reports, JW 20.11.1962; WH 2.3.1972; WH 17.11.1980

43 DA, Market Reports, WH 29.7.1972; JW 2.3.1980; Brazil, JW 11.3.1968; JW 24.10.1970; 1.11.1982

44 DA, Market Reports, JW 17.11.1963; JW 11.11.1971

45 DA, JW&S Minute Book No. 4, 31.10.1947

46 DA, Market Reports, JW 15.11.1977

47 DA, Market Reports, WH 13.5.1985; DA, JW&S Minute Book No. 8, 31.10.1973

48 *Pittsburgh Press*, 10.12.1964; *San Bernardino County Sun*, 7.6.1941; *Tampa Bay Times*, 1.9.1951; American Tobacco also had a 'Piper Heidsieck Chewing Tobacco' launched around 1919.

49 DA, DCL Management Committee, 21.2.1940, 28.6.1949, 23.5.1951, 4.2.1953; JW&S Minute Book No. 4, 26.1.1940, 10.6.1949; JW&S Minute Book No. 5, 10.6.1960

50 For various 'Johnnie Walker shoes', see *Alton Evening Telegraph*, 6.3.1936;

[*Streator*] *Times*, 15.6.1950; *San Bernardino Sun*, 14.6.1964; DA, DCL Management Committee, 18.6.1946; JW&S Minute Book No. 5, 19.7.1950, 14.7.1954

51 DA, JW&S Minute Book No. 6, 11.9.1961, 16.2.1962, 4.7.1962, 15.2.1963; *Lime Springs Herald*, 20.2.1958

52 *Charlotte Observer*, 8.8.1969; 'Real Johnnie Walker gets Motel Out of its Hair', *Orangeburg Times & Democrat*, 8.8.1969

53 DA, JW&S Minute Book No. 6, 17.4.1964; DCL Management Committee, 12.9.1962

54 '*Whisky Galore!* sounds like a toper's vision of utopia – having no connection with present day austerity. It is not however a dream, but a delightful comedy.' *Lincolnshire Echo*, 21.6.1949. The film was later described by one of its producers as 'the longest unsponsored advertisement ever to reach cinema screens the world over', Hume and Moss, *The Making of Scotch Whisky*, p. 190

55 DA, JW&S Minute Book No. 8, 12.1.1973, 16.3.1973, 26.3.1976

56 Ripley, *Whisky for Tea*, pp. 113–68. For racing sponsorships, see for example DA, JW&S Minute Book No. 6, 3.5.1973

57 Kate Bassett, *In Two Minds: A Biography of Jonathan Miller* (London, 2012), pp. 169, 369; DA, JW&S Minute Book No. 4, 8.3.1968

58 DA, JW&S Minute Book No. 6, 20.11.1969, No. 5, 14.10.1971; DCL Management Committee, 28.4.1971; *Kent & Sussex Courier*, 29.10.1971; *DCL Gazette*, December 1971, p. 22

59 DA, JW&S Minute Book No. 7, 14.1.1972

60 DA, JW&S Minute Book No. 6, 25.6.1965, 11.4.1969; No. 8, 19.3.1975; No. 9, 24.5.1979; No. 11, 19.3.1985

61 DA, JW&S Minute Book No. 4, 6.3.1939, 1.5.1939, 8.1.1941; No. 5, 28.5.1959, 23.6.1959

62 DA, JW&S Minute Book No. 5, 18.8.1955, 23.2.1956

63 DA, JW&S Minute Book No. 5, 16.6.1958, 16.12.1958; No. 6, 13.1.1967, 19.5.1967, 27.9.1967, 9.11.1967

64 DA, DCL Management Committee, 17.10.1967, 14.11.1967, 16.12.1969, 29.1.1970, 25.5.1970

65 DA, DCL Management Committee 14.12.1982

66 DA, DCL Management Committee, 12.10.1965, 19.11.1966. 'There is a surprisingly wide spread distribution of Malt Whiskies . . . all these Malt Whiskies on the market are very light in colour, and this has a certain appeal to the Italian public. There are good prospects for sales of Cardhu, which will be on the shelves by late October.' DA, Market Reports Italy, JW, 19.9.1965

67 DA, DCL Management Committee, 17.10.1967, 14.11.1967, 25.8.1968

68 DA, DCL Management Committee, 8.6.1971; JW&S Minute Book No. 5, 16.1.1970, 16.3.1970

69 *Illustrated London News*, 25.7.1981, 7.12.1981, 6.12.1982, 27.8.1983, 26.11.1983; *Press & Journal*, 10.5.1983, 18.5.1985

70 DA, DCL Management Committee, 16.11.1982, 16.10.1984. Walker argued that 'greater use could be made of the public relations potential offered by that distillery and had requested that improved reception facilities should be provided. Walker had also requested that Talisker whisky should be offered for sale on the premises.'

71 DA, JW&S Minute Book No. 5, 28.11.1949, 18.8.1954

72 DA, JW&S Minute Book No. 5, 21.9.1955; *Illustrated Sporting & Dramatic News*, 19.9.1956; *DCL Gazette*, Winter 1965, pp. 193–9. The contractors on the project were Melville Dundas & Whitson.

73 DA, JW&S Minute Book No. 6, 24.7.1964, 1.11.1964, 25.1.1965, 25.6.1965, 15.9.1965, 13.1.1967, 14.6.1968

74 DA, JW&S Minute Book No. 6, 9.7.1970

75 DA, DCL Management Committee, 9.6.1970, 14.12.1971, 13.6.1972, 13.4.1973

76 DA, JW&S Minute Book No. 6, 20.11.1969, 16.1.1970

77 *DCL Gazette*, August 1970, pp. 6–7

78 *Illustrated London News*, 30.5.1970

79 DA, DCL Management Committee, 10.6.1975, 17.5.1977, 12.7.1977, 2.11.1977, 13.12.1977; *The Times*, 19.12.1977, 22.12.1977

80 DA, DCL Management Committee, 17.1.1978; *The Times*, 23.12.1978; Hugh Ripley, *Whisky for Tea* (Lewes, 1991), p. 182

81 *Illustrated London News*, 29.1.1979, 30.8.1980, 25.7.1981; *Coventry Evening Telegraph*, 20.6.1979, 5.10.1979; *Liverpool Echo*, 4.9.1979, 22.9.1980; *Belfast Telegraph*, 17.9.1979

82 DA, DCL Management Committee, 14.2.1978, 14.3.1978, 13.6.1978, 12.9.1978

83 Ripley, *Whisky for Tea*, p. 183

84 *The Times*, 4.4.1978

85 DA, DCL Management Committee, 15.4.1980, 13.7.1982, 12.3.1985, 27.3.1985, 16.7.1985

86 DA, DCL Management Committee, 1.10.1980, 4.3.1981, 29.4.1981

87 DA, DCL Management Committee, 14.12.1982

88 DA, DCL Management Committee, 24.9.1981; *The Times*, 21.2.1984, 8.8.1984

89 'Distillers bring back Red Label to halt the long slide', *The Times*, 17.11.1983

90 Subsequently Guinness Chairman Ernest Saunders and a number of leading British business figures were jailed for having conducted an illegal share-support operation. For two accounts of the takeover see Nick Kochan and Hugh Pym, *The Guinness Affair* (London, 1987) and Peter Pugh, *Is Guinness Good for You? The Bid for Distillers – The Inside Story* (London, 1987)

Epilogue: 'Keep Walking'

1   *Printers' Ink*, 15 September 1909, p. 29
2   For Tom Jago, see *The Times*, 26.10.1918
3   DA, JW&S Letter Book A11/2, Blaikie to Gibbs, Bright & Co., Melbourne, 25.1.1889
4   'A new nip in the air', *Aberdeen Evening Express*, 24.8.1992
5   *Press & Journal*, 26.4.1990
6   *New York Times*, 12.12.1978
7   'Big prizes but no Price in paradise: The world's best have not all fallen for the attractions of the Johnnie Walker World Championship', *Independent*, 16.12.1993
8   *The Times*, 13.5.1997, 30.10.1997
9   'That fun-loving Frenchman, Bernard Arnault, has told the boards of Guinness and Grand Met that there is no sense in keeping hamburgers and hard drink in one combine but they have shunned his advice.' *The Times*, 12.11.1997
10 *The Times*, 18.12.1997
11 Amitava Chattopadhyay, 'Johnnie Walker: Reigniting Growth' (Insead Case Study, 2017), passim; IPA Effectiveness Awards Study, *Johnnie Walker – From Whisky Producer to Global Icon: The Story of 'Keep Walking'*, 2008, p. 5
12 IPA, *Johnnie Walker*, pp. 7–33
13 'Closure could turn Kilmarnock into a ghost town', *Glasgow Herald*, 2.7.2009; *The Times*, 2.7.2009, 5.7.2009, 10.9.2009

INDEX

References to images are in *italics*.

315

INDEX